Pennsylvania
HIKING TRAILS

KEYSTONE TRAILS ASSOCIATION

Pennsylvania HIKING TRAILS

13TH EDITION

Ben Cramer, Editor

Region Editors
Henry Frank, Wayne Gross,
Joe Healey, Lorraine Healey, Mike Lipay, Richard Mitchell,
Jim Ritchie, Ralph Seeley, and Tom Thwaites

STACKPOLE
BOOKS

Published by
STACKPOLE BOOKS
5067 Ritter Road
Mechanicsburg, PA 17055
www.stackpolebooks.com

Conditions in the natural world are constantly changing. Fallen trees, flash floods, forestry practices, human developments, and myriad other phenomena often necessitate the rerouting, closing, or abandonment of hiking trails. Any of these can happen at any time and are beyond the control and often the knowledge of the persons or clubs that maintain trails. Changes to any of the trails described herein may have been made after the publication of this book, and the publisher and contributors must disclaim any liability whatsoever for the condition of the trails, occurrences on them, or accuracy of any data or material set forth. This book is based on the best knowledge available to the publisher and contributors at the time of its publication. All persons using this book do so at their own risk, and this guide should not be used without adequate maps and other commonsense precautions, which should be practiced by all outdoorspersons.

Printed in United States of America

Cover design by Wendy Reynolds

Front cover: Hikers on the Loyalsock Trail, Endless Mountains Region. WAYNE GROSS
Back cover: Barbour Rock Vista on the West Rim Trail, Pennsylvania Wilds Region.
CURT WEINHOLD

Library of Congress Cataloging-in-Publication Data

Pennsylvania hiking trails / Keystone Trails Association ; Ben Cramer, editor. – 13th ed.
    p.   cm.
    Includes bibliographical references and index.
    ISBN-13: 978-0-8117-3477-6 (pbk.)
    ISBN-10: 0-8117-3477-3 (pbk.)
    1. Hiking–Pennsylvania. 2. Trails–Pennsylvania. I. Cramer, Ben. II. Keystone Trails Association.
GV199.42.P4P46   2008
796.5109748–dc22

                                                                          2007033227

Contents

Acknowledgments

This book is entirely the work of volunteers, and the information herein is brought to you by far more people than the editors listed in the credits. The editors have benefited greatly from the contributions of dozens of different hiking clubs, many helpful state officials, hundreds of individual hikers and trail maintainers, and the editors of and contributors to previous editions of this book. The community of Pennsylvania hiking enthusiasts has made this book possible.

This book is a project spearheaded by Keystone Trails Association and was made possible by the group's volunteer leaders, including President Thyra Sperry, Publications Chairman Wayne Gross, Glenn Oster, and the KTA Publications Committee. The editors would also like to express great thanks to KTA Executive Director Paul Shaw and the staff of Stackpole Books, especially Kyle Weaver and Brett Keener.

The thirteenth edition of *Pennsylvania Hiking Trails* is dedicated to the many hundreds of volunteers who collectively contribute more than 30,000 hours each year to build and maintain the state's wonderful hiking trails. Through their selfless efforts, the splendor of Pennsylvania's natural world can be gently explored by all who appreciate the outdoors for generations to come.

Introduction

Pennsylvania hikers are blessed with thousands of miles of maintained trails, from short interpretive walks in city parks to major backpacking treks through vast tracts of forested wilderness. These footpaths are spread over a varied terrain rich in natural resources and historic interest. Hiking opportunities have been expanding robustly in recent years, thanks to the efforts of a growing community of enthusiasts. Most of these trails are on public lands and are the result of an extraordinary cooperative effort between ordinary outdoor lovers and several governmental land management agencies.

Although Pennsylvania has a reputation for being a densely populated industrial state, it contains vast tracts of remote forested areas that are sparsely inhabited and teeming with wildlife. Much of Pennsylvania features rugged terrain that can test even the most experienced hiker. These areas of great scenic beauty and secluded wilderness have received relatively little publicity from the nationwide hiking community, so Pennsylvania's trails are still somewhat unused and under-appreciated. On many of the state's long-distance backpacking trails, it is still possible to hike for days and never meet another person.

The hiking opportunities in Pennsylvania are vast, exciting, and diverse. This book is meant to create interest among hikers in the trails described and lead them to explore more hiking opportunities. Even though this book features hundreds of trails throughout Pennsylvania, they are not even close to all the hiking opportunities in the commonwealth. All enthusiastic hikers should consider joining a hiking club to meet like-minded persons, share favorite experiences, and learn about new opportunities.

The trails and outings detailed here do not need to be hiked in isolation. For an ambitious day of fun, consider exploring several short trails that are near each other. Conversely, Pennsylvania's many long-distance trails need not be appreciated only by backpackers who have days or weeks available. Day hikers are free to explore sections of longer trails that are within reach of their cars, and in-and-out hikes on long trails can be surprisingly rewarding. Many Pennsylvania hikers have completed the state's long-distance trails one section at a time over an extended hiking season, or even several years, and they can claim bragging rights just like the through-hikers.

In this age of poor health and a car-obsessed culture, hiking is becoming recognized more and more as a beneficial exercise regimen for people of all ages. Simple walking for an ample distance has many well-known cardiovascular benefits. Persons of all levels of ability and physical fitness can begin their hiking hobby on interpretive and nature trails, not to mention a quickly growing network of flat and easy rail-trails. Those hikers who are looking for a physical challenge and a true sense of exploration can choose from thousands of miles of backcountry trails, often with strenuous climbs and long distances that encourage serious exercise and physical fitness.

And finally, in our modern American culture, kids are severely deprived of exercise and fitness opportunities. Hiking is easy and almost always free of charge, and every family in Pennsylvania has hiking opportunities within a short driving distance. Hiking is perfect for getting kids the exercise they need and to help them develop a love for the outdoors.

Philosophy of the Book

Pennsylvania is lucky to have more hiking opportunities than could be contained in a single book. The basic goal of the thirteenth edition of *Pennsylvania Hiking Trails* is to provide a robust list of available hiking areas and trails. For each trail, the general description includes the geographic location and how to get there, the distance of self-contained hikes or the combined distance of a trail network, special features of natural or historical interest, and contact information (when available) for obtaining maps and other pertinent planning information.

This is not a typical hiking guide, but an introduction to resources that can keep the enthusiastic hiker occupied for years to come. The point of this book is not to compete with existing trail guides and maps, which by nature are able to provide much more information on their specific trails of interest than could be provided in a comprehensive book like this. Accordingly, for most of the trails introduced here, information is given on existing guides or maps that can help you plan an outing. For many of the shorter trails, the information presented here will suffice, but you are encouraged to obtain specific maps and brochures via the contact information given under each entry.

As a comprehensive introduction to Pennsylvania hiking, this book is not meant to provide point-by-point trail descriptions. Most long-distance trails are served by very informative guidebooks created by their clubs and maintainers, and these books are essential for anyone using those trails. This book introduces the trails and gives information on obtaining these detailed guides when available. It provides detailed point-by-point hiking descriptions only for three long-distance backpacking trails for which no other such descriptions are available: the Chuck Keiper Trail, Bucktail Path, and the Donut Hole Trail, all in the Pennsylvania Wilds Region. These trails do not have their own up-to-date detailed guidebooks, making them anomalies among Pennsylvania's premier backpacking resources. In the coming years, Keystone Trails Association intends to support the creation of guidebooks for the long-distance trails that still need them.

A Note on Contact Information. Since the last edition of this book in 1998, the Internet has revolutionized the way hikers and clubs share and receive information. With a few exceptions, the trail descriptions in this book avoid personal phone numbers, mailing addresses, and e-mail addresses. Contact information for larger hiking clubs or state agencies is given in most cases, as are general website addresses. In most cases, if you wish to contact an individual, you can find up-to-date information on the appropriate website.

Hiker Health and Safety

The climate and terrain of Pennsylvania are not especially demanding, compared with many of the world's more dangerous outdoor destinations. Regardless, there are certain risks that may present a challenge but can be handled by hikers exercising common sense.

Most importantly, dress with the expectation of changing weather. Even on very pleasant days, the weather has been known to change abruptly in the Pennsylvania backcountry, particularly at high elevations. Always take along a few pieces of extra clothing that will help when the rain starts or the temperature drops. For winter hiking, dress sensibly for the cold temperatures and snowy conditions. Be prepared especially for harsh winds, as the windchill factor is often considerably more severe than the ambient temperature; and for bright sunlight reflected off snow, because snowblindness is a very real possibility.

Backcountry water sources should be treated with suspicion by all hikers in Pennsylvania. Experienced outdoorspersons may feel comfortable drinking from mountain streams and springs, but even those are potential sources of acid contamination and waterborne pathogens. Never drink from a low-lying lake or stream that has many tributaries or any stream in an agricultural or urbanized area. Backcountry hikers should treat all water with filters or other purification devices. Day hikers can simply pack their water at home before setting out; make sure to take enough based on the distance of your hike and the day's levels of heat and humidity.

Another crucial item for the Pennsylvania hiker is insect repellent. Mosquitoes and gnats can be a severe nuisance in the summer and fall, and ticks carrying

Lyme disease have been noted in the state. For most hikers, a strong retail insect repellent will be sufficient; look for products containing DEET. Check for ticks after any hike through overgrown areas, and seek medical attention immediately if any are found to be attached to your skin.

Conscientious hikers should refrain from disturbing wildlife. There are some potentially dangerous animals in Pennsylvania, including black bears, eastern timber rattlesnakes, copperheads, and porcupines. Coyotes are common but usually keep to themselves, as do the rare bobcats and elk found occasionally in the north-central region.

None of these animals attack humans without provocation. In most cases, if you leave them alone, they'll leave you alone. This includes very uncommon encounters with spoiled black bears. Back away peacefully from a surprise encounter, and do not give the animal a reason to try to defend itself. Some of these creatures have been known to ransack untended campsites, and porcupines sometimes damage the brake systems of cars in a quest for salt. Make sure that food at campsites is appropriately hidden or made inaccessible.

A Note on Hiking in State Game Lands. Many of the hikes in this book are on state game lands, which are dedicated to managing game for hunters and fishermen. Most of these areas preserve the wilderness and should not be discounted by the hiker simply because of the presence of sportsmen. However, hikers must exercise caution in the presence of hunters. Keystone Trails Association, the publisher, and the trail maintainers and hiking clubs that have contributed to this book disavow all responsibility for the danger in which hikers may place themselves within state game lands or other areas with hunters. Do not hike on state game lands during the big-game-hunting seasons in the fall and early winter, except on Sundays, when hunting is prohibited in Pennsylvania at the time of this writing. Big-game hunting also takes place in certain portions of state forests and state parks. The Pennsylvania Game Commission manages hunting seasons for many types of small game throughout the rest of the year, and these seasons present less risk for the hiker. Anyone hiking in a state game land or any other area frequented by hunters is strongly advised to wear at least one prominent piece of safety orange clothing for visibility.

Hiking Etiquette

So that hiking is an enjoyable experience for everyone, you should follow certain simple guidelines when venturing into the woods. These guidelines will help protect the natural qualities of the backcountry, ensuring that you and others who follow may continue to find the pleasant conditions that you expect.

- Stay on the trail. No matter how steep or muddy, do not contribute to erosion and plant loss by beating your own path.

- Use streams and ponds as water supplies only. Do all washing away from water sources, and dispose of wastewater at a safe distance.

- Dispose of human waste properly wherever toilet facilities are not available. For solid waste, dig a hole six to eight inches deep at least 200 feet from any open water source.

- For all campfires, use nearby dead and fallen wood; never cut live wood. At campsites, use existing fire rings or fireplaces. Extinguish all fires completely. During dry seasons, use a portable stove and check ahead to see if open campfires are prohibited.

- Carry out all trash. Conscientious hikers can assist trail maintainers by picking up litter.

- Whenever possible, hike in small groups of ten or fewer people. To minimize impact on the local ecosystem, there should never be more than ten people at a backcountry campsite.

- Respect the natural world. Do not litter, vandalize rocks, remove tree or plant specimens, or disturb wildlife. Practice Leave No Trace ethics—take only photographs; leave only footprints.

When hiking on trails that travel along or through private property, always respect the wishes of the landowner. Behave courteously and observe any posted requirements. These trails are allowed to exist thanks to a lot of hard work by volunteers in negotiating with landowners. Cooperate with landowners and refrain from trespassing or engaging in other behaviors that you wouldn't condone on your own property. When in doubt, inquire with the appropriate parties before setting out on your hike. All relevant private land boundaries are described in this guide.

A Note on Backcountry Camping. Primitive camping by backpack is generally permitted throughout Pennsylvania's state forests, except in certain ecologically sensitive spots such as state natural areas. All state forests require that campsites be sufficiently removed from roads, trails, and water sources. In most cases, camping permits are not required for individuals or small groups who spend only one night in a given location. Permits are required for large groups and under certain specific circumstances for individuals and small groups. Consult the appropriate state forest office in advance, and supply your expected camping locations and dates. It's better to make sure ahead of time that you really don't need a permit. Backcountry camping without a permit is also allowed throughout Allegheny National Forest, except for some restricted areas. (See the Northwest and Allegheny National Forest chapter for more details).

At state parks, backcountry camping typically is prohibited, with camping allowed only at official campgrounds for a fee. During busy times of the year, you should make state park campground reservations in advance by contacting the Department of Conservation and Natural Resources (DCNR) or the park office. Camping and campfires are prohibited in state game lands, except for those through which the Appalachian Trail passes (some restrictions apply).

Organization of the Book

Because of the vast quantity of hiking opportunities in Pennsylvania, this book divides the state into nine hiking regions for clarity. Each region's name should not be considered a summary of all that the region has to offer. On the other hand, each has been designated based on recognizable ecosystem types and regionwide natural phenomena. Pennsylvania natives will easily recognize the distinct natural features of these regions, and outdoor enthusiasts visiting from out of state will marvel at the scenic variety found in these different parts of the commonwealth.

A separate chapter focuses on each of the following nine regions, shown on the accompanying outline map of Pennsylvania: Piedmont and Great Valley; Blue Mountain; Seven Mountains; Laurel Highlands; Three Rivers; Northwest and Allegheny National Forest; Pennsylvania Wilds; Endless Mountains; and Pocono Highlands. Each chapter begins with a detailed introduction describing the territory included and giving a summary of the region's natural resources and hiking opportunities.

The nine regions are designed to coincide with large trail systems whose component parts have a natural relationship to each other. The majority of Pennsylvania's long-distance trails are contained within a single region, but some extend across multiple regions. Breaking these trails up into sections, with partial descriptions found in different chapters, would make it difficult for the hiker interested in extended trips. Therefore, this book begins with a chapter describing these long-distance trails.

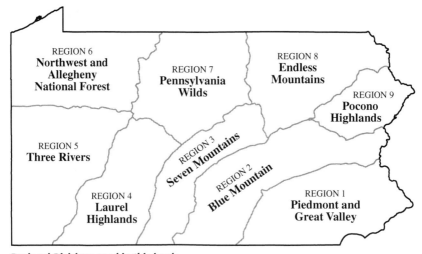

Regional Divisions used in this book

Information on Maps

Hikers may be surprised to find few trail maps in this book. There are several important reasons for this. Because this book serves as an introduction to hiking opportunities for which more information is often available elsewhere, providing maps for many or all of the trails described would present serious logistical challenges. Since the last edition of this book, the availability of detailed public-use maps for Pennsylvania's public lands has increased significantly, and most such maps have become available online. Modern mapmaking and topographic software have also allowed hiking clubs and trail maintainers to create detailed maps for many longer trails. Meanwhile, travelers have long known that the largest and most detailed map is the most useful, especially if you are covering great distances on foot. Hikers know that a map for any long-distance trail that is reduced to fit on a portion of one page in a book is not useful for much more than finding a trailhead.

The major challenge for any hiking guide is presenting maps that are sufficiently detailed. Fortunately for Pennsylvania hikers, detailed large-scale maps are almost always available from state agencies or hiking clubs, and you are highly encouraged to go to the source for maps that will be more useful than what could be printed here. Most of the trail introductions herein conclude with contact information for obtaining maps and descriptive brochures. Many are available online or can be obtained at little to no cost.

This book does contain maps for some trails for which detailed maps are not available elsewhere, or in some cases for excursions that have been designed by the editors for maximum enjoyment of an area that has many interconnecting trails. Each chapter of this book also begins with a general locator map marking the locations of each trail described in that region in relation to major cities and highways, so that you can plan trips to trails that are in your general areas of interest.

Many of the lands traversed by the hiking trails in this book are managed by the Department of Conservation and Natural Resources (DCNR), which includes the Pennsylvania Bureau of Forestry (state forests), Bureau of State Parks, and Game Commission (game lands). These agencies produce maps with varying degrees of detail that can be useful for the hiker. Since the last edition of this book in 1998, the commonwealth has made most of its maps and public lands information available online, revolutionizing the availability and robustness of data for hikers.

State forest maps almost always show the routes of hiking trails, and some of the state forest districts produce more specific maps that focus on the routes of long-distance trails (especially in the Pennsylvania Wilds region). These maps are generally available at state forest offices and nearby state parks, and in recent years many have become available online in downloadable formats. Use the State Forests section of the DCNR website at www.dcnr.state.pa.us. Each state forest district has its own page with links to maps when available. The trail-specific maps generally are not available online at the time of this writing, but they usually can be obtained for free from the appropriate state forest office.

State park maps and brochures have improved greatly in recent years, combining thorough recreational information with detailed maps of all of the park's trails. Most state park maps also feature the routes of long-distance backpacking trails that pass through the park's boundaries. These brochures are now mostly available online as well and can be downloaded and printed without the need to contact or travel to the park in question. Use the State Parks section of the DCNR website at www.dcnr.state.pa.us. Each state park has its own page with links to maps and brochures. Individual parks that are known for many hiking trails also provide detailed trail descriptions.

The Pennsylvania Game Commission (PGC) publishes its own series of informative and detailed maps for all of the hundreds of game lands under its management. Maps can be obtained from regional PGC offices in Franklin, Jersey Shore, Dallas, Reading, Huntingdon, and Bolivar, as well as numerous local field offices. For any game land described in this book, hikers may visit the PGC website at www.pgc.state.pa.us. The contact information for the regional and field offices is available at the website, and in recent years the commission has also made the maps and recreational brochures for most of its game lands available online. You now can download a map for every state game land from the regional pages at the PGC website.

The United States Geological Survey (USGS) also publishes outstandingly detailed topographic quadrangle maps covering all of Pennsylvania, including longitude and latitude, elevation, and natural and cultural features, plus roads, towns, and individual buildings in rural areas. These maps often display hiking trails as well. Just note that given the vast requirements of the USGS mission for mapping the entire country, the quadrangle maps for particular areas are updated only every several years, during which time conditions can change. Regardless, the maps are indispensable for learning about the local terrain and for planning exploratory hikes on trails that may not appear on maps from other sources. USGS maps are widely available at map and outdoor recreation stores and can also be purchased from the USGS website at www.usgs.gov. For more information, contact the USGS headquarters and eastern region office at USGS National Center, 12201 Sunrise Valley Drive, Reston, VA 20192, (703) 648-4000.

About Keystone Trails Association

Keystone Trails Association (KTA), a volunteer-directed public service organization, is a federation of membership organizations and individuals dedicated to providing, preserving, protecting, and promoting recreational hiking trails and hiking opportunities in Pennsylvania, and to representing and advocating the interests and concerns of the Pennsylvania hiking community.

Founded in 1956, KTA coordinates the efforts of walking and hiking groups in and around Pennsylvania and develops, builds, and maintains hiking trails and trail support facilities. Trail lands are protected through support and advocacy, as well as by acquisition when desirable and feasible. Educating the public in the responsible use of trails and the natural environment is a prime objective.

Members are kept informed about hiking issues and activities through a quarterly newsletter and semiannual meetings. The KTA website at www.kta-hike.org has also become a premier source of information for all Pennsylvania hikers. For more information, contact Keystone Trails Association, 101 North Front Street, Harrisburg, PA 17101; (717) 238-7017.

The KTA Awards program recognizes individuals who have hiked eligible trails with awards presented at the KTA Annual Meeting every autumn. To learn more about these awards and their requirements, visit the Awards page on the KTA website. Trail guides, maps, and other items are available for sale on the website.

Perhaps the best known activity undertaken and coordinated by KTA is its trail care program, which organizes numerous weekend and week-long trail construction and maintenance trips each year. These trips are open to all interested persons and provide opportunities to learn trail construction skills, preserve hiking trails, and enjoy the camaraderie of other volunteers. Trail maintenance activities are listed in the KTA newsletter and on the website. Annual Trail Care Awards recognize individuals who perform trail work.

Individuals and hiking clubs are welcome to become members of Keystone Trails Association by using the membership application form on the KTA website at www.kta-hike.org. Donations to KTA are always welcome.

KTA Member Organizations

Keystone Trails Association coordinates the efforts of many different local and regional hiking clubs to promote and protect the hiking trails of Pennsylvania. Consider joining a club in your area dedicated to one of your favorite trails to meet other hikers and learn about opportunities for exploring and maintaining trails. KTA member organizations and their contact information are listed below. Note that this information is subject to change.

Allegheny Outdoor Club, Warren, PA www.alleghenyoutdoorclub.org
Allegheny Trails Hiking Club, Pittsburgh, PA www.alleghenytrails.org
Allentown Hiking Club, Allentown, PA www.allentownhikingclub.org
Alpine Club of Williamsport, Williamsport, PA
   www.lycoming.org/alpine
Appalachian Mountain Club–Delaware Valley Chapter, Philadelphia, PA
   www.amcdv.org.
Asaph Trail Club, Wellsboro, PA
   www.wildasaphoutfitters.com/asaphtrailclub.html

Batona Hiking Club, Glenside, PA members.aol.com/batona
Berks Community Hiking Club, 40 South Miller St., Shillington, PA 19607
Blue Mountain Eagle Hiking Club, Reading, PA www.bmecc.org
Boy Scout Troop 733, 232 Beechwood Rd., New Wilmington, PA 16142
Butler Outdoor Club, Butler, PA www.butleroutdoorclub.org
Camp Swatara, Bethel, PA www.campswatara.org
Central Pennsylvania Conservancy, Harrisburg, PA www.centralpaconservancy.org
Chester County Trail Club, West Chester, PA www.cctrailclub.org
Cleveland Hiking Club, Cleveland, OH www.clevelandhikingclub.com
Cumberland Valley Appalachian Trail Club, Boiling Springs, PA www.geocities.com/cvatclub
Explorers Club of Pittsburgh, Pittsburgh, PA www.pittecp.org
Forest Coalition, www.paforestcoalition.org
Friends of the Wissahickon, Philadelphia, PA www.fow.org
Horse-Shoe Trail Club, Birchrunville, PA www.hstrail.org
Lancaster Hiking Club, Lancaster, PA www.community.lancasteronline.com/lancasterhikingclub
Lebanon Valley Hiking Club, 504 Margin Rd., Lebanon, PA 17042
Mason-Dixon Trail System, Wrightsville, PA www.masondixontrail.org
Mid State Trail Association, Boalsburg, PA www.hike-mst.org
Mountain Club of Maryland, Baltimore, MD www.mcomd.org
North Country Trail Association, Lowell, MI www.northcountrytrail.org
North Country Trail Association–Wampum Chapter, Wampum, PA www.northcountrytrail.org/wam
Philadelphia Trail Club, Huntington Valley, PA www.m.zanger.tripod.com/index.htm
Pocono Outdoor Club, East Stroudsburg, PA www.poconooutdoorclub.org
Potomac Appalachian Trail Club, Vienna, VA www.potomacappalachian.org
Potomac Appalachian Trail Club–North Chapter, 3050 Bullfrog Rd., Taneytown, MD 21787
Quehanna Area Trails Club, Morrisdale, PA www.westbranch.org/community%20pages/quehanna%20trail/quehanna%20trail.htm
Rachel Carson Trails Conservancy, Pittsburgh, PA www.rachelcarsontrails.org
Ridge & Valley Outing Club, Bellefonte, PA 16823 www.rvoc.centreconnect.org
Schuylkill County Conservancy, Orwigsburg, PA www.schuylkillconservancy.org

Schuylkill River National & State Heritage Area, Pottstown, PA
www.schuylkillriver.org
Shenango Outing Club, PO Box 244, Greenville, PA 16125
Sierra Club–Allegheny Group, Pittsburgh, PA www.alleghenysc.org
Sierra Club–Otzinachson Group, Orangeville, PA
www.pennsylvania.sierraclub.org/Otzinachson
Sierra Club–Pennsylvania Chapter, Harrisburg, PA www.sierraclub.org/pa
Springfield Trail Club, 605 Prospect Ave., Secane, PA 19018
Standing Stone Trail Club, Lewistown, PA www.hike-sst.org
Susquehanna Appalachian Trail Club, Harrisburg, PA www.satc-hike.org
Susquehanna Trailers Hiking Club, Laflin, PA
www.susquehanna_trailers.tripod.com
Susquehannock Trail Club, 5003 US 6 West, Ulysses, PA 16948
Tiadaghton Forest Fighters Association, PO Box 5091, South
Williamsport, PA 17702
Venture Outdoors, Pittsburgh, PA; www.ventureoutdoors.org
Warrior Trail Association, Inc., PO Box 103, Waynesburg, PA 15370
Wilderness First Aid, Alexandria, VA www.wfa.net
Wilmington Trail Club, Wilmington, DE www.wilmingtontrailclub.org
Woodbourne Forest & Wildlife Preserve, Montrose, PA
www.woodbourneforest.org
Wyoming Valley Wellness Trails Partnership, Wilkes-Barre, PA
www.wvwellnesstrails.org
York Hiking Club, New Freedom, PA www.yorkhikingclub.com

Long-Distance Trails

Region Editor: Richard Mitchell

Contributors: Ben Cramer, Chris Firme, Henry Frank,
Tom Kelliher, Bill Metzger, Tom Thwaites

Pennsylvania hikers and backpackers have been blessed with several long-distance backpacking trails that stretch across one or more regions. This chapter provides descriptions of these trails in their entirety, so that you do not have to piece together information from multiple chapters for all of the regions visited by a particular trail.

The trails described in this chapter are only a few of the long backpacking trails in Pennsylvania. There are many other trails that are dozens or even hundreds of miles long and offer extended trips for both beginning and experienced backpackers. Most of the other long-distance trails in the commonwealth are contained within one region and are covered in the appropriate chapters. Long-distance trails, just like all hiking trails of any length, also offer rewarding day hikes for those who wish to explore particular trail sections that are within reach of their cars.

Appalachian Trail

232 miles in Pennsylvania

Undoubtedly America's most famous hiking path, the Appalachian Trail (AT) rambles 232 miles through the Blue Mountain Region of southeastern and eastern Pennsylvania. This 2,174-mile-long footpath extends from Georgia to Maine, and its midpoint is currently at Pine Grove Furnace State Park in Cumberland County. The Pennsylvania portion of the AT enters from Maryland atop South

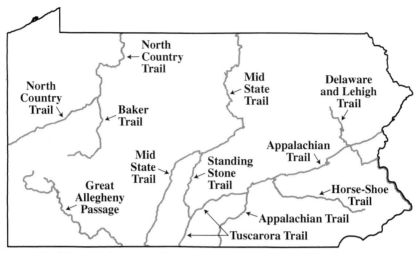

Pennsylvania's Long-Distance Trails

Mountain and then plunges down into Cumberland Valley at Boiling Springs. After several miles of unique rural walking, the AT climbs Cove Mountain above Carlisle and proceeds to the Susquehanna River at Duncannon. After crossing the river on a highway bridge, the AT continues northeast toward New Jersey, almost exclusively following the crests of Peters Mountain, Blue Mountain, and Kittatinny Ridge. Near Stroudsburg, the AT descends into Delaware Water Gap National Recreation Area before continuing into New Jersey.

The Appalachian Trail is marked by 2-by-6-inch white blazes. Road crossings are frequently marked by signs installed by the Pennsylvania Department of Transportation. Shelters and campsites are found throughout the trail's length, with space available on a first-come, first-served basis. Hikers are advised to carry their own camping equipment, as the shelters are often full, especially on weekends and during the prime long-distance hiking season. Camping in state game lands is prohibited except for through-hikers on the Appalachian Trail. Some restrictions apply. Contact the Pennsylvania Game Commission or the Appalachian Trail Conservancy office in Boiling Springs in advance to ensure that specific regulations are met.

Founded in 1925, the Appalachian Trail Conservancy (formerly Conference) is a nonprofit educational organization that built the AT and now maintains it in conjunction with member clubs and various local, state, and federal agencies. The construction and continuing maintenance of this long-distance recreational trail is perhaps the largest volunteer effort of its type in American history.

The ATC publishes guidebooks and other educational literature about the AT. For membership or publication information, contact Appalachian Trail Conservancy, P.O. Box 807, Harpers Ferry, WV 25425, www.appalachiantrail.org. The ATC also maintains a regional office to coordinate activities on the AT in Pennsylvania and the surrounding states. For specific information, contact ATC Mid-Atlantic Regional Office, 4 E. First St., P.O. Box 625, Boiling Springs, PA 17007, (717) 258-5771.

The *Pennsylvania Appalachian Trail Guide,* published by KTA, contains detailed trail information and maps for the Pennsylvania section of the AT. You can purchase the guidebook at bookstores, outfitters, or directly from ATC or KTA.

Tuscarora Trail
92 miles in Pennsylvania

The Tuscarora Trail is a spur of the Appalachian Trail (AT) that travels through four states and offers serious backpacking opportunities of its own. The trail enters Pennsylvania's Ridge and Valley Region from Maryland, south of McConnellsburg, and joins the Appalachian Trail north of Carlisle.

The Tuscarora Trail in Pennsylvania and Maryland and the Big Blue Trail in Virginia and West Virginia were conceived in the late 1960s. The two trails were built to bypass development pressures along the AT in northern Virginia. If the AT had not received protection under the National Scenic Trails Act of 1968, the Tuscarora and Big Blue would likely have become the new AT route starting in northern Virginia. When the AT received federal protection, however, Keystone Trails Association and Potomac Appalachian Trail Club (PATC) decided to maintain the Tuscarora and Big Blue as AT spur trails.

By the early 1980s, several years of gypsy moth defoliation and other factors led to heavy tree mortality along the ridges of mountainous south-central Pennsylvania. The Tuscarora Trail was exposed to full sunlight, resulting in explosive growth of thicketlike plants and bushes. This change in the forest, coupled with a loss of trail maintainers, made much of the Tuscarora Trail all but inaccessible to hikers.

In 1990, the North Chapter of Potomac Appalachian Trail Club was asked to assist a maintainer in opening a particularly bad section of the trail in Franklin and Fulton Counties. Even after several years of work to get the section open, there were rumors that the Tuscarora Trail in Pennsylvania would be abandoned. Since the North Chapter's section of the AT was in excellent condition, the group decided to take on the challenge of the Tuscarora. The trail officially reopened in 1995.

In 1997, the 110-mile Tuscarora and 142-mile Big Blue were unified to become a single trail known as the Tuscarora Trail. The complete 252-mile route is now maintained by PATC. The trail is blazed blue to match the standard color for side trails in the AT system. A guidebook and maps for the entire trail are available; the north section, including Pennsylvania, is covered by maps J and K, and the south half is covered by maps F, G, and L.

Hikers on the Tuscarora Trail must be aware that the trail traverses a significant amount of private land. Always respect landowners' rights and privileges, and remember that it is their kindness that allows an unbroken route for the Tuscarora Trail. For more information, contact Potomac Appalachian Trail Club, 118 Park St. SE, Vienna, VA 22180-4609, (703) 242-0693 or (703) 242-0965 for the activities tape, or visit patc.net.

Horse-Shoe Trail
140 miles

This premier long-distance trail through the Piedmont and Great Valley Region of southeastern Pennsylvania was constructed for hikers and horseback riders. The Horse-Shoe Trail begins at Valley Forge National Park, outside of Philadelphia, and runs westward to the Appalachian Trail on top of Stony Mountain, about 12 miles north of Hershey. The western end of the trail is accessible from PA 325 via 3.3 miles of the AT. The Horse-Shoe Trail exists largely through the generosity of landowners who have allowed the trail route to cross their property. Public parks and state game lands are also utilized. Trail users should exercise proper care and respect on both private and public land. Dogs must be leashed at all times.

The Horse-Shoe Trail is marked with yellow blazes; side trails to points of interest are blazed white. Relocations of the trail's route have been frequently necessary in recent years, so you should consult the latest edition of the trail guidebook for route changes. Trail users who desire to camp on private land must obtain permission from landowners. Camping, for a fee, is allowed in French Creek State Park; camping is not permitted on state game lands. The trail guidebook provides information on other types of accommodations, campgrounds, stores, parks, and intermediate road access points. The guidebook, which comes with a trail patch, is available from Horse-Shoe Trail Club, Inc., P.O. Box 182, Birchrunville, PA 19421, or visit hstrail.org.

Mid State Trail System
261 miles (420 kilometers)

The Mid State Trail System (MST) is Pennsylvania's longest hiking and backpacking trail, traveling 261 miles, and rising, through the Seven Mountains and Pennsylvania Wilds Regions. The system also features several lengthy side trails. The main route of the Mid State Trail is marked by 5-by-15-centimeter rectangular orange blazes. Side trails are marked with blue blazes.

The original section of the trail, heading northeast from Alexandria on US 22, was built beginning in 1969 by the Penn State Outing Club and other groups. The Mid State Trail was the first major hiking trail in America to be laid out and measured with the metric system. The MST guidebook and all its maps are described with metric measurements.

The southern end of the MST now connects with Maryland's Green Ridge Trail at the Mason-Dixon line, providing a connection to the C&O Canal Towpath trail and the Great Allegheny Passage. At the time of this writing, the official northern end of the MST is at the West Rim Trail in Pine Creek Gorge, Tioga County. A northern extension to the New York state line is under construction, however, and will connect the MST to New York's Finger Lakes Trail, thus creating a continuous three-state backpacking route. The northern extension will traverse Tioga-Hammond Lakes, Hills Creek State Park, and State Game Land 37.

The MST is almost entirely on public land and passes through one roadside rest, two scout camps, four state wild areas, four state forest picnic areas, five state forests, eight state natural areas, and nine state parks. Other points of interest are Stone Valley Recreation Area in Centre County and the Woolrich Factory Outlet Store in Clinton County. A portion of the route in Blair County currently follows the Lower Rail-Trail, but a relocation has been planned through State Game Land 118. From the Little Juniata River to Centre County, the MST consists largely of rocky ridgetop trail that makes for a rugged and demanding hike, with many outstanding vistas. Beyond Centre County, the MST follows many old trails and road or railroad grades, making for easier hiking, but with less frequent views and greater possibility of incursions by horses, bikes, and all-terrain vehicles. The trail also crosses several major rivers, usually via road or railroad bridges, including the Raystown Branch of the Juniata at Everett, the Frankstown Branch of the Juniata at Alfarata, the Little Juniata at Barree, the West Branch of the Susquehanna at McElhattan, and Pine Creek at Ramsey.

The rocky ridges and thick forests provide an illusion of remoteness and solitude that is surprising for the second most industrialized state in the nation. The MST is rarely more than 1.25 miles (two kilometers) from the nearest road, however. The level of usage on the MST is still low, and if you hike alone, you may meet more bears than people. The MST also intersects more than seventy-five side trails, over thirty of which are blue-blazed. One notable side trail is Greenwood Spur in Centre and Huntington Counties, which connects to the Standing Stone Trail, which leads south to the Tuscarora Trail, which in turn ultimately leads to the Appalachian Trail.

State park campgrounds along the Mid State Trail are available for a fee at Greenwood Furnace, Penn Roosevelt, Poe Valley, Poe Paddy, Reeds Gap, R. B. Winter, Little Pine, and Hills Creek State Parks. Primitive camping is available in many areas along the trail, and state forest camping rules apply. Camping is *not* permitted in any state game lands, state forest natural areas, or along Penns Creek between Poe Paddy and Cherry Run. Camping permits are not required for one-night stays by backpackers on state forest lands, except in Pine Creek Gorge. If you wish to camp more than one night at the same location, contact the relevant state forest office to obtain a permit. Public-use maps for the state forests traversed by the MST—Buchanan, Rothrock, Bald Eagle, Tiadaghton, and Tioga—illustrate the trail's route. You can obtain a full trail guide and map set for the MST from Mid State Trail Association, P.O. Box 167, Boalsburg, PA 16827, www.hike-mst.org.

Standing Stone Trail
71 miles

Known as the Link Trail until early 2007, the Standing Stone Trail (SST) connects the Mid State and Tuscarora Trails and traverses the Blue Mountain and Seven Mountains Regions. The trail is orange-blazed and maintained by Standing Stone Trail Club. The new name derives from a tradition among the Native Americans of what is now south-central Pennsylvania to maintain tribal genealogies on a "standing stone" displayed in each village, inspiring early settlers to use the term as a general name for the region. In 2007, the former Link Trail Club changed the name of the club and the trail to the more historically poetic Standing Stone.

The northern end of the SST is at Greenwood Furnace State Park, where it meets Greenwood Spur, a side trail of the Mid State Trail System that leads 6.7 miles north to the MST. The southern end of the SST is near Cowans Gap State Park, where it meets the Tuscarora Trail. The long-distance hiker can travel from the Mid State Trail in Centre County to the Appalachian Trail in northern Virginia by using the Greenwood Spur, the SST, and the Tuscarora Trail.

From its northern trailhead, the SST follows the top of Stone Mountain south. After crossing PA 655, it climbs over Jacks Mountain, descending on the famous Thousand Steps Trail and crossing US 22 and the Juniata River at Mapleton. The trail continues south, passing Jacks Mountain Fire Tower and continuing to Three Springs. South of Meadow Gap, there are private land issues at the time of this writing, so you must use a blue-blazed side trail to reach US 522. South of US 522, the SST tunnels under the Pennsylvania Turnpike to reach Buchanan State Forest, where it joins the Tuscarora Trail.

You can purchase a guidebook from Keystone Trails Association or Standing Stone Trail Club. To download digital maps, visit the club's website at www.hike-sst.org.

North Country National Scenic Trail
195 miles in Pennsylvania
(partially complete at time of writing)

When Congress passed the National Trails System Act in 1968, the system included two existing trails and fourteen proposed trails. One of those proposals, the North Country National Scenic Trail (NCNST), was approved by Congress in 1980. When completed, the NCNST is expected to reach 4,600 miles, from Crown Point, New York, on the southwest shore of Lake Champlain, to Lake Sakakawea State Park in North Dakota. At the time of this writing, about 1,800 miles of the total trail route have been completed, including more than two-thirds of the 195-mile route that has been proposed through Pennsylvania.

The NCNST snakes its way through the northwestern corner of Pennsylvania, entering from New York into Allegheny National Forest in the north and exiting near Negley, Ohio, in the southwest. Completed sections include 96 miles in Allegheny National Forest; a portion of the preexisting Baker Trail to Cook Forest State Park; a section through state game lands in Clarion, Butler, Lawrence, and Beaver Counties; and sections within Moraine and McConnells Mill State Parks. The remainder of the proposed NCNST route includes various sections from the southern boundary of Cook Forest State Park to the Ohio state line.

The completed 96-mile segment in Allegheny National Forest, signed and marked with blue blazes, is the longest trail in the national forest. The trail enters from the New York state line north of Willow Bay Recreation Area, on the eastern shore of Allegheny Reservoir. The NCNST travels south through old-growth forests in the Tionesta Natural and Scenic Areas, and then westward through Cherry Run and Henrys Mills. The trail briefly joins the northern end of the Minister Creek Trail, continues westward to Dunham Siding near Heart's Content Scenic Area, and then heads south again through Kellettville. The NCNST joins the Baker Trail at the national forest boundary south of Muzette. For the backpacker, seven national forest campgrounds are located on or near the trail. Primitive camping is permitted nearly anywhere within the national forest, except at a few designated areas.

For more information about the NCNST, or to help with its implementation in Pennsylvania, contact one of the state chapters of the North Country Trail Association (NCTA), described at www.northcountrytrail.org/pa. You can also contact North Country Trail Association, 229 E. Main St., Lowell, MI 49331, (866) 445-3628, www.northcountrytrail.org. The North Country Trail website also has maps to view or purchase, including descriptive guides for the completed section in Allegheny National Forest.

Baker Trail

141 miles

The Pittsburgh Council of American Youth Hostels, now known as Hostelling International, established the Baker Trail in 1950. A portion of the trail in the Pittsburgh area was cut off by suburban development and was later rechristened the Rachel Carson Trail (see the Three Rivers Region chapter). The Baker Trail begins at Garver's Ferry along the Allegheny River near Freeport, between Pittsburgh and Kittanning, and passes through farmland and woods heading northward to Crooked Creek Park, Mahoning Creek Reservoir, and Cook Forest State Park. There the North Country National Scenic Trail has been added to the existing route of the Baker Trail, eventually reaching Allegheny National Forest. Much of the Baker Trail's route follows gas lines, power lines, and unpaved country roads. The route is yellow-blazed.

In addition to long backpacking trips, the Baker Trail offers rewarding day hikes and short nature walks. Along the trail are five Adirondack-style shelters with raised wooden floors, each with space for six to eight people. There are no signs directing hikers to the shelters, so you must consult the Baker Trail guidebook. You will also find many primitive campsites and several fee-based campgrounds in close proximity to the trail, including sites at Crooked Creek, Milton Loop, and Cook Forest.

The Baker Trail guidebook describes the trail and shelter locations and contains a full set of topographic maps. Because of private land and access challenges, it is strongly recommended that you have a copy of the guidebook, which is available from Rachel Carson Trails Conservancy, Inc., P.O. Box 35, Warrendale, PA 15086, www.rachelcarsontrails.org/bt.

Note: Hikers are prohibited from using the railroad bridge to cross the Kiskiminetas River, about a mile north of the Garver's Ferry trailhead. Crossing the tracks in Schenley is also prohibited. At the time of this writing, camping is no longer permitted at Schenley Shelter. Accordingly, it is advisable to avoid hiking in this vicinity. Because of private land issues, it is recommended that northbound hikers begin at Taylor Run, about 10 miles north of Garver's Ferry, or at Crooked Creek Dam, about 5 miles north of Taylor Run. Hiking south from these points is not recommended. Finally, because of an issue with a landowner on the one-mile trail segment between Gravel Lick Bridge and Cook Forest State Park, you should check with Rachel Carson Trails Conservancy well in advance of hiking in this area to learn the current situation.

Great Allegheny Passage

165 miles in Pennsylvania

The Great Allegheny Passage was completed in 2006 and now connects Pittsburgh with Cumberland, Maryland, via a network of multiuse hiking trails that primarily follow old railroad grades. One interesting aspect of the trail system, particularly in the Laurel Highlands Region, is that the old railroad line went through ridges and not over them, via a multitude of tunnels and bridges. One impressive engineering feat was the half-mile-long Salisbury Viaduct. Another highlight is Ohiopyle State Park, where you can easily see several waterfalls and some of the best whitewater in the eastern United States. In the Laurel Highlands Region, the Great Allegheny Passage has been added to the preexisting and very popular Youghiogheny River Trail.

The last section of the trail to be completed was Big Savage Tunnel in Somerset County, which opened in early 2007. The network now connects with the historic C&O Canal Towpath in Cumberland, creating a continuous 318-mile nonmotorized corridor all the way from Pittsburgh to Washington, D.C. The Great Allegheny Passage and the C&O Canal Towpath are included in the Potomac Heritage National Scenic Trail, and in Pennsylvania the Great Allegheny Passage consists of seven preexisting trails and new connectors managed by Allegheny Trail Alliance. The Pennsylvania section is approximately 113 miles from the Maryland border to McKeesport; a 52-mile spur, the Montour Trail, leads from McKeesport to Pittsburgh International Airport. The Montour Trail also has a spur of its own, the Panhandle Trail, which reaches 29 miles from Carnegie to Weirton, West Virginia. At McKeesport, the Great Allegheny Passage connects with the Three Rivers Heritage Trail, leading into downtown Pittsburgh.

Several trail guides and informational publications are available. To learn more about the Great Allegheny Passage in Pennsylvania, contact Allegheny Trail Alliance, P.O. Box 501, Latrobe, PA 15650, (888) 282-2453, www.atatrail.org. You can find very informative maps and trail information at the website. For more information on the Montour and Panhandle spur trails in the Pittsburgh area, contact Montour Trail Council, 304 Hickman St., Suite 3, Bridgeville, PA 15017, (412) 831-2030, www.montourtrail.org.

Delaware & Lehigh Canal National Heritage Corridor and State Heritage Park

150 miles (partially complete at time of writing)

Established by Congress in 1988, this National Recreation Trail and State Heritage Corridor links Wilkes-Barre to Bristol via canal towpaths and rail-trails. The corridor parallels the Lehigh River from near Wilkes-Barre to Easton, and then parallels the Delaware River from Easton to Bristol. The section along the

Delaware is the longest surviving section of canal from the great towpath era of the early to mid-nineteenth century.

Planners are in the process of creating the continuous 150-mile Delaware & Lehigh (D&L) Trail through the corridor. Most of the route is open to hikers, but maintenance standards are not uniform because sections are owned and maintained by many different agencies and municipalities. Individual segments of the corridor have their own listings in various chapters of this book. See the entries for Delaware Canal State Park (Bristol to Easton) in the Piedmont and Great Valley Region chapter, Lehigh Canal Towpath (Easton to Jim Thorpe) in the Blue Mountain Region chapter, and Lehigh Gorge State Park and Ashley Planes in the Pocono Highlands Region chapter. Other portions of the trail are under development. More than thirty other trails, offering interesting side trips or leading to other long-distance trails, are projected to intersect the D&L Trail, creating enough hiking opportunities to keep you busy for weeks.

The Complete Guide to the Delaware and Lehigh National Heritage Corridor: Where to Go, What to See and Do (1994), by Willis M. Rivinus, provides then-current details about the corridor area and its activities and events. For further information, contact Delaware & Lehigh National Heritage Corridor, 2750 Hugh Moore Park Rd., Easton, PA 18042, (610) 923-3548, www.delawareandlehigh.org.

Great Eastern Trail

In 2005, the American Hiking Society proposed a major new trail system connecting more than 10,000 miles of footpaths in the eastern United States. The project's goal is to promote lesser-known trails and encourage long-distance exploration on foot. The proposed network is largely made up of existing long-distance backpacking trails found from New England to Florida, with lengthy new connecting trails planned, particularly in New York and Alabama. The network will create a continuous footpath considerably longer than the Appalachian Trail and will also connect to other long-distance trails, such as the Florida National Scenic Trail, which leads to the Everglades, and the North Country National Scenic Trail, which leads to the Midwest. A very intrepid hiker who completes the Florida and North Country Trails, plus the proposed Great Eastern Trail, will have hiked from North Dakota to New England to Florida almost completely on footpaths. In Pennsylvania, the Mid State, Standing Stone, and Tuscarora Trails will be included in the network. For more information, visit www.greateasterntrail.org.

REGION 1

Piedmont and Great Valley

Region Editor: Henry Frank

The Piedmont and Great Valley Region consists of southeastern Pennsylvania from Blue Mountain to the Philadelphia metro area. The region is bounded on the east by the Delaware River, on the south by Delaware and Maryland, on the west by US 15 from Maryland to Harrisburg, and on the north by I-81 and I-78. In addition to Philadelphia, the region contains several other large metro areas, including Allentown/Bethlehem, Reading, Harrisburg, Lancaster, and York.

This region is a portion of the piedmont that rises gently from the Atlantic Ocean to the foothills below the long and steep ridges of the Appalachian Mountains. The most noteworthy geographic feature of southeastern Pennsylvania is a portion of the Great Appalachian Valley, the wide corridor that stretches from Georgia to New Jersey along the base of the eastern edge of the Appalachians, known in Pennsylvania as Cumberland Valley or Great Valley.

Southeastern Pennsylvania offers great variety in its hiking opportunities. Several longer trails satisfy the hiker's hunger for an extended day hike or backpacking trip. Hiking through the region's many historic areas combines exercise with a close-up look at life in other eras. Wildlife management and preservation areas, public arboreta, and botanical gardens enhance the urbanite's love for the outdoors. Converted canal towpaths and rail-trails offer easy and scenic walking.

The almost continuously urbanized Boston-to-Washington corridor passes through this region, and the rest of the region is challenged by urban sprawl. Nevertheless, the hikers and outdoor lovers of southeastern Pennsylvania have been rewarded with a robust and well-maintained collection of walking-oriented

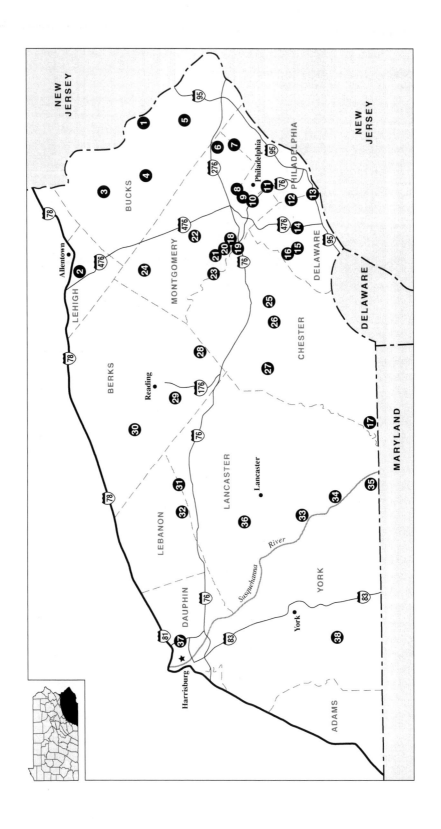

parks and long-distance trails. The vast hiking opportunities available in this region might not lead very far from civilization, but they are not to be overlooked by hikers and outdoor lovers.

1

Delaware Canal State Park

The Delaware Canal, paralleling the river for 60 miles in Bucks and Northampton Counties, was built in 1831–32 for transporting coal. After the canal was closed in 1931, the state took ownership and in 1940 designated the corridor Theodore Roosevelt State Park. In 1989, the park was renamed Delaware Canal State Park. The southern terminus of the canal is at Bristol, but because the area from Bristol to Yardley is heavily industrialized, you might prefer to begin at Washington Crossing State Park. Although often within sight of roads, the towpath offers pleasant walking with great historical interest.

Between Easton and Bristol, this diverse park contains the historic canal towpath, many miles of river shoreline, and eleven islands. From riverside to farm fields to historic towns, visitors enjoy the ever-changing scenery. Other features include canal boat rides, community festivals, shopping, arts and crafts, and tiny historical museums.

Together, Delaware Canal State Park on the Pennsylvania side and Delaware & Raritan Canal State Park on the New Jersey side use five bridges to form a series of loop trails connecting the two states. The connection bridges are found in Uhlerstown, Lumberville, Center Bridge, Washington Crossing, and Morrisville. From any of several parking areas along the loop trail, you have easy access to the towpaths in both states and can hike the main loop of 30 miles or smaller loops of varying lengths. For a perfect extended weekend, consider hiking the loop trails by day and staying overnight at one of the area's many bed-and-breakfasts.

At Easton, the Delaware Canal connects to the Lehigh Canal. These trails are part of the Delaware and Lehigh Trail (D&L Trail), which will soon stretch 150 miles from Easton to Wilkes-Barre (see the Long-Distance Trails chapter for details). *The Guide to the Delaware Canal: Along the Delaware between Bristol and Easton, Pennsylvania* (1994), by Willis M. Rivinus, provides interesting commentary. For a park brochure and map, contact Delaware Canal State Park, 11 Lodi Hill Rd., Upper Black Eddy, PA 18972, (610) 982-5560, www.dcnr.state.pa.us/state parks/parks/delawarecanal.aspx.

Pool Wildlife Sanctuary

Located along Little Lehigh Creek just north of Emmaus, Pool Wildlife Sanctuary is administered by Wildlands Conservancy, a nonprofit land preservation and environmental education organization. The wooded sanctuary has five short interlocking trails that permit you to design a variety of hikes of approximately 1.5 to 2 miles. Conservancy offices at the sanctuary are open on weekdays.

From Allentown, follow Cedar Crest Boulevard (PA 29) south from the I-78 exit. Go 1.3 miles to Riverbend Road and turn left. Take the first right onto Orchid Place and proceed down the hill. Turn right and cross the bridge into the sanctuary. From Bethlehem, travel through Fountain Hill on Emmaus Avenue. One mile past I-78, turn right at the Y onto Harrison Street. At the third stop sign, turn right onto Macungie Avenue, which later becomes Orchid Place. At the bottom of the hill, turn left and cross the bridge into the sanctuary. For further information or a brochure with map, contact Wildlands Conservancy, 3701 Orchid Place, Emmaus, PA 18049, (610) 965-4397, www.wildlandspa.org.

Nockamixon State Park

Located in northern Bucks County, the 5,000-acre Nockamixon State Park features a series of hiking, biking, and equestrian trails surrounding the southern and western shores of its large lake. An environmental study area with 3.5 miles of hiking trails is located in the southwestern portion of the park. A 2.8-mile paved bicycle path and 20 miles of equestrian trails complete the system. Nockamixon State Park is located on PA 563, 5 miles east of Quakertown and 9 miles west of Doylestown. The main entrance on PA 563 can be easily reached from PA 309 and PA 313, or from the north via PA 412. For further information or a park map, contact Nockamixon State Park, 1542 Mountain View Dr., Quakertown, PA 18951, (215) 529-7300, www.dcnr.state.pa.us/stateparks/parks/nockamixon.aspx.

4

Peace Valley Nature Center

Peace Valley Nature Center is a Bucks County park that promotes understanding and respect for nature and offers hands-on educational experiences. More than 250 species of birds have been sighted at the center. Fourteen miles of nature trails meander through woods and meadows, via footpaths on mowed grass or gravel, with bridges or stone steps at creek crossings. The paved Hike & Bike Path leads around Lake Galena.

Guided nature walks are conducted on Sundays and summer evenings. The Solar Building, featuring displays and a gift shop with nature-oriented items, is open Tuesday through Sunday. The park is northwest of Doylestown. From PA 313, turn left onto New Galena Road. At Chapman Road, turn left to the Solar Building and parking lot. For further information or a trail map, contact Peace Valley Nature Center, 170 Chapman Rd., Doylestown, PA 18901, (215) 345-7860, www.peacevalleynaturecenter.org.

5

Tyler State Park

Neshaminy Creek zigzags through Tyler State Park's 1,700 acres, dividing the land into several interesting sections. The park features 10.5 miles of paved bicycle trails, 9 miles of dirt bridle trails, and 4 miles of gravel hiking trails. All are open to hikers. Trails on the west side of the creek are hilly, but the rest of the park area is predominantly level and easy. Because the trails intersect so many times, it is possible to construct endless loops of various lengths. Parking is available at several picnic areas, allowing for different starting points. Two park buildings provide overnight hostel-style lodging, and Spring Garden Mill is used for performances by a local theater company. Several old stone dwellings in the park date back to the early 1700s.

Access Tyler State Park via I-95 at Exit 49 (Newtown/Yardley). Drive west on the four-lane bypass around Newtown. The park entrance is on the left at the intersection of Swamp Road and the bypass. For a recreational guide with map, contact Tyler State Park, 101 Swamp Rd., Newtown, PA 18940, (215) 968-2021, www.dcnr.state.pa.us/stateparks/parks/tyler.aspx.

6

Pennypack Preserve

Pennypack Preserve is hidden away along the upper reaches of Pennypack Creek in southeastern Montgomery County. Three miles of creek are protected in the preserve, and more than 9 miles of trails wind through its 725 acres. The stream valley features a floodplain forest, meadows, several groves of conifers, and an upland forest with old-growth stands of tulip and oak trees. Pennypack Preserve also encompasses a farm whose expansive fields are gradually being converted to native grasslands to provide habitat for meadow-nesting birds. Several abandoned agricultural fields are being actively reforested, with clusters of deerproof tree shelters. Blue and green herons and eastern bluebirds are frequently seen at the preserve.

The Pennypack Ecological Restoration Trust is interested in developing a trail connection with Lorimer Park, which would result in a trail along Pennypack Creek from the Delaware River to Hatboro. A visitors center, located in a renovated barn off Edge Hill Road, contains natural history displays. No fires, pets, or camping are permitted in the preserve, and picnicking is allowed only at the visitors center.

To reach the preserve, take I-95 to the Woodhaven Road exit (PA 63 West). Proceed to the junction with US 1, and at the end of Woodhaven Road immediately after that interchange, turn left onto Evans Street. Travel one block; then turn right (north) onto Byberry Road. Travel 5 miles on Byberry Road; then turn left onto Mason's Mill Road. At the end of Mason's Mill Road, turn left onto Huntingdon Road. At the rise of the hill, turn right onto Edge Hill Road. The preserve entrance is on the left. For further information or a map and trail guide, contact Pennypack Ecological Restoration Trust, 2955 Edge Hill Rd., Huntingdon Valley, PA 19006, (215) 657-0830, www.pennypacktrust.org.

7

Pennypack Park

Running 9 miles from Montgomery County to the Delaware River, Pennypack Park is now a greenbelt but was once the industrial heart of Philadelphia. In the early 1900s, the city bought the land along Pennypack Creek and removed the obsolete old mills. The Pennypack is a place of firsts: the first gristmill, the first stone arch bridge (built in 1697 and still used to carry traffic on Frankford Avenue), and the first environmental center established within a park.

The park consists of gently sloping land that is partially covered with large trees, including many spectacular tulip trees. Other areas feature grassy meadows running down to the water's edge. Wild raspberries and blackberries grow along the edges of the woods, and you may see deer.

Perhaps the best way to start a hike is to park on any street that crosses the Pennypack, walk down to one side of the creek, and find the trail running on that side. Hike until you are ready to turn around, find a bridge crossing the creek, and then hike back on the trail on the other side. The western side of the creek features a bike trail most of the way, and some areas have more than one trail. If you take a trail that ends at a street, backtrack to the creek. Pennypack Park is also connected by trail to nearby Lorimer Park, which features 6 miles of its own hiking trails.

Two points of interest are the grave of William Penn's surveyor general, next to Holme Avenue, and an environmental center where Verree Road crosses the creek. On the west side of Pine Road is Fox Chase Farm, under lease to the school district of Philadelphia to show students a large working farm. Pennypack Park is open Monday through Friday except major holidays, and trails are open from dawn to dusk.

Several maps of Pennypack Park are available. You can obtain trail maps by sending a self-addressed, stamped envelope to Pennypack Environmental Center, 8600A Verree Rd., Philadelphia, PA 19115. You can also call (215) 685-0470 or visit www.fairmountpark.org/pennypackec.asp for information. Some maps can be obtained for a donation to Friends of Pennypack Park, P.O. Box 14302, Philadelphia, PA 19115, (215) 934-7275, www.balford.com/fopp. Full-color maps of Pennypack Park and Wissahickon Valley are available for a donation by writing Fairmount Park Commission, Attn: Trail Maps, One Parkway, 1515 Arch St., Floor 10, Philadelphia, PA 19102, or calling (215) 934-7275.

8
Morris Arboretum of the University of Pennsylvania

Arboreta and public gardens provide walking experiences that differ sharply from hiking through natural landscapes, because the designed environment emphasizes education. Morris Arboretum, in the Chestnut Hill section of Philadelphia, consists of 92 acres of woodlands, fields, and gardens. Included is one of the western hemisphere's finest collections of Asian trees. More than 6,000 trees and shrubs are labeled for identification.

To reach the arboretum, take the Blue Route (I-476) to the Plymouth Meeting exit. Turn east onto Germantown Pike and continue for just over 3 miles. Turn left onto Northwestern Avenue; the arboretum entrance is about a quarter mile on the right. For an alternate route from downtown, take Kelly Drive northwest to Lincoln Drive. At the end of Lincoln Drive, turn right on Allens Lane, then left on Germantown Avenue. Drive through Chestnut Hill, and turn right onto Northwestern Avenue.

Except for major holidays, the grounds are open daily with an admission fee. For maps and more information, contact Morris Arboretum, 100 E. Northwestern Ave., Philadelphia, PA 19118, (215) 247-5777, www.business-services .upenn.edu/arboretum.

9

Green Ribbon Trail

Wissahickon Valley Watershed Association was formed in the 1950s to protect upper Wissahickon Creek with a continuous band of public open space. Located in southern Montgomery County, this area was formerly farmland, then wealthy estates, and now consists of housing developments bordering on the creek.

The Green Ribbon Trail runs through this open space for nearly 20 miles, starting in Philadelphia at the confluence of Wissahickon Creek and the Schuylkill River (at the Schuylkill River Trail in Manayunk) and ending in Upper Gwynedd Township in Montgomery County. Wissahickon Valley Watershed Association negotiated easements with landowners and built the walking path. This trail offers both the tranquil experience of hiking along a meandering stream in woods and meadows and the feeling of walking through urban backyards. Frequent creek crossings use everything from old arched stone bridges to strategically placed stepping stones.

The trail is divided into two sections. The southern part, about 5 miles long, starts in Whitemarsh Township where Stenton Avenue crosses the creek. Heading generally north, this section passes through Fort Washington State Park, the grounds of Germantown Academy, and the Wissahickon Valley Watershed Association's small nature museum, and ends at Mount Pleasant Avenue. Morris Arboretum (see separate entry above) is one block to the east via Northwestern Avenue.

The northern section of the trail, about 3.5 miles long, starts in Lower Gwynedd Township where Blue Bell Pike crosses the creek at Penllyn. The Penllyn Natural Area has a self-guided nature trail. The creek in this area changes character, becoming smaller and flowing through more open fields. In a quarter mile, upon reaching overhead power lines, you exit onto a side trail, which in a few feet becomes a blacktop trail with a split-rail fence on both sides. It goes between two houses at the cul-de-sac on West Prospect Avenue.

Because the trail passes along or through private property and sensitive floodplains, parking is limited mainly to the Fairmount Park trailhead on Northwestern Avenue in Chestnut Hill or the Militia Hill section of Fort Washington State Park in Whitemarsh Township. There also is some parking in the West Valley

Green Road/Stenton Avenue area and along West Valley Green Road at the Philadelphia Cricket Club. Since this trail is in the Wissahickon Green Ribbon Preserve, no camping, fires, or unleashed animals are allowed, but picnicking is permitted. A detailed trail map covering the Montgomery County portion of the Green Ribbon Trail is available from Wissahickon Valley Watershed Association, 12 Morris Rd., Ambler, PA 19002, (215) 646-8866, www.wvwa.org.

10

Schuylkill Center for Environmental Education

The Schuylkill Center for Environmental Education (SCEE) is in the Roxborough section of Philadelphia with 340 acres and more than 3 miles of hiking trails, many of which traverse the low hills overlooking the Schuylkill River, offering beautiful vistas. The trails are marked and self-guiding and include a nature trail for persons with disabilities.

From the Schuylkill Expressway (I-76), take Exit 338 (Green Lane/Belmont Avenue). Turn onto Green Lane, cross the river bridge, and continue to Ridge Avenue. Turn left on Ridge Avenue, travel 2.2 miles, and then turn left onto Port Royal Avenue. Travel .2 mile and turn right onto Hagys Mill Road. The SCEE driveway is ahead on the left.

The trails are open daily, with variable hours, and the main building is open Monday through Saturday. There is no admission fee, but visitors are encouraged to become members. For maps and further information, contact Schuylkill Center for Environmental Education, 8480 Hagys Mill Rd., Philadelphia, PA 19128, (215) 482-7300, www.schuylkillcenter.org.

11

Wissahickon Gorge Trail

Wissahickon Creek Gorge, in Fairmount Park within the city limits of Philadelphia, features more than 50 miles of often rugged trails crisscrossing the valley. The park provides a surprising feeling of remoteness within America's fifth-largest city. In the eighteenth century, the Wissahickon was an important industrial area, supplying waterpower for grist, paper, saw, and textile mills. The city acquired the gorge to protect the water supply, and it has been a park since 1868.

Many of the trees on the northern slopes are beech and hemlock, while the southern and western slopes contain oaks with mountain laurel underneath. The steep slopes feature rugged rock outcroppings, many studded with garnets. Old dams, covered bridges, deserted quarries, and statutes of William Penn and the Indian leader Tedyuscung dot the area.

Along the west side of the creek is the gravel Forbidden Drive, favored by joggers, bikers, dog walkers, horse riders, and even an occasional horse carriage. On the other side of the creek is a popular hiking trail. There are also many trails higher up on the banks offering spectacular views and more solitude. Many of the small brooks flowing into the Wissahickon are surrounded by parklands that jut like fingers into the adjacent city landscape. These brooks all have trails along them and offer different ways to enter the gorge. Cooking fires are permitted at several stone fireplaces along the creek.

Andorra Natural Area and Tree House Visitor Center are in the northwest corner of the park, off Northwestern Avenue. This area was once a commercial nursery, and there are specimen plantings along its trails. Valley Green, the last of the old inns, still operates a restaurant and snack bar.

Start your hike at either end of Forbidden Drive. The southern end is at a small parking lot off Lincoln Drive; the northern end is on Northwestern Avenue. On foot from the northern end, follow Forbidden Drive south until you reach Bells Mill Road. Just after, a trail rises steeply to the right, which you can follow south for about 5 miles. You can also go left at Bells Mill Road and then take the first trail to the right, which follows Wissahickon Creek on the western side.

Maps of the Gorge are available at Valley Green Inn, or contact Friends of the Wissahickon, 8708 Germantown Ave., Philadelphia, PA 19118, (215) 247-0417, www.fow.org.

12
Cobbs Creek Park

Cobbs Creek Park is on the western edge of Philadelphia. This 7-mile-long narrow strip of land follows the creek, with undeveloped trails along the banks. The park is bounded by Market Street to the north, Mount Moriah Cemetery to the south, Cobbs Creek Parkway to the east, and the Stonehurst neighborhood to the west. The preferred hiking areas are on the east side of the creek north of Baltimore Avenue and on the west side of the creek south of Baltimore Avenue.

For many in West Philadelphia, Cobbs Creek is a premier hiking and recreation attraction. Because of its numerous outdoor attractions and abundance of picnic spaces, the park is extremely popular with families during summer weekends. For more information, contact Fairmount Park Conservancy, 1617 John F. Kennedy Blvd., Suite 1670, Philadelphia, PA 19103, (215) 988-9334, www.fair mountparkconservancy.org.

The Works Progress Administration (WPA) constructed the Cobbs Creek Stable in 1936 as a park guard headquarters and public comfort station. Following a $2.6 million restoration, the building reopened in 2001 as the Cobbs Creek Community Environmental Education Center, which now showcases a magnificent naturalist mural, community rooms, classrooms, and laboratories. The center is open Monday through Friday except major holidays. For more information, contact Cobbs Creek Community Environmental Education Center, 700 Cobbs Creek Parkway, Philadelphia, PA 19143, (215) 685-1900.

13
John Heinz National Wildlife
Refuge at Tinicum

Within the borders of Philadelphia is the John Heinz National Wildlife Refuge, with several miles of trails past ponds, marshes, fields, and woods. Wildlife abounds in this urban oasis. Various mammals such as white-tailed deer and fox, as well as reptiles and amphibians, reside here year-round, and 280 species of birds have been observed. This 1,200-acre freshwater tidal marsh is located near Philadelphia International Airport and is open daily from sunrise to sunset. Cusano Environmental Education Center is free of charge and is open daily except for federal holidays.

To reach Cusano Environmental Education Center and the main entrance of the refuge, use the PA 291 exit from I-95 northbound or the exit to Bartram Avenue from I-95 southbound. Follow Bartram Avenue back toward Philadelphia and away from the airport, and turn left onto South 84th Street. At the second light, turn left onto Lindbergh Boulevard; then from that street take the first right into the wildlife refuge. For maps and further information, contact John Heinz National Wildlife Refuge at Tinicum, 8601 Lindbergh Blvd., Philadelphia, PA 19153, (215) 365-3118, www.fws.gov/northeast/heinz.

14
Springfield Trail
4.5 miles

The Springfield Trail is a yellow-blazed circuit through Springfield Township, Delaware County, conveniently located near US 1 and I-476. The trail goes through Smedley Park (hub of the adjacent 2.2-mile Leiper-Smedley Trail), Lownes Park, and several smaller parks along Crum Creek and Whiskey Run. Most of the trail passes through woodlands containing large sycamores, oaks,

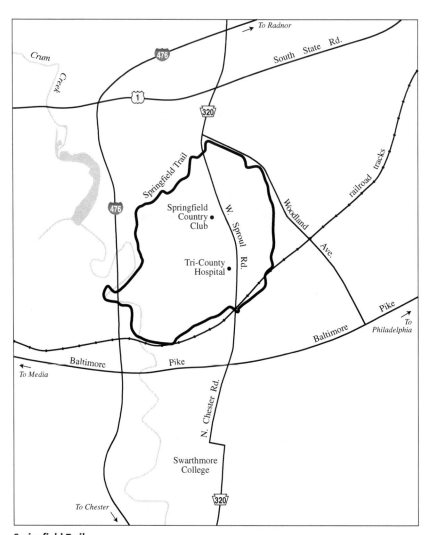

Springfield Trail

and tulip trees. Part of the trail is on private land; please respect the rights of landowners. Confusingly, several cross trails also have been marked with yellow blazes, so watch for the Springfield Trail's 2-by-6-inch blazes. *Caution:* A section of the trail is near trolley tracks; do not walk on the tracks. For more information, contact the Springfield Township Parks and Recreation superintendent at (215) 836-7600 or visit www.springfield-montco.org/parks-recreation.asp.

15

Tyler Arboretum

The Tyler Arboretum is a 650-acre tract about 4 miles northwest of Media. Amazingly, the small arboretum contains 20 miles of foot trails through woodlands, wetlands, and meadows, with seven marked trails ranging from .9 to 8.5 miles. Guided hikes are available throughout the year. There are more than 200 acres of fields and cultivated collections of flora, with 15 acres devoted entirely to rhododendron. The older plantings include twenty-three trees noted for their size or rarity, including a giant sequoia planted before 1860 and a Cedar-of-Lebanon that is more than 15 feet in circumference. The ornamental plantings were started around 1830 by Quaker naturalists Minshall and Jacob Painter. Originally known as Painter Arboretum, the name was changed in memory of their nephew, John J. Tyler, when the property was bequeathed to trustees for scientific and educational purposes in 1944.

From the Blue Route (I-476), take Exit 5 for US 1 (Springfield/Lima). Take US 1 southbound to PA 352. Turn right onto PA 352 northbound and pass Granite Run Mall. At the first intersection after the mall, turn right onto Barren Road. Follow Barren Road past Penncrest High School on the right; then turn left at the next intersection. Follow Painter Road about 1 mile to the arboretum entrance on the right. The arboretum is open year-round, except on Thanksgiving and Christmas. Admission is free for members and children under three. Dogs are prohibited. A guide and map are available at the visitors center. For further information, contact Tyler Arboretum, 515 Painter Rd., Media, PA 19063, (610) 566-9134, ext. 200, www.tylerarboretum.org.

16

Ridley Creek State Park

The 2,606-acre Ridley Creek State Park, northwest of Media in Delaware County, provides ample opportunities for hiking. The gently rolling terrain contains woodlands and meadows, and Ridley Creek bisects the park. Twelve miles of hiking trails pass through a variety of habitats. There are also a 5-mile multiuse trail and a 5-mile horse trail. The Colonial Pennsylvania Plantation, a reconstruction of a farm originally built in 1776, provides you an opportunity to observe farm tools, clothing, furniture, and period meals. Colonial chores and crafts are demonstrated. There is an admission fee to the plantation.

From the Blue Route (I-476), take Exit 5 for US 1 (Springfield/Lima). Take US 1 southbound to PA 352. Take PA 352 northbound for about 3.5 miles; then turn right onto Gradyville Road. Proceed about 1.5 miles to the first stop sign;

then turn right through the park gate. For further information, contact Ridley Creek State Park, 1023 Sycamore Mills Rd., Media, PA 19063, (610) 892-3900, www.dcnr.state.pa.us/stateParks/parks/ridleycreek.aspx. Friends of Ridley Creek State Park is a nonprofit organization dedicated to preserving, protecting, and enhancing the park, and the group coordinates a wide variety of volunteer activities. Visit www.friendsofrcsp.org.

17
Nottingham County Park

The 651-acre Nottingham County Park is located 6 miles south of Oxford, off the US 1 Bypass in southwestern Chester County. The park sits atop an outcropping of serpentine, a pale green stone once used as a building material, and contains a unique area of pitch pine forest and prairie grass savanna. There are eight named trails that vary in length from .2 to 2.7 miles. The longest is the Buck Trail, which provides spectacular views of the valleys to the north.

From the US 1 Bypass south of Oxford, take the exit for PA 272 and turn south toward Nottingham. Proceed a quarter mile and turn right on Herr Drive. Then turn right on Old Baltimore Pike, and shortly thereafter turn right again onto Park Road. Follow the signs to the park entrance at left. Camping and picnicking are available in the park. For further information, contact Nottingham County Park, 150 Park Rd., Nottingham, PA 19362, (610) 932-2589, www.chesco.org/ccparks.

18
Schuylkill River Trail
22 miles

The Schuylkill River Trail offers an enjoyable hike from Independence Hall in historic downtown Philadelphia to Valley Forge National Historic Park. From Independence Hall, you follow city streets to the Philadelphia Art Museum, where the trail splits into two possible routes, one on either side of the Schuylkill River. From Lock Street in Manayunk, the trail follows the towpath of the Manayunk Canal, completed in 1819. Here you see old factories with doors opening directly onto the canal for easy loading and unloading of barges, plus Flat Rock Dam, old locks, and the abandoned granite Roxborough water intake plant. The next section of the trail runs along the old freight line of the Penn Central Railroad to Betzwood and Valley Forge. Along the way are Conshohocken and Norristown, where Riverfront Park offers a convenient resting spot, and the Schuylkill Valley Nature Center at Spring Mills.

At the time of this writing, plans are in place for a continuous trail along the Schuylkill River from downtown Philadelphia to Pottsville. An extension from Phoenixville to Pottstown is under construction, and a section in Berks County known as the Thun Trail is being developed. For more on the status of the Schuylkill River Trail beyond Reading, see the Blue Mountain Region chapter. For further information, contact Schuylkill River Greenway Association, Schuylkill River National & State Heritage Area, 140 College Dr., Pottstown, PA 19464, (484) 945-0200, www.schuylkillriver.org.

19

Valley Forge
National Historic Park

The historically significant Valley Forge National Park is a great place to hike, with 28 miles of multipurpose trails and 19.5 miles of hiking trails. The 6.6-mile Joseph Plumb Martin Trail connects key historic and interpretive sites. The long-distance Horse-Shoe Trail begins near Washington's Headquarters and runs 140 miles to the Appalachian Trail near Harrisburg (see the Long-Distance Trails chapter). Other hiking trails include the relatively flat River and Valley Creek Trails and the hilly trails on Mount Joy and Mount Misery. Pets must be leashed at all times, and hikers should stay on established trails. You can access the Schuylkill River Trail (see separate entry above) by crossing PA 23 near the Welcome Center and following the signs.

To reach the park, take the Schuylkill Expressway (I-76) toward King of Prussia. Take US 202 south for a short distance; then exit onto US 422 westbound. From US 422, take the Valley Forge exit (PA 23 West). Turn right off the exit ramp and merge into the center lane. The park entrance is straight through the first set of traffic lights, at the intersection with North Gulph Road. The park grounds are open daily year-round. The Welcome Center, Washington's Headquarters, and Washington Memorial Chapel are also open year-round with varying hours. The Welcome Center shows a film every half hour. Reconstructed soldier huts, monuments, and interpretive signs throughout the park provide insight into the Revolutionary War period. For maps and further information, contact Valley Forge National Historical Park, 1400 N. Outer Line Dr., King of Prussia, PA 19406, (610) 783-1077, www.nps.gov/vafo.

20

John James Audubon Center
at Mill Grove

Mill Grove is a sanctuary north of Valley Forge National Park that contains the first American home of artist and naturalist John James Audubon, which is now a small museum. The sanctuary contains five blazed loop trails totaling about 7 miles, which all overlap and eventually return to the museum. Features along the trails are an old copper mine and smokestack, an unmarked miner's grave, Lover's Rock, and Perkiomen Creek. The rich diversity of the sanctuary lands is well worth exploring. The sanctuary is also an access point for the county trail system, with connections to the Perkiomen Trail and the Schuylkill River Trail (see separate entries in this chapter). Pawlings Road provides further parking access for this trail system.

The museum is open Tuesday through Sunday. The sanctuary grounds are open daily from 7 A.M. to dusk, except for major holidays. From US 422 west of Valley Forge, take the Audubon exit. At the first light, turn left onto Audubon Road, which leads to the sanctuary entrance at Pawlings Road. For more information, contact John James Audubon Center at Mill Grove, 1201 Pawlings Rd., Audubon, PA 19403, (610) 666-5593, pa.audubon.org/centers_mill_grove.html.

21

Perkiomen Trail
20 miles

The Perkiomen Trail is an easy, hard-surfaced rail-trail extending from Green Lane to Valley Forge National Park in Montgomery County. There are many trailheads, from Green Lane Park in the north to Pawlings Road in the south. Users must remember that much of the trail passes private property, so you should always stay on the trail, leaving it only at access points that are clearly marked for public use. For maps and further information, contact Perkiomen Trail Coalition, P.O. Box 23, Schwenksville, PA 19473, trails.montcopa.org/trails/cwp/view,a,1455,q,30899,trailsNav,%7C.asp, or phone Central Perkiomen Valley Park at (610) 287-6970.

22
Evansburg State Park

Evansburg State Park is hidden between Norristown and Collegeville. Skippack Creek bisects the land into ridges and valleys that create enclosed solitude and scenic views, with more than 6 miles of trails. Most of the trails are easy, with some sections of moderate difficulty.

The 5-mile Skippack Creek Loop Trail roughly parallels the picturesque course of the creek for 2.5 miles on each side. This hike offers streamside walking, mature oak forest, open fields, grassy glades, and unexpected isolation. There is half a mile of steep sidehill trail looking down through hemlock trees to the stream below. The trail includes historic structures and ruins from early German settlements.

The 1-mile Mill Race Trail, a loop on the south side of Pines Picnic Area, uses half a mile of the Skippack Creek Loop Trail. It runs along an old millrace through a dense pine forest. A 1-mile loop extension of the Overlook Trail, near the southern boundary of the park, is accessed from Meadows Picnic Area. This trail features a spectacular view of the stream valley and an old woods road along an attractive rock-bed brook.

Environmental education and interpretive programs are offered from March through November. The Friedt Visitor Center, once a homestead built by German Mennonites in the early 1700s, features exhibits on pioneer lifestyles. Adjacent to the house are a well, root cellar, and herb garden. An exhibit room is devoted to the natural history of the area, with displays of local flora and fauna. From Collegeville, you can reach the park via Germantown Pike, Skippack Creek Road, and May Hall Road. For further information, contact Evansburg State Park, 851 May Hall Rd., Collegeville, PA 19426, (610) 409-1150, www.dcnr.state.pa.us/stateparks/Parks/evansburg.aspx.

23
Black Rock Sanctuary

Black Rock Sanctuary, about 1 mile north of Phoenixville, is dedicated to wildlife habitat and public use. It consists of 119 acres of wetlands, woodlands, and meadows, and one of many desilting basins found along the Schuylkill River. The sanctuary offers a wonderful opportunity to relax and learn about the history, geology, wildlife, plant life, and habitats of the basin. The sky over Black Rock is a flyway for birds that migrate up and down the East Coast. The wetlands attract waterfowl and nurture other plants and animals.

To savor and enjoy the rich natural wonders of Black Rock Sanctuary, hike the .8-mile, ADA-accessible Interpretive Trail through the wetlands. Seasonal changes affect water levels, plants, and wildlife, so return often to see how nature varies throughout the year. The sanctuary is open daily except for Christmas. For more information, visit dsf.chesco.org/ccparks/cwp/view.asp?a=1550&q=616465&ccparksNav=|34716|.

24
Green Lane Reservoir Park

The 3,400-acre Green Lane Reservoir Park, near Green Lane in Montgomery County, features three lakes and four recreational areas. The Deep Creek Lake area offers fifty overnight campsites for family camping, and nature trails attract hikers, mountain bikers, and equestrians. Green Lane Park is the home of the Montgomery County Environmental Education Center, which holds programs year-round for both children and adults.

From the intersection of PA 29 and PA 63 in Green Lane, go north on PA 29 for 1.3 miles; then turn left on Knight Road. Proceed about 1.5 miles to the reservoir and park area. For further information, contact Green Lane Park, P.O. Box 249, 2144 Snyder Rd., Green Lane, PA 18054, (215) 234-4528, www2.montcopa.org/parks/cwp/view,A,1516,Q,26377.asp.

25
Chester Valley Trail
1.4 miles open; 15 miles proposed

The 1.4-mile demonstration section of the Chester Valley Trail offers a relaxing route through one of Chester County's busiest areas. The planned Phase One extension is from Exton Park east to Merion Township, and the Phase Two extension will lead west to Downingtown. The trail surface will be crushed limestone. The trail is in various states of development, so inquire before traveling.

To access the demonstration section of the trail, take the PA Turnpike to Exit 312 (Downingtown). Follow PA 100 south to Swedesford Road and turn left. Continue on Swedesford Road approximately 2.75 miles to Phoenixville Pike. Turn left on Phoenixville Pike and travel about a quarter mile to the trailhead at Battle of the Clouds Township Park on the right.

Montgomery and Chester Counties are working jointly to extend the route; the trail is planned to ultimately stretch from Downingtown to Norristown, where it will connect with the Schuylkill River Trail (see separate entry above). The route will pass through King of Prussia and Bridgeport, cross the Schuylkill River on DeKalb Pike, and cross the Schuylkill Expressway (I-76) on a bridge to be built by PennDOT. At the time of this writing, construction is in progress or will soon begin on various sections of the route. For further information, contact Chester Valley Trail, Chester County Parks and Recreation Dept., Government Services Center, 601 Westtown Rd., Suite 160, West Chester, PA 19382, (215) 344-6415.

26
Robert G. Struble Trail
2.6 miles open; 16 miles proposed

The paved and white-blazed multiuse Robert G. Struble Trail is a work in progress. When completed, it will be 16 miles long. Part of the trail follows the east branch of the Brandywine River. At about 1.8 miles, it connects with the Uwchlan Trail for access to the Eagleview residential area, corporate campus, and retail shops. The trail was built on an abandoned Pennsylvania Railroad bed, extending about 3 miles from west of Kerr Park in Downingtown to Dorlan Mill Road. This hiking and biking trail was dedicated in 1979 and is named for Bob Struble, an active Chester County conservationist.

A large parking area, marked with a sign, is .2 mile from PA 282 on Norwood Road in Downingtown. Several bridges across feeder streams into the Brandywine date from 1916. A full-color trail map is currently being produced and will be available at Springton Manor Farm Park Office, 860 Springton Rd., Glenmoore, PA 19343, (610) 942-2450. For further information, contact Chester County Department of Parks and Recreation, 601 Westtown Rd., Suite 160, West Chester, PA 19380, (610) 344-6415, dsf.chesco.org/ccparks/cwp/view.asp?a =1552&q=621757.

27
Hibernia County Park

Hibernia County Park, in West Caln Township, Chester County, 4 miles north of Coatesville has five named trails ranging in length from .7 to 2.4 miles and in difficulty from ADA-accessible to steep and rocky. Several historic buildings in the park are open for tours. Reach the park from the US 30 Bypass by taking PA 82 north approximately 2 miles to Cedar Knoll Road. Turn left and go 1.3 miles to the park entrance on your left. For maps and further information, contact Hibernia County Park, 1 Park Rd., Wagontown, PA 19376, (610) 383-3812, dsf.chesco.org/ccparks/cwp/view.asp?A=1550&Q=616010.

28
French Creek State Park

French Creek State Park offers hikers an outstanding selection of trails that wind through mature hardwood forests and around two scenic lakes. Numerous park trails and a portion of the Horse-Shoe Trail (see the Long-Distance Trails chapter) provide endless possibilities for unique and customized hikes. There are nine named trails within the park, ranging in length from 1 to 8 miles and in difficulty from moderate to strenuous. Some of the trails are rocky and steep in sections, so sturdy footwear is recommended. Hopewell Furnace National Historic Site, a well-preserved early American ironmaking community, is adjacent to French Creek State Park and easily reached via the trail network.

French Creek State Park is located off PA 345, south of Birdsboro and north of PA 23 in Berks and Chester Counties. For more information and a detailed map with trail descriptions, contact French Creek State Park, 843 Park Rd., Elverson, PA 19520, (610) 582-9680, www.dcnr.state.pa.us/stateparks/parks/frenchcreek.aspx.

29
Nolde Forest Environmental Educational Center

Nolde Forest was the first state park in Pennsylvania devoted entirely to environmental education. The Nolde Forest Environmental Education Center covers 665 acres of beautiful and diverse deciduous woodlands and coniferous plantations, providing programs that help develop a sound environmental ethic. A network of trails connects the center's streams, ponds, and habitats. Teaching stations offer places for students to learn and benches for those who wish to sit and enjoy the natural world. Nolde Mansion was renovated to provide offices, meeting rooms, and a library. A short loop trail accessible to wheelchairs begins at the mansion. Pets must be leashed at all times.

Nolde Forest is in Berks County on PA 625, 2 miles south of PA 724 and 3 miles north of PA 568. The office and mansion are open Monday through Friday. All other areas are open seven days a week, sunrise to sunset. A recreational guide with trail map is available from Nolde Forest Environmental Education Center, 2910 New Holland Rd., Reading, PA 19607, (610) 796-3699, www.dcnr.state.pa.us/stateparks/parks/noldeforest.aspx.

30

Blue Marsh Lake
and Recreation Area

Blue Marsh Lake and Recreation Area is reached via PA 183 in Berks County, approximately 7 miles north of Reading and just south of Bernville. The lake was developed by the U.S. Army Corps of Engineers for flood control, water supply, and recreation. At present, there are more than 30 miles of multiuse hiking and nature trails, with numerous access points around the lake. Trail maps are available at the visitors center and at trailheads.

The multiuse trails are open year-round for nonmotorized recreation. The Blue Marsh Lake Hiking Trail is 30 miles long, circling the lake along easy to moderate terrain, with brown posts marked with white directional blazes. Other hiking possibilities include an orienteering trail, several shorter loop trails, and three self-guided nature trails. Two of the nature trails are located within Dry Brooks Day Use Area, and one of these is ADA-accessible; the third nature trail can be accessed from State Hill Boat Ramp. In addition, the Boat Trail begins at the Church Road access.

The visitors center, located in Bern Township on Palisades Road, is open every day of the year except Christmas. From May to September, there is a fee for the main day use area. For more information, contact U.S. Army Corps of Engineers, Blue Marsh Lake, 1268 Palisades Dr., Leesport, PA 19533, (610) 376-6337, www.nap.usace.army.mil/sb/bm_guide.htm.

31

Middle Creek Wildlife Area

The 6,000-acre Middle Creek Wildlife Area offers both diversified outdoor recreation and undisturbed habitat for wildlife. The preservation area is located in Lancaster and Lebanon Counties, north of Lititz and east of PA 501. The southern portion has a public hunting area with developed hiking trails. The public recreation area includes a visitors center with wildlife exhibits and a theater (open from March 1 through November 30). The remainder of the reserve consists of wildlife propagation areas where entry is prohibited and a controlled-hunting area that is open to permit holders. The large artificial lake attracts geese, ducks, and swans during the migration season; one flock of five thousand geese remains at the lake all year.

The Millstone Trail leads up to the ridge that carries the Horse-Shoe Trail, about 9 miles of which are on Middle Creek property (see the Long-Distance Trails chapter). These trails and some of the dirt roads offer a good figure-eight loop hike of about 10 miles. A map and brochure with trail information are available. The Conservation Trail, a 1.4-mile loop from the visitors center, has its own trail guide. Contact Middle Creek Wildlife Management Area, P.O. Box 110, Kleinfeltersville, PA 17039, (717) 733-1512, www.pgc.state.pa.us/pgc/cwp/view.asp?a=487&q=159288.

32
Conestoga Trail System
63 miles

The "up-close and personal" hike along the Conestoga Trail System through the panoramic beauty of Pennsylvania Dutch Country is far better than a harried auto tour. The orange-blazed Conestoga Trail bisects Lancaster County from north to south. The northern terminus is at the intersection of the Horse-Shoe Trail (see the Long-Distance Trails chapter) and US 322, 4 miles west of Brickerville. The Conestoga Trail then follows Hammer, Cocalico, Conestoga, and Pequea Creeks to the Susquehanna River. It continues to Lock 12 in York County, connecting with the Mason-Dixon Trail (see separate entry below) near PA 74.

The trail starts in wooded rolling hills in the north, but it soon gives way to the rich farm meadows of Pennsylvania Dutch Country. The Conestoga Trail passes five covered bridges, numerous old mills, and historic houses. You will encounter some rural road walking in the central section before reaching Lancaster County's Central Park. The southern 15 miles are hilly, with vistas overlooking the Susquehanna River. Along the gorge rim of Lake Aldred, the trail is within Pequea Creek Recreation Area.

Camping is permitted only at Central Park, Pequea Family Campground, and the primitive camping area at Reeds Run. The Conestoga Trail System crosses much private property, and continued permission to cross will depend on respectful hiker behavior. For maps and further information, contact Lancaster Hiking Club, P.O. Box 7922, Lancaster, PA 17604, community.lancasteronline.com/lancasterhikingclub.

33
Atglen-Susquehanna Trail

The Pennsylvania Railroad's Atglen-Susquehanna Line (also known as the Low Grade Line) traversed southern Lancaster County from Atglen to Safe Harbor. The 23-mile line featured stone bridges, brick-lined tunnels, and the 600-foot-long, 130-foot-high Martic Forge Trestle. An organization called Friends of the

Atglen-Susquehanna Trail is working to turn this corridor into a rail-trail to provide open space and recreational opportunities in a developed area. For information on the status of this developing path, contact Friends of the Atglen-Susquehanna Trail Inc., P.O. Box 146, Quarryville, PA 17566, (717) 786-9055, www.fasttrail.org.

34

Holtwood Environmental Preserve

Lake Aldred, owned by Pennsylvania Power and Light Company, provides diverse lakeside recreational opportunities on 5,000 acres on both shores of the Susquehanna River in Lancaster and York Counties. The area is also managed for soil conservation, timber production, wildlife habitat, and agriculture. The Holtwood Recreation Area in Lancaster County features two day-use pavilions, an arboretum, and the Face Rock Observation Site, with a panoramic view of the river, dam, and power plant. This site also features the Oliver Patton Trail, a .8-mile loop named after the original farmer of this tract of land.

Thirty-nine miles of hiking trails around Holtwood Environmental Preserve lead to scenic overlooks, historic sites, and unique woodlands. Bird watchers will see migrating warblers in early spring, nesting bald eagles and ospreys in late spring, and herons in August. Shenk's Ferry Wildflower Preserve is nationally known for its large variety of spring woodland flowers.

On the east bank of the river, the Conestoga Trail is a rugged pathway designed for experienced hikers; on the west bank, the Mason-Dixon Trail provides a beautiful but difficult day hike (see separate entries in this chapter). Kelly's Run–Pinnacle Trail System consists of 6 miles of loop trails leading to a scenic vista overlooking the river. Urey Overlook Trail leads to another spectacular vista. The 1-mile Pinnacle Trail connects Kelly's Run Trail to the Pinnacle Overlook Day Use Area. This trail climbs 500 feet on an old logging road and leads through an old farm that has been reforested with pine trees. Two interconnected loop trails, the Pine Tree Trail and the Fire Line Trail, plus the Kelly's Run Return Trail, allow you to design treks of varying lengths.

The Lock 12 Historic Area in York County, containing another section of the Mason-Dixon Trail, preserves numerous artifacts from a bygone canal era. The Pequea Creek Area in Lancaster County and the Otter Creek Area in York County offer camping facilities. The Conestoga Trail connects Holtwood Recreation Area with Pequea via Kelly's Run Trail and an abandoned trolley line in picturesque Pequea Creek gorge.

From Lancaster, take PA 272 south to Buck, then turn right onto PA 372. Take PA 372 west for 6 miles and turn right onto River Road. Go .5 mile and turn left onto Old Holtwood Road. Go .5 mile more and turn left onto New Village

Road. The Holtwood Environmental Preserve Office is the first building on the right, and the Environmental Center is the first building on the left. From York, take PA 74 south, turn left onto PA 372, go across the Susquehanna River, and then take the first left onto Pinnacle Road. Follow this road for about 1 mile, along which it becomes New Village Road. The Holtwood Environmental Preserve Office is on the left before Old Holtwood Road, and the Environmental Center is on the right.

The Holtwood Environmental Preserve Office is open by appointment only. Information is available at both campgrounds and at the office. For hiking leaflets with maps, contact Holtwood Environmental Preserve, 9 New Village Rd., Holtwood, PA 17532, (800) 354-8383, www.pplweb.com/holtwood.

35

Mason-Dixon Trail
113 miles in Pennsylvania

The 193-mile, blue-blazed, long-distance Mason-Dixon Trail starts at Chadds Ford near the Delaware border. It heads south to Newark, Delaware, then enters Maryland, passing through Elk Neck State Park and crossing the Susquehanna River to Havre de Grace. The trail then follows the west bank of the river for 65 miles north to Wrightsville, Pennsylvania. In this stretch, it passes Conowingo Dam, Peach Bottom, Lock 12, Otter Creek Family Campground, Holtwood Dam, and Long Level. From Wrightsville, the trail heads west to Gifford Pinchot State Park and ends at the Appalachian Trail near Mount Holly Springs.

Hiking along backroads in Delaware and Maryland takes you past beautiful old homes, farms, and rural scenery. In York County, the river bluffs rise about 800 feet above the Susquehanna, providing spectacular views as well as aerobic exercise. Maps and a guidebook are available, with information on parking, water, camping, food, and motels. For more information or to purchase the guidebook, contact Mason-Dixon Trail System Inc., 719 Oakbourne Rd., West Chester, PA 19382, www.masondixontrail.org.

36

Lebanon Valley Rail-Trail

The Cornwall and Lebanon Railroad, built by the Coleman family to haul iron from their iron furnaces to the Pennsylvania Railroad, was abandoned after Hurricane Agnes in 1972. It was acquired by Lancaster County in 1981 and converted into the Lebanon Valley Rail-Trail. In 2007, the trail was renovated to ameliorate severe drainage problems, repair trail structures, provide safer road crossings, and construct a new compacted stone dust surface. With the renovation of this very popular trail, tens of thousands of park patrons can enjoy themselves in a safe environment. The trail features creek views, shady woods, cornfields, and open meadows.

The Conewago Recreation Trail parallels Conewago Creek, running 5 miles from PA 230 (starting 2 miles east of Elizabethtown) to Mount Gretna Road near PA 241 at the Lancaster-Lebanon County line. Here the trail links with the Lebanon Valley Rail-Trail, which runs another 8 miles to Cornwall. At the time of this writing, plans have been made for a continuous 20-mile rail-trail from Elizabethtown to Lebanon, a project undertaken by Lebanon Valley Rails to Trails.

From the PA 283 expressway, take the exit for PA 230. After the short access road to PA 230, turn left (east) and continue for 3 miles to the Conewago Recreation Trailhead. Parking is available on PA 230. For maps and further information, visit Lebanon Valley Rails to Trails at www.lvrailtrail.com.

37

Capital Area Greenbelt
20 miles

The 20-mile Capital Area Greenbelt encircling Harrisburg was conceived and partially constructed in the early 1900s. After falling into disuse, the greenbelt was revitalized with the formation of the Capital Area Greenbelt Association in 1991. The greenbelt uses parks and trails to loop around the city.

In the words of the greenbelt website, the trail network "is designed to provide its visitors an opportunity to hike, ride bicycles, skate, jog, walk their dog, practice up on flora and fauna identification and generally appreciate nature." This linear park connects Riverfront Park, Paxtang Park, Reservoir Park, the grounds of the State Hospital, Harrisburg Area Community College, and Wildwood Lake. The greenbelt network has several trailheads and access points. For maps and further information, contact Capital Area Greenbelt Association Inc., P.O. Box 15405, Harrisburg, PA 17105, (717) 921-4733, www.caga.org.

38
Heritage Rail Trail County Park
21 miles

The Heritage Rail Trail is a rails-to-trails project following the bed of the Northern Central Railroad, which linked Washington, D.C., with upstate New York. Abraham Lincoln rode the line on his trip to Gettysburg, stopping in Hanover Junction, where Matthew Brady took a famous picture of the president at the station. Today the rails coexist with a multiuse trail, providing hiking, biking, and cross-country skiing opportunities during the day. Once a month, small railcars run the tracks.

The 21 miles of trail in Pennsylvania extend from the Mason-Dixon line north to the Colonial courthouse in downtown York. At the Mason-Dixon line, the trail joins the 25-mile right-of-way in Maryland, forming an extended interstate hiking and biking system. There are two historic train station museums at New Freedom and Hanover Junction, which are open in the summer.

To reach Hanover Junction, take I-83 to the Glen Rock exit. Follow PA 216 west to PA 616, and then go north on PA 616 to Hanover Junction. To reach New Freedom, exit I-83 at Shrewsbury. Follow PA 851 west to New Freedom; then turn left on Penn Street to Front Street. For museum hours and other information, contact the managers of the Heritage Rail Trail County Park via the York County Department of Parks and Recreation, 400 Mundis Race Rd., York, PA 17406, (717) 840-7440, www.york-county.org. Or contact York County Rail-Trail Authority, P.O. Box 335, Seven Valleys, PA 17360, (717) 428-0999, ycwebserver.york-county.org/Parks/RailTrail.htm. Maps, photos, and directions are available at the website. You can visit the office, by appointment only, at 45 Cherry Street in Seven Valleys.

REGION 2

Blue Mountain

Region Editor: Henry Frank

The Blue Mountain region is dominated by its namesake ridge and its parallel sister ridges, stretching above the Great Appalachian Valley from Maryland in the south to Delaware Water Gap in the northeast. This region is bounded on the east by the Delaware River; on the southeast by I-78, I-81, and US 15; on the south by the Maryland border; on the west by US 522 to Selinsgrove then US 15 to Northumberland; and on the north by US 11, PA 93, US 209, and I-80 to the Delaware River.

The Blue Mountain region makes up the southern portion of the dramatic Ridge and Valley Province of central and eastern Pennsylvania. An eons-old collision between Africa and North America formed the Appalachians as a series of long, steep, and roughly parallel ridges, as if the continental shelf were a carpet kicked on one edge by a giant. One can tell how long ago this was in the scheme of continental drift, as Africa and North America are now moving away from each other. Despite eons of erosion downward from their once-commanding heights, these ridges are still very steep and extremely rocky, resulting in challenging hikes for the outdoor lover.

Traveling northwest from the Atlantic seaboard, the first embodiment of the Appalachians is a nearly continuous knife-edged ridge running just beyond the Great Appalachian Valley. Both the ridge and the valley run nearly uninterrupted from northern Georgia to New Jersey, with the ridge only occasionally breached by rivers that offered the only viable routes for the early westward expansion of America. In Pennsylvania, most of this ridge is known as Blue Mountain, with some sections carrying the original name of Kittatinny Ridge. Blue Mountain

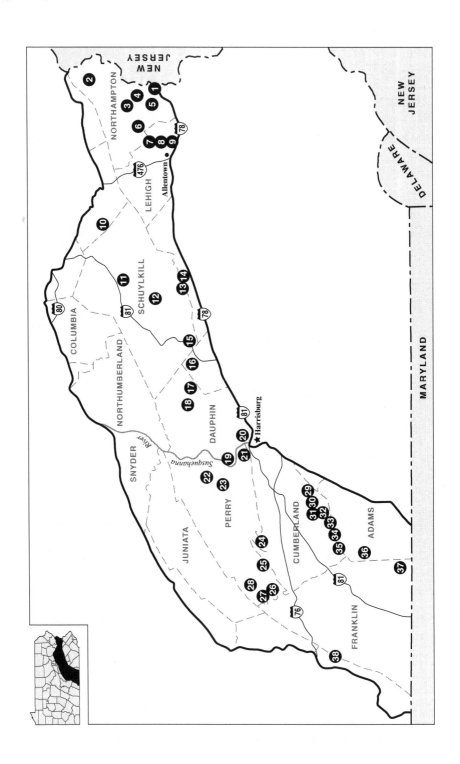

forms a sharp and abrupt boundary between geographic and geologic regions. This region also encompasses several ridges that are parallel to Blue Mountain and almost as long, including Tuscarora, Shade, Blacklog, Second, Peters, Sharp, and Mahantango Mountains. These roughly parallel ridges form the unique eastern and central Pennsylvania landscape of narrow valleys separated by steep ridges that continue uninterrupted for dozens or even hundreds of miles.

Because the ridges are steep and rocky, they have generally escaped the farming and other development activities that filled the parallel valleys. Recovery from mining and lumbering has returned much of the ridgelines to a wild forested condition. Hikers often see historic remnants such as forts and military roads from before the Revolution, charcoal and iron industry artifacts, and ghost towns from the coal-mining era. The ridges also constitute a major raptor migration flyway. Hawks and other birds of prey are sighted in large numbers, particularly in the autumn.

The Appalachian Trail traverses this entire region, primarily following the top of Blue Mountain and occasionally the tops of some of its sister ridges. The Tuscarora Trail follows the top of the equally sharp ridge of the same name before jumping over some intervening ridges to meet the AT on Blue Mountain. (See the Long-Distance Trails chapter for more on these trails).

1

Lehigh Canal Towpath
60 miles

Once trod by mule teams pulling cargo-laden boats, the 60-mile Lehigh Canal towpath is used today by hikers, joggers, bicyclists, cross-county skiers, and bird watchers. Two Rivers Landing in Easton and Old Mauch Chunk Landing in Jim Thorpe provide visitor information and interpretive exhibits. The National Canal Museum in Easton is the only museum in the country dedicated to America's historic towpath canals.

Planners are in the process of adding the Lehigh Canal Corridor to the continuous 150-mile Delaware & Lehigh Trail (D&L Trail). Conditions vary along the corridor, because ownership of the canal right-of-way is in the hands of many local municipalities, clubs, and private owners. Some sections are cleared and well maintained, but other sections are not. *The Complete Guide to the Delaware and Lehigh National Heritage Corridor: Where to Go, What to See and Do* (1994), by Willis M. Rivinus, provides then-current details about the corridor area and its activities and events. For information about individual sections of the corridor, contact Delaware & Lehigh National Heritage Corridor, 1 S. Third St., 8th Floor, Easton, PA 18042, (610) 923-3548, www.nps.gov/dele/contacts.htm.

See the Piedmont and Great Valley Region chapter for the Delaware River section from Bristol to Easton. For the continuation of the corridor into Lehigh

Gorge, see the Pocono Highlands chapter. This chapter provides details starting in Easton, where the Lehigh Canal meets the Delaware Canal, and continuing to the north and west. There are numerous access points along the length of the corridor.

Easton to Chain Dam (3 miles): This section through Hugh Moore Park is in excellent condition, with canal boat rides and a museum. A popular hike combines this segment with the 9 northernmost miles of the Delaware Canal.

Chain Dam to Allentown (14 miles): The route is in excellent condition, taking you through Allentown and Bethlehem, the most urbanized section of the entire corridor.

Allentown to Lehigh Gap (18 miles): Some mileage is privately owned, and other stretches are poorly maintained. Well-maintained sections are found in Walnutport and Northampton. Sections owned by Three Mile Boating Association and Tri-Borough Sportsmen's Club are in good condition.

Parryville to Jim Thorpe (6 miles): This section is in good condition.

2

Minsi Lake

Minsi Lake is a Northampton County park in Upper Mount Bethel Township, leased from the Pennsylvania Fish Commission. The woods surrounding the small artificial lake and the adjacent Bear Swamp are the last natural habitat of the black bear in the county. Waterfowl congregate on the lake, and the swamps and bogs produce many wildflowers not commonly seen in the region.

The 4-mile Minsi Lake Trail loops around the lake and passes through a mature forest. The Swamp Trail leads from the parking lot through the swamp to the nature area. Elevated walkways allow close-up observation of natural swamp vegetation. Because of the wet areas, mosquitoes can be a problem for part of the year. Hunting is permitted, so caution and safety orange clothing are advised during hunting seasons.

To reach the park, take PA 191 north from Bethlehem through Bangor and Roseto. One mile north of Roseto, turn right onto Lake Minsi Drive. Cross Fox Gap Road and turn left at the T intersection, still following Lake Minsi Drive. Pass the archery range and turn left onto Blue Mountain Drive; then immediately turn right to the parking lot. For maps and further information, contact Northampton County Parks, RD 4, Greystone Building, Nazareth, PA 18064, (610) 746-1975.

3

Jacobsburg Environmental Education Center

Jacobsburg Environmental Education Center is a 1,167-acre unit of the state park system located in Bushkill Township, Northampton County. The area is named for the Jacobsburg Settlement, an eighteenth-century community with a tannery, gristmill, iron forge, and sawmill. Additional points of historical interest include the nearby Henry family estate, the site of a factory that provided guns for the War of 1812. Structural remains and ruins are evident throughout the grounds. The center conducts interpretive programs, bird walks, and other nature programs throughout the year. The 18.5-mile network of trails makes the center's fields, woodlands, and streams accessible to both students and casual visitors. These facilities are for use by hikers, bicyclists, horseback riders, and cross-country skiers. Wear safety orange during hunting seasons.

From PA 33, take the Belfast exit. Turn east on Henry Road and go a short distance to Belfast Road. Turn left and proceed .6 mile to the main parking lot in Jacobsburg State Park. The park office is half a mile farther, at the junction of Belfast and Jacobsburg Roads. To obtain a park brochure with map, contact Jacobsburg Environmental Education Center, 835 Jacobsburg Rd., Wind Gap, PA 18091, (610) 746-2801, www.dcnr.state.pa.us/stateparks/parks/jacobsburg.aspx.

4

Plainfield Township Trail

6.7 miles

This rail-trail traverses the length of Plainfield Township, Northampton County. The line was originally designed to transport slate from nearby quarries. Today the right-of-way provides scenic walking in a rural area. Highlights include five bridges over Bushkill Creek, a view of a 70-foot drop into the creek gorge, and unique rural scenery.

To reach to the Belfast parking lot, take the Stockertown exit off PA 33. Take PA 191 north a short distance into Stockertown. Where that highway turns left, instead turn right onto Main Street and proceed to the next traffic light. Turn left onto East Center Street, which soon becomes Sullivan Trail Road, and travel .8 mile. The trailhead parking lot is on the right, just after a power station. You also can access the trail at the northern terminus in Pen Argyl, or via the 4th Street exit off US 22 in Easton, by following PA 611 north to Winchester Drive, which connects to the bike path. For more information, contact Plainfield Township, 6292 Sullivan Trail, Nazareth, PA 18064, (610) 759-6944.

5

Louise W. Moore Park

The beautiful 100-acre Louise W. Moore Park in Northampton County features hiking trails, tennis courts, community gardens, a playground, and a softball field. Located in Lower Nazareth and Bethlehem Townships, the park is popular with hikers, joggers, and cross-country skiers. Several loops depart from the parking lot and allow hikes of various lengths. The park consists mostly of rolling open terrain; from the high spot, a 20-mile view is possible. One half-mile loop goes through a mature wooded area. A bulletin board park map shows the trails, but the open nature of the area makes a map unnecessary.

To reach the park entrance, use PA 33. Take the Hecktown Road exit, and go west on that road for .2 mile. Turn left onto Country Club Road. The park straddles this road, and the hiking section is on the right side. The section to the left contains the picnic, sports, and playground areas. For further information, contact Northampton County Parks, RD 4, Greystone Building, Nazareth, PA 18064, (610) 746-1975.

6

Nor-Bath Recreation Trail
7 miles

Nor-Bath Recreation Trail is a rail-trail in Northampton County that connects the boroughs of Northampton and Bath. The pathway is the original railroad ballast with a mix of cinders, stone, dirt, and grass. Shade is abundant. The right-of-way is used also for cross-country skiing in winter. Parking is available at Jacksonville Park. From US 22, take PA 987 north, and then follow the combined PA 987 and PA 329. Where that road bears left in Jacksonville, continue straight onto Jacksonville Road. Parking is on the left just after the trail crossing. For further information, contact Northampton County Parks, RD 4, Greystone Building, Nazareth, PA 18064, (610) 746-1975.

Ironton Rail Trail
9.2 miles

Ironton Rail Trail, on the former Ironton Railroad in Lehigh County, is owned by Whitehall Township and Coplay. The line was used to haul coal, iron ore, and limestone to the blast furnaces of the Thomas Iron Works. Today the right-of-way provides a setting for recreational pursuits, and the trail highlights many historic sites. Of special interest are Troxell-Steckel House, one of the earliest surviving log homes in the county, and Saylor Park Cement Industry Museum. The trail also passes through Whitehall Parkway, a 110-acre township park laced with trails.

The Ironton Rail Trail includes a 5.3-mile loop segment through Coplay and Hokendauqua. A section of the trail parallels the Lehigh River. The total trail length is 9.2 miles including the loop; at the time of this writing, 7.8 miles of the total distance is paved and open for all uses, as is the loop segment. The remainder of the trail is made of crushed and rolled stone in excellent condition.

Trail users are encouraged to park at the trailhead. From US 22 in Allentown, drive north on PA 145 (MacArthur Road) 3.9 miles to Chestnut Street. Turn right on Chestnut Street and proceed .5 mile to the trailhead on the right. The Charles Neff Trail leads to the Ironton Rail Trail and the parkway trail system. For further information, contact Whitehall Township Parks and Recreation, 3219 MacArthur Road, Whitehall, PA 18052, (610) 437-5524, ext. 160.

8

Jordan Creek Parkway

Jordan Creek Parkway is a Lehigh County park offering two short, connected trails. Though just north of US 22 and west of MacArthur Road, most of the area is shady woods. The trail along Jordan Creek is surprisingly isolated, even though you can hear US 22 through the trees. The longest possible loop hike is just over 3 miles. There are a number of other "volunteer" trails throughout the park, and all trails are shared with bicyclists. From US 22, take the exit for MacArthur Road (PA 145), and turn north. After about half a mile, turn left on Mickley Road and proceed to the park grounds. Parking is available at the creekside near the red barn or at the Parks and Recreation building.

9

Allentown City Parks

The city of Allentown, in Lehigh County, maintains an impressive park system. Two parks in the western part of the city offer extended walking and hiking opportunities.

Little Lehigh Parkway, accessed by M. L. King Parkway or Fish Hatchery Road, is a long, narrow park that follows Little Lehigh Creek for 3 miles. Parking is available at each end and at two intermediate points. Paths line both sides of the creek, permitting you to hike a complete loop of 6 miles or a shorter route. This park features the covered Bogerts Bridge and a fish hatchery.

Cedar Creek Parkway lies east of Cedar Crest Boulevard and north of Hamilton Street. This is also a long, narrow park surrounding a stream. Features of the park include Lake Muhlenberg and its waterfowl, the Rose Garden, and developed areas for swimming, tennis, and basketball. Dogs are not permitted in the Rose Garden area, and feeding waterfowl is prohibited. The park is cut in half by Ott Street, but you can go under that street's bridge over the creek. A 2.5-mile loop hike can begin at the Rose Garden, the swimming pool, or the lake.

For further information on hiking at these or other city parks, contact Allentown Recreation Department, 3000 Parkway Blvd., Allentown, PA 18104, (610) 437-7757; or Allentown Parks Department, 2700 Parkway Blvd., Allentown, PA 18104, (610) 437-7628.

10
Switchback Railroad Trail System

The Switchback Railroad Trail System is a rail-trail with a unique history. To solve the problem of transporting coal from the mines on Summit Hill to the Lehigh Canal at Jim Thorpe, industrialists constructed a gravity railroad consisting of a downhill track for the loaded cars, a separate return track using two inclined planes (with steam engines), and a gravity line. The two tracks crossed twice, at Five Mile Tree and on the Mount Jefferson Inclined Plane. When the system opened in 1827, it was the second railroad in America. The railroad stopped hauling coal in 1872, and the line became one of the country's leading tourist attractions until 1937, when the rails were sold for scrap. The railroad ride, with its inclines and descents, is said to have been the inspiration for the roller coaster. In 1977, the abandoned right-of-way was purchased and converted into a trail.

Several hikes are possible. One 8-mile hike from Summit Hill to Jim Thorpe is all downhill and mostly through woods. The lower section along the stream is especially delightful. The second hike starts in Jim Thorpe and ascends the Mount Pisgah Inclined Plane, with great views at the top. You can make a round-trip hike by returning on the downward track when you reach the crossing at Five Mile Tree. A third option is to use the trails in Mauch Chunk Lake Park. The Switchback Trail goes through the 2,300-acre park and connects with its trails. The Shoreline Trail is a 1.5-mile self-interpretive trail along the lake through woods and open shoreline with rhododendron, laurel, and hemlock. The 3.5-mile Fireline Trail along the top of Mauch Chunk Ridge follows a shale roadway through predominantly oak forest. The Woods Trail provides access to a swampy area at the west end of the lake. In winter, the Switchback Railroad can be ideal for cross-country skiing.

Parking is available in Jim Thorpe, Summit Hill, and at Mauch Chunk Lake Park. A brochure, with maps of both the park and Switchback Railroad route, is available from Mauch Chunk Lake Park Office, Carbon County Parks and Recreation, 625 Lentz Trail, Jim Thorpe, PA 18229, (717) 329-3669.

11

Locust Lake State Park

Locust Lake State Park offers several miles of hiking trails traversing both woodlands and open areas. Situated at the western end of Locust Valley near the headwaters of Locust Creek, the park encompasses 1,144 acres, including a 52-acre lake. With the exception of some 60 acres near the dam, the entire park is forested. A loop trail system begins near the amphitheater at the western side of the lake. The blue-blazed Ridge Trail winds for .8 mile along a creek, through a mature forest and a young woodland. The yellow-blazed Hemlock Trail is a 2-mile hike through a mature stand of hemlocks, partially along Locust Creek. The 4-mile white-blazed Oak Loop Trail encircles a ridge in a mature deciduous forest.

The park is 7 miles north of Pottsville, 3 miles south of Mahanoy City, 8 miles west of Tamaqua, and 6 miles west of Tuscarora State Park, which also features some hiking opportunities. To reach the park, follow the signs leading 2 miles southwest from the Hometown (PA 54) exit off I-81. For more information and a trail map, contact Locust Lake State Park, c/o Tuscarora, Barnesville, PA 18214, (570) 467-2404, www.dcnr.state.pa.us/stateparks/parks/locustlake.aspx.

12

Schuylkill River Trail
(Bartram Trail)

A long-distance network of rail-trails is being developed along the Schuylkill River from Philadelphia to Pottsville in Schuylkill County. At the time of this writing, the trail is complete in the Philadelphia area (see the Piedmont and Great Valley Region chapter for details). A 12-mile section in Schuylkill County known as the Bartram Trail is being developed in the Blue Mountain Region. For further information, contact Schuylkill River Greenway Association, Schuylkill River National and State Heritage Area, 960 Old Mill Rd., Wyomissing, PA 19610, (610) 372-3916, www.schuylkillriver.org.

13

Tom Lowe Trail

2.8 miles

The Tom Lowe Trail, constructed in 1977 by the ELCO Hiking Club of Eastern Lebanon County High School, is named in memory of a charter member of the club. This path, located on game lands north of Shartlesville, Berks County, when combined with the Sand Spring Trail (see separate entry below), the Appalachian Trail, and game land service roads, creates a challenging and scenic loop hike. The Tom Lowe and Sand Spring Trails together make up their own loop of about 5 miles. The Tom Lowe Trail starts along a beautiful stream for about 800 feet before crossing it. The trail passes through a mixed forest and over rocky terrain to its junction with the Sand Spring Trail at the top of the mountain.

To reach the trailhead parking area, take Exit 23 (Shartlesville) from I-78 and drive north on Mountain Road for .3 mile. Bear left onto Forge Dam Road, and

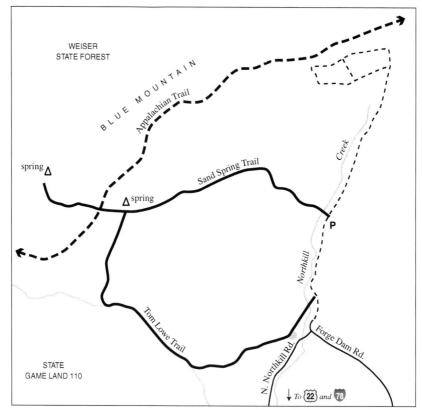

Tom Lowe and Sand Spring Trails

continue 1.5 miles (past the intersection with Northkill Road) to the parking area. The orange-blazed trail, marked by a sign, begins near the south end of the parking area.

14
Sand Spring Trail
2.2 miles

The Sand Spring Trail is a blue-blazed spur of the Appalachian Trail that leaves the AT on Blue Mountain, 5.3 miles north of PA 183. In about 200 yards, it descends to the east to Sand Spring, a fine walled spring, where it connects with the orange-blazed Tom Lowe Trail (see separate entry above). No camping is permitted at or near the spring. The Sand Spring Trail continues another 1.7 miles to gated Shartlesville Road, 100 yards north of a Game Commission parking area. The Sand Spring Trail then continues northwest to a Game Commission road that was the former route of the AT. For directions to the parking area, see Tom Lowe Trail above.

15
Swatara State Park

Swatara State Park is located in Lebanon and Schuylkill Counties, 14 miles north of Lebanon and 3 miles west of Pine Grove. The park is easily accessible from I-81 at Exit 90 (PA 72) or Exit 100 (PA 443). The park is undeveloped, with 3,520 acres of rolling fields and woodlands between Second and Blue Mountains. Seven miles of scenic Swatara Creek wind through the park. The park has no facilities, but there are plans for five trailheads with parking and restrooms.

A short section of the Appalachian Trail traverses the southern portion of the park between PA 443 and Swatara Creek, which you cross via the historic iron Waterville Bridge. Several easy hunting trails and logging roads take you through beautiful hemlock groves with scenic views of the surrounding mountains and Swatara Creek. State Road, deteriorated and rarely used by vehicles, runs past a fossil dig, and nearby is a stone lock of the old Union Canal system. The lock is especially interesting in April, when a loud crescendo of music emanates from the resident frogs. State Road is ideal for cross-country skiing. For further information, contact Swatara State Park, c/o Memorial Lake, Grantville, PA 17028, (717) 865-6470, www.dcnr.state.pa.us/stateparks/parks/swatara.aspx.

16
State Game Land 211

State Game Land 211 encompasses four parallel mountain ridges north of Harrisburg and east of the Susquehanna River: Peters Mountain (just east of the US 22/322 bridge), Stony Mountain, Sharp Mountain, and Second Mountain. Roads in the valleys between the ridges provide access to numerous trails, including the game land service road on the old bed of the Schuylkill and Susquehanna Railroad. Some of the other access roads are gated to prevent vehicular traffic. PA 325 and PA 443 (to the south of the area) offer vehicular access to trailheads. The western end of the game land can be reached via Stony Creek Road, 9 miles from Dauphin. Some trails in the eastern section of the game land can be reached via Goldmine Road, which begins at PA 443, 2 miles east of the junction with PA 72 at Green Point; goes north over Second, Sharp, and Stony Mountains; and ends at PA 325 at its intersection with Greenland Road.

The Appalachian Trail (see the Long-Distance Trails chapter) is the main trail in the area. It runs in a generally west-east direction following the ridge of Peters Mountain from the Susquehanna River, entering State Game Land 211 just east of the Victoria Trail, and passing Shikellimy Rocks. It then descends to PA 325 west of Dehart Reservoir, crosses Clarks Creek, and ascends steadily for 3 miles on a fire road to the top of Stony Mountain. A short distance beyond is the old site of Stony Mountain Fire Tower, since moved west to near the Water Tank Trail. Here the yellow-blazed Horse-Shoe Trail (see the Long-Distance Trails

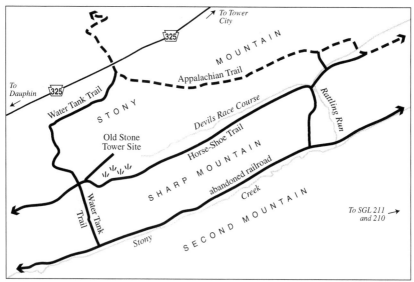

SGL 211

chapter) comes in from the south. After crossing the shallow valley between Stony and Sharp Mountains, the AT follows an old stagecoach road along the crest of Sharp Mountain to Rausch Gap, in what is locally known as St. Anthony's Wilderness. The AT then turns southeast up and over Second Mountain to PA 443 near Green Point.

State Game Land 211 also has a large network of connecting trails. Many of these trails are blazed but receive minimal maintenance. Some are seldom used, but others are hiked by adventurous and experienced hikers who like the more challenging terrain of these mountains. Some of the trails lead to historic ruins from the lumbering and mining eras. You can most easily follow the many hiking trails of the area by using a map and compass. The color KTA map for the AT, sections 7 and 8 (Susquehanna River to Swatara Gap), shows most of the trails and the distances between points. Game land sportsmen's recreation maps are also available.

Schuylkill and Susquehanna Railroad Grade (19.5 miles): This old railroad was built in the 1850s as a link between Schuylkill County's coal and timber resources and industrial centers in southern and western Pennsylvania. It operated between Pottsville and Dauphin until 1933. The tracks and ties were removed in 1946, shortly after the Game Commission acquired a large tract of surrounding land. Today the railroad bed is a popular 17.5-mile recreational path between Ellendale Forge on the west and Gold Mine Road on the east. Both ends are gated to prevent vehicular traffic. Another 2 miles are open east of Gold Mine Road to the Lebanon Reservoir. Many of the other connecting trails can be accessed from this railroad bed, which is also a Game Commission service road.

Shikellimy Trail (.9 mile): This blue-blazed access trail goes south from the AT on Peters Mountain to PA 325, at a point 2.3 miles west of where the AT crosses the highway.

Water Tank Trail (2.4 miles): This blue-blazed trail leaves the AT just south of its junction with PA 325 and a large game land parking area. It bears right after crossing Clarks Creek and heads south up Third Mountain/Stony Mountain, where it crosses Rattling Run Road (which carries the Horse-Shoe Trail) before dropping very steeply to the old railroad bed.

Rattling Run Trail (8.6 miles): This trail, an old stagecoach road, diverges from the AT on Sharp Mountain, heading west where the AT turns east. It crosses Rattling Run and continues on Third Mountain, passing near the new site of the mysterious Stony Mountain Fire Tower (the old site was on the AT) and a radio tower, before dropping down to Ellendale Forge in Stony Creek Valley. This trail is now used by the Horse-Shoe Trail and is blazed yellow.

Yellow Springs Trail (1.5 miles): This blue-blazed trail connects the ruins of Yellow Springs village on the AT with the stone tower. It then arches to the south and back to the AT on Sharp Mountain before descending to the old railroad bed and the site of the former Yellow Springs Station. The section of the trail that descends to the Stony Creek railbed is impassable due to severe erosion from flooding. The trail is being relocated by the Susquehanna Appalachian Trail Club.

Stone Tower Trail (2 miles): This red-blazed trail can be found along PA 325 just east of PennDOT marker 380 and 6 miles east of Carsonville Road. A double red blaze is found on the south side of the road, and the trail leads up the rocky slope of Stony Mountain to the site of the old stone tower. Just before reaching the tower, it meets the blue-blazed Yellow Springs Trail.

Sand Spring Trail (1.6 miles): This blue-blazed trail leaves PA 325 at a point 6.8 miles east of Carsonville Road, near PennDOT marker 400. The trail climbs steeply up Stony Mountain to connect with the AT .3 mile west of Cold Springs Trail. A yellow-blazed trail at the crest of Stony Mountain leads east .3 mile to a vista.

Cold Springs Trail (.9 mile): Starting 2.3 miles west of Rausch Gap Shelter Trail (an AT side trail), this well-worn but unblazed trail drops down the south slope of Sharp Mountain to the old railroad bed and the site of the former Cold Springs Station.

Rausch Gap and Goldmine Area Trails: Trails in the area between Rausch Gap and Goldmine Road to the east allow loop hikes around Sharp Mountain.

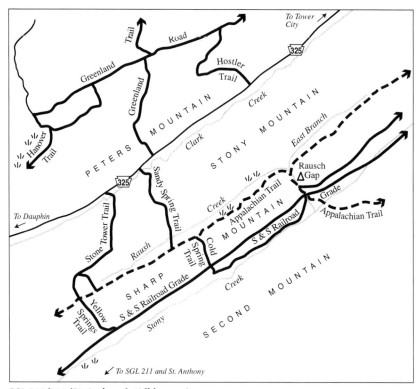

SGL 210/211 (St. Anthony's Wilderness)

Most are unmarked and follow Game Commission access roads or old railroad grades. Rausch Gap was the site of a thriving mining community in the 1850s, but it was abandoned by the end of the century as a result of the closure of the mine and the relocation of the railroad offices to Pine Grove. The remains of many stone foundations are still visible at the former Rausch Gap Station. A small community cemetery is nearby. The AT descends from Sharp Mountain through the gap; a short side trail leads to the Rausch Gap Shelter.

Old Stage Trail (3.1 miles): This trail connects with the AT in Rausch Gap and travels east across Sharp Mountain to Goldmine Run and Goldmine Road. The trail is red-blazed for a short distance from the AT.

Old Railroad Siding Grade (2.3 miles): This trail connects with the AT in Rausch Gap. It follows the lower south slope of Sharp Mountain east to Goldmine Run and the railroad breaker ruins, and then proceeds to Goldmine Road.

Chinese Wall (.3 mile): The gated access road and Game Commission parking area for this interesting site are on the east side of Goldmine Road 4.4 miles north of its intersection with PA 443. The "wall" is a spectacular outcrop of Sharp Mountain quartz-pebble conglomerate, also known as Boxcar Rocks or High Rocks.

17

State Game Land 210

State Game Land 210, with more than 11,000 acres, is just north of Game Land 211 (see separate entry above) across Clark's Valley. It covers portions of Peters and Broad Mountains and is adjacent to two tracts of Weiser State Forest. Greenland Road, the main artery through Game Land 210, is gated at its western end at SR 4013, about halfway between Lykens and Carsonville, and at its eastern juncture with Weiser State Forest. This is a Game Commission maintenance road leading to wildlife feed plots. The trails off Greenland Road are not blazed and follow service roads. They are identified with wooden signs at their junctions with Greenland Road, which is marked with orange diamond blazes as a snowmobile trail. Except during hunting seasons, hiking is pleasant because the feed plots provide opportunities for wildlife viewing.

Hanover Trail (2.5 miles): This trail starts at the western end of Greenland Road near a large State Game Land 210 sign. Parking is located across paved SR 4013. The trail bears right toward wildlife food plots and in .4 mile bears right again to cross and parallel the South Fork of Powell Creek.

Greenland Trail (4 miles): This trail leaves PA 325 at a point 7.9 miles east of the AT crossing, just east of PennDOT marker 400. The trail goes up the bank on the north side of the road, opposite a double yellow blaze on the south side of the road. The trail is blazed yellow as it ascends Peters Mountain but is not blazed all the way to Greenland Road. A 2-mile extension to the north along Nine O'Clock Run is found by jogging a short distance east on Greenland Road.

Hostler Trail (2.2 miles): This unblazed trail is inconspicuous at its starting point on PA 325 between PennDOT markers 400 and 450, .1 mile east of the junction with Stahls Road. It ascends Peters Mountain on a somewhat rocky footpath, until it becomes a road near the top and connects to Greenland Road. After turning right (east) on this road for a short distance, the Hostler Trail bears off to the north for 1.2 miles to connect with Larch Road.

18

Weiser State Forest, Haldeman Tract

Haldeman Tract, a beautiful remote area on top of Broad Mountain near Elizabethville and Lykens, is one of eight noncontiguous tracts in Weiser State Forest. This area is west of State Game Land 210 (see separate entry above). Hiking in this tract is mostly on gated old woods roads, now designated as snowmobile trails and marked with orange diamonds, which form pleasant loop hikes on gentle grades. The trails and dirt forest roads are shown on the Weiser State Forest public-use map and on the KTA Appalachian Trail Map (see the Long-Distance Trails chapter). There is no overnight camping in the Haldeman Tract. Two picnic areas (without water or toilet facilities) make good starting points for hikers.

To reach Rowland Picnic Area, take PA 225 south from Elizabethville for .9 mile to Quarry Road, just past the Elizabethville Quarry. Turn left and follow Quarry Road for 1 mile to Deitrich Road. Turn right and take this road .9 mile to White Oak Road, and turn right again. Follow White Oak Road for .3 mile past the forest headquarters to a parking area on the right. The picnic area is a short distance ahead on the road. To reach Minnich Hit Picnic Area, take SR 4013 (Market Street/Glen Park Road/Powells Valley Road) south from Lykens about 3 miles to Lykens Road and turn right. Drive 4 miles and bear left onto White Oak Road. Continue 1.2 miles on this road to Minnich Hit on the left.

From Minnich Hit Picnic Area, Split Rock Trail is a .5-mile, yellow-blazed loop, and Minnich Hit Trail (a snowmobile trail) leads northwest 1 mile. From .9 mile south of Minnich Hit, Lukes Trail (a snowmobile trail) leads 3.3 miles east from White Oak Road to a State Game Land 210 parking lot on SR 4013. The unmarked Wolf Pond Trail leads 2.4 miles northwest from White Oak Road to a snowmobile trail in Deep Hollow.

For more information, contact Weiser State Forest, P.O. Box 99, Cressona, PA 17929-0099, (717) 385-7800, www.dcnr.state.pa.us/forestry/stateforests/weiser.aspx.

19
Susquehanna Trail

The Susquehanna Trail, a blue-blazed spur of the Appalachian Trail, leads to a good spring and the site of the former Susquehanna Shelter. The trail can be used in conjunction with the AT to form a strenuous and outstandingly scenic 4.1-mile loop hike. From the Clark's Ferry Bridge (US 22/322) on the east side of the Susquehanna River, about 15 miles north of Harrisburg, take the exit ramp to PA 147. Parking is found below the bridge's access ramps. Across the railroad tracks and at the bottom of a stone retaining wall, a trailhead bulletin board marks the route of the AT up the steep slope of Peters Mountain. At about .5 mile, after the AT briefly levels out, the Susquehanna Trail departs to the left (northeast). It leads close to the spring and former shelter site before ascending the steep, rocky side of the mountain to again intersect with the AT on top. Turn right and return down the mountain on the AT, passing several magnificent views over the Susquehanna River.

This side trail and the adjacent section of the AT are maintained by York Hiking Club. Susquehanna Trail is shown on the KTA map for the Appalachian Trail, sections 7 and 8. For further information, visit the York Hiking Club website at www.yorkhikingclub.com.

20
Wildwood Lake Sanctuary

Wildwood Lake Sanctuary is a 228-acre nature preserve operated by Dauphin County Parks and Recreation. It encompasses a variety of habitats, including wetland, forest, meadow, and stream. A network of trails features two ADA-accessible boardwalks, complete with benches, bird blinds, and spotting scopes. Benjamin Olewine III Nature Center is at the southern end of the park, with an interactive exhibit hall, classroom, and nature shop.

Formerly known as Wetzel's Swamp, this unique preserve has a large concentration of American lotus plants, a Pennsylvania endangered species, and an abundance of wildlife. The 3.1-mile Wildwood Way Trail begins at a picnic pavilion along Industrial Road at the north end of the sanctuary. The first mile is a level canal towpath covered with wood chips; the subsequent 2 miles are paved pathways following the rolling hills of the bluff. Side trails and boardwalks lead off the main path. Wildwood Way Trail can be reached from all three parking lots along Industrial Road or from the nature center parking lot.

The park is open from dawn to dusk. The nature center is open to the public Tuesday through Sunday, except holidays. Admission is free for both the center and the park. Wildwood Lake Sanctuary is on the north side of the Harrisburg metro area. From I-81, take Exit 66 and proceed north on Front Street. At the first traffic light, turn right on Linglestown Road (PA 39). At the next traffic light, turn right on Industrial Road and continue for a little more than 1 mile, then turn left on Wildwood Way at the sign for the nature center. The area is shown on the KTA map for the Appalachian Trail, sections 7 and 8. For more information, contact Wildwood Lake Sanctuary, 100 Wildwood Way, Harrisburg, PA 17110, (717) 221-0292, or visit Friends of Wildwood at www.wildwoodlake.org.

21
Darlington Trail
7.7 miles

The Darlington Trail, on top of Blue Mountain, extends from Tower Road in the east to a junction with the Appalachian Trail and Tuscarora Trail (see the Long-Distance Trails chapter) in the west. The trail is named for area missionary Bishop Darlington and was constructed in about 1908 by the long-defunct Pennsylvania Alpine Club, of which the bishop was secretary. In 1954, the Susquehanna Appalachian Trail Club took responsibility for the trail. The original AT was superimposed on the Darlington route until the 1940s, when operations at Fort Indiantown Gap Military Reservation made it necessary to relocate the AT. The two trails now meet 2.4 miles east of Sterretts Gap. The Darlington Trail is marked with orange blazes.

The eastern trailhead is found by following Tower Road south .8 miles from New Valley Road. Look for the Game Commission gate on the right. You can find additional access to the Darlington Trail at Millers Gap and Lambs Gap, via mountain roads leading from PA 944 to Game Commission parking areas on top of the mountain. The trail passes through both game land and private land. Camping and fires are not permitted.

For information on trail conditions, and a trail map, contact Susquehanna Appalachian Trail Club, P.O. Box 61001, Harrisburg, PA 17106, www.satc-hike.org.

22
Little Buffalo State Park

The scenic 830-acre Little Buffalo State Park in Perry County is reached via PA 34, 1 mile south of Newport, and then Little Buffalo Road westbound. The 88-acre Holman Lake and adjacent rolling hills are visible from this road. The park maintains 7 miles of hiking trails, including a 1.5-mile self-guided trail. Multiple

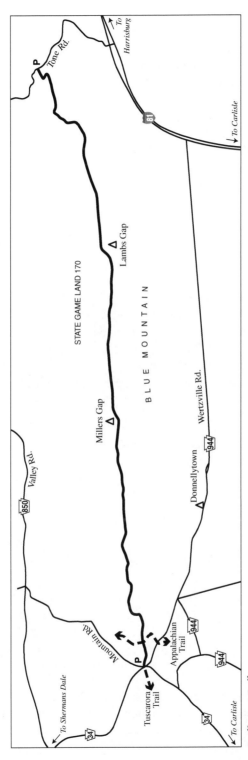

Darlington Trail

trails create a loop hike around the lake. On the north side of Little Buffalo Road, the red-blazed North Side Trail meanders up and down a roller coaster of small hills for a moderately strenuous hike. The park features Shoaff Grist Mill, built in the mid-1800s, Burr Arch covered bridge, the abandoned narrow-gauge bed of the Newport and Sherman's Valley Railroad, and Blue Ball Inn, a late-1700s tavern. For more information, contact Little Buffalo State Park, 1579 State Park Rd., Newport, PA 17074, (717) 567-9255, www.dcnr.state.pa.us/stateparks/parks/littlebuffalo.aspx.

23
Box Huckleberry Natural Area

Box Huckleberry Natural Area, an isolated 10-acre tract in Tuscarora State Forest near New Bloomfield and south of Little Buffalo State Park, features a rare colony of box huckleberry, a single plant estimated to be more than thirteen hundred years old. The "single plant" grows over a wide area, and an interpretive trail loops through the site. To reach the natural area, drive 1.5 miles southeast from New Bloomfield on PA 274/PA 34. Turn right at the interpretive trail sign at Huckleberry Road. Travel .5 mile to a small turnoff at the entrance sign. For a trail guide and map, contact Tuscarora State Forest, RR 1, Box 486, Blain, PA 17006, (717) 536-3191, www.dcnr.state.pa.us/forestry/stateforests/tuscarora.aspx.

24
Colonel Denning State Park

Colonel Denning State Park is on PA 233 in Doubling Gap, 8 miles north of Newville and 9 miles south of Landisburg. This small, 273-acre park is surrounded by Tuscarora State Forest. At Doubling Gap, Blue Mountain doubles back on itself, forming a deep reverse S shape. The park's location in the valley formed by the hairpin bend makes for scenic hiking, and it is a good starting point for the extensive trail system nearby. Many of the trails lead to the summit of Blue Mountain at the south end of its S-curve, where Flat Rock Overlook provides a tremendous view over Cumberland Valley—one of the premier vistas in all of Pennsylvania. On a clear day, South Mountain, which carries the Appalachian Trail, is visible dozens of miles to the south.

More than 18 miles of hiking trails are accessible from the state park, including a portion of the Tuscarora Trail (see the Long-Distance Trails chapter). Other trails can be combined with the Tuscarora Trail to form short or long loop hikes. One point of reference on Blue Mountain is Wagon Wheel Junction, where five trails intersect. At the turn of the century, a barrel stave mill operated somewhere nearby; the staves were carried down the mountain by horse and wagon on what is now the Tuscarora Trail.

Flat Rock Trail (2.5 miles): This red-blazed trail begins at the park's nature center and leads to the top of Blue Mountain at the Wagon Wheel. It then coincides with the blue-blazed Tuscarora Trail to Flat Rock Overlook.

Warner Trail (2.5 miles): This trail starts at the Wagon Wheel and follows the northern side of the ridge, overlooking the park. The trail then crosses over to the south side and meets the Tuscarora Trail.

Woodburn Trail (1.6 miles): This trail begins on PA 233, 1 mile south of the park office, near a large pull-off at an old shale bank. The trail ascends Blue Mountain rather steeply and terminates at the Tuscarora Trail near the Wagon Wheel.

Lehman Trail (.5 mile): This short connector trail was once a section of the Tuscarora Trail before that trail was rerouted to Flat Rock Overlook. From the Wagon Wheel junction, the Lehman Trail follows an old logging road across Wildcat Ridge and meets the present Tuscarora Trail at the head of Wildcat Hollow.

Cider Path Trail (1.2 miles): This trail begins on Old Doubling Gap Road, just east of the park boundary. It climbs steeply to the summit of Blue Mountain, then dips over the other side to meet the Warner Trail.

There are several other trails in the park and just to the east. All are shown on the park map and hiking brochure, which also displays surrounding areas of Tuscarora State Forest. The guide can be obtained from Colonel Denning State Park, 1599 Doubling Gap Rd., Newville, PA 17241, (717) 776-5272, www.dcnr .state.pa.us/stateparks/parks/coloneldenning.aspx.

25

Frank E. Masland Natural Area

The 1,270-acre Frank E. Masland Natural Area, in Tuscarora State Forest, is reached via Laurel Run Road, 9 miles west of its intersection with PA 233. That intersection is about 4 miles south of Landisburg. The natural area was designated primarily to protect a tract of old second-growth timber and contains the finest oak forest in the state. The trees are commonly 32 to 40 inches in diameter and more than 100 feet tall.

The area has several unmarked trails. From Laurel Run Road along the southern boundary of the natural area, Deer Hollow Trail and Turbett Trail proceed northeast to the North Branch of Laurel Run. They are joined there by a trail running along the stream. You may also enter the natural area from Phoenix Bridge Access Point, located at the Laurel Run Road crossing of the North Branch. Follow the North Branch into the natural area on unmarked and rarely used paths. The farther in you go, the larger the trees become, particularly the hemlocks and white oaks. The Boiler Trail, connecting Laurel Run Road with Blain-McCrea Road, starts near this access point and forms a portion of the southwestern boundary of the natural area. These trails are not blazed and do not receive much maintenance. They may be quite overgrown, especially in summer. For a map and information, contact Tuscarora State Forest, RR 1, Box 486, Blain, PA 17006, (717) 536-3191, www.dcnr.state.pa.us/forestry/stateforests/tuscarora.aspx.

26
Hemlocks Natural Area

Hemlocks Natural Area is located off Hemlock Road in Tuscarora State Forest and within Big Spring State Park, 10 miles west of Blain via PA 274. From the park, drive about 4 miles up unpaved Hemlock Road to a parking area, and watch for trailhead signs. No camping is allowed in the natural area. The 120-acre area preserves a virgin hemlock forest and was designated a national natural landmark in 1973. The magnificent original white pine and hemlock forests that once covered this region have nearly disappeared except for this stand in Hemlocks Natural Area.

Three miles of trails traverse the area, providing you with a glimpse of the giant hemlock forest as it appeared centuries ago. You can combine two trails to form a 1.4-mile loop hike. The red-blazed Hemlock Trail follows a rocky footpath through moss and ferns along Patterson Run, crossing the stream five times. The yellow-blazed Rim Trail is on the steep slope to the southeast of Patterson Run. Laurel Trail and Patterson Run Trail allow further exploration of the natural area. For a brochure describing the natural area, contact Tuscarora State Forest, RR 1, Box 486, Blain, PA 17006, (717) 536-3191, www.dcnr.state.pa.us/forestry/stateforests/tuscarora.aspx.

27
Big Spring State Park

Big Spring is a small state park along PA 274, 5.5 miles southwest of New Germantown in western Perry County. The park is named for a nearby spring, the waters of which form scenic Sherman's Creek. The park can also be used as a hub for many of the hiking trails in Tuscarora State Forest.

Tunnel Trail (1 mile): From PA 274, turn onto Hemlock Road just west of the main parking area for the state park. The trailhead is located at a display case.

This blue-blazed loop trail leads to the ruins of two narrow-gauge railroads, and to the site of a partially-completed railroad tunnel that was intended to carry the Path Valley Railroad through Conococheague Mountain.

Iron Horse Trail (9.9 miles): This red-blazed loop trail has two trailhead parking areas. One is located at the upper parking lot along Hemlock Road at Big Spring State Park. The other is located two miles southwest of New Germantown, and four miles east of Big Spring, on the south side of PA 274. Tuscarora State Forest headquarters is .8 mile east of this trailhead. The Iron Horse Trail has two sections. The section on the north side of PA 274 mostly follows the old Path Valley Railroad grade, and the section on the south side follows the remains of the Perry Lumber Company Railroad. The trail is relatively level, but does have some rocky footway on the old railroad beds. The north section follows Eby Ridge and the lower slopes of Conococheague Mountain. Portions of this section of the trail have suffered from low maintenance in the past. The south section meanders along Sherman's Creek, with repeated stream crossings on Youth Conservation Corps footbridges. For current conditions and a map of the trail, contact Tuscarora State Forest, as in the preceding entries, or visit www.dcnr .state.pa.us/stateparks/parks/bigspring.aspx.

28

Tuscarora State Forest

The 90,000-acre Tuscarora State Forest encompasses classic ridge-and-valley topography, with parallel ridges running southwest to northeast. The majority of the forest is located in western Perry County, with additional lands northwest of PA 35 along the Juniata–Perry County line and a smaller tract on Tuscarora Mountain near the Juniata River. The forest is managed under the multiple-use concept, with recreational activities becoming increasingly popular. Three state parks, four state forest picnic areas, three state forest natural areas, and one wild area are included in this forest district. The forest contains many short local hiking trails, most marked by signs at the starting and ending points. There are proposals to change the existing regulations to allow "foot travel only" on designated hiking trails, but at the time of this writing, most trails are multiuse.

Twenty-seven miles of the Tuscarora Trail (see the Long-Distance Trails chapter) traverse the ridges and valleys of the state forest, from Doubling Gap near Colonel Denning State Park in the eastern portion of the forest to Rising Knob Mountain ridge in the southwest. The Tuscarora can be combined with some of the short local trails or forest roads to form loop hikes. A state forest public-use map displaying the natural areas and trails is available. For more information, contact Tuscarora State Forest, RR 1, Box 486, Blain, PA 17006, (717) 536-3191, www.dcnr.state.pa.us/forestry/stateforests/tuscarora.aspx.

29
White Rocks Ridge Trail
1.3 miles

White Rocks Ridge and its namesake trail are on the north rim of South Mountain, 2 miles southeast of Boiling Springs. This blue-blazed spur of the Appalachian Trail follows the ridge northeasterly, winding through and over outcroppings of hard quartzite rock before descending to Kuhn Road. The trail is rough and rocky; use extra caution during inclement weather. There are fine views north across Cumberland Valley to Blue Mountain from the high points on the rocks. This trail meets the AT 100 yards south of the point where the AT starts descending Center Point Knob. You can create a loop hike by using the AT south from Boiling Springs, climbing up to Center Point Knob, then traversing the ridge on White Rocks Ridge Trail and descending to Kuhn Road. From there, a 2-mile road walk on Creek Road and Leidigh Drive returns you to the AT. Follow the AT north into Boiling Springs, where parking is available at the township historical park.

The White Rocks Ridge Trail and surrounding roads are shown on the Potomac Appalachian Trail Club map of the AT (map 1, Cumberland Valley). For more information, contact Cumberland Valley Appalachian Trail Club, P.O. Box 395, Boiling Springs, PA 17007, www.geocities.com/cvatclub.

30
Holly Gap Preserve

The 913-acre Holly Gap Preserve is located just south of Mount Holly Springs in Cumberland County. The nature preserve borders on 1,500-foot Mount Holly, one of the endless knobs that make up the South Mountain range, and Mount Holly Gap, through which Mountain Creek flows. South Mountain is one of the principal components of the Appalachian system of long, parallel ridges that stretch from Georgia to New Jersey, though South Mountain is unusual for its abrupt end in southern Pennsylvania.

The habitat at the preserve varies from a 200-acre wetland of open marsh and seepage swamp to upland forest on the mountain. The land was purchased by The Nature Conservancy in conjunction with grassroots land acquisition efforts of local citizens and politicians, to protect the endangered bog turtle and the globally rare purple flowered spurge. The trails are mostly old woods roads that are marked with rectangular blazes and painted can lids of various colors. In addition, green, diamond-shaped Nature Conservancy markers help guide visitors.

Marsh Trail (1.5 miles): From the parking lot, this violet-blazed loop trail follows a wide road along Mountain Creek and then along the marsh wetlands. After 1 mile, a half-mile loop climbs to meet the Ridge Trail and then returns.

Creek Trail (1.6 miles): This red-blazed loop trail branches off the Marsh Trail and follows Mountain Creek south for about half a mile, before turning away from the creek upslope and returning.

Ridge Trail (2.3 miles): This yellow-blazed loop trail branches off the Marsh Trail to ascend Mount Holly through an upland forest environment. The trail loops around the crest of the mountain with a lookout point on the southeast side.

Lamberton Trail (.8 mile): This trail starts near the parking area just past the point where Ridge Road bears right to ascend Mount Holly. (The road continuing ahead is private). The trail, marked with white dots, ascends the southeastern flank of the mountain rather steeply using a number of switchbacks. After a 500-foot climb, the trail joins the Ridge Trail at a vista. There is an optional .4-mile loop near the top.

To reach Holly Gap Preserve, use I-81 south of Carlisle. Take Exit 47 (PA 34), and go south about 6 miles through Mount Holly Springs. Just beyond Deer Lodge on the right, turn right onto the driveway at Mount Holly Marsh Preserve, marked by a sign. Follow the dirt road .1 mile to the parking lot on the left. For further information, contact The Nature Conservancy, 2101 N. Front St., Harrisburg, PA 17110, (717) 232-6001; or Susquehanna Appalachian Trail Club, P.O. Box 61001, Harrisburg, PA 17106, www.satc-hike.org.

31

Kings Gap Environmental Education and Training Center

Sitting astride South Mountain, Kings Gap offers a stunning panoramic view of Cumberland Valley. The Kings Gap Environment Education and Training Center, housed in a stately mansion, offers a variety of educational programs from preschool natural awareness to environmental problem solving. Sixteen miles of hiking trails interconnect three main areas and are open year-round. Trailheads are located at the three day-use areas.

Boundary Trail (1.5 miles): This easy to moderate trail skirts the western boundary of Kings Gap through an oak and pitch pine forest with an understory of blueberries and huckleberries.

Forest Heritage Trail (1.6 miles): This easy to moderate loop trail connects several prominent charcoal hearths. Although the hearths have been inactive for more than 100 years, most remain fairly free of vegetation because of soil damage.

Kings Gap Hollow Trail (1.7 miles): This is an easy and inviting trail lined with a lush understory of ferns, winding along Kings Gap Hollow Run and following the gap in the mountain. The terrain changes noticeably as you approach the mountaintop.

Locust Point Trail (1 mile): This easy to moderate side loop of the Boundary Trail travels through a ridgetop forest of chestnut oak and pitch pine. A clearing created by fallen locust trees offers a view of Cumberland Valley and Kings Gap Hollow.

Maple Hollow Trail (1.3 miles): This easy to moderate trail travels through a maple hollow with plentiful water, then loops back to the parking lot through the drier, less fertile forest of chestnut oak that covers much of Kings Gap.

Pine Plantation Trail (.6 mile): A short, easy loop that highlights the management techniques used in thinning the 42-acre plantation.

Ridge Overlook Trail (.8 mile): A moderate to difficult ridgetop trail for the hiker looking for a challenge, with boulder outcrops and a view of the valley below.

Rock Scree Trail (1.9 miles): Beginning in the pine plantation, this easy to moderate trail leads past the ridge where stone cutters quarried the rock used to construct the mansion. The trail continues up the mountain to the mansion and a magnificent view of the valley.

Scenic Vista Trail (2.5 miles): As the name suggests, this easy to moderate trail offers an inspiring view. Benches are strategically placed for relaxation and enjoyment.

Watershed Trail (1.8 miles): This easy to moderate loop encompasses the headwaters of Kings Gap Hollow Run. You will see the circular colonies of Allegheny mound-building ants.

Whispering Pines Trail (.3 mile): This paved trail loops through the interior of the pine plantation, with signs in both Braille and script describing the coniferous forest.

White Oaks Trail (.3 mile): This paved loop uses signs in both Braille and type to describe the deciduous forest.

Woodland Ecology Trail (.6 mile): Informational signs on this easy trail help you identify forest plants and interpret the ecology of the chestnut oak forest.

The center's entrance is on Pine Road, 1 mile east of the Huntsdale Fish Hatchery. From I-81, take Exit 37 for PA 233. Follow PA 233 south for about 2.5 miles. Turn left onto Pine Road and continue 2.5 miles. The entrance to the center is on the right, and the mansion is at the end of the road on top of the mountain. For more information, contact Kings Gap State Park, 500 Kings Gap Rd., Carlisle, PA 17015, (717) 486-5031, www.dcnr.state.pa.us/stateparks/parks/kings gap.aspx.

32
Michaux State Forest

Michaux State Forest, with more than 85,000 acres, is located in portions of Adams, Cumberland, and Franklin Counties. It extends in an arc from just southwest of Mount Holly Springs almost to the Maryland state line near Rouzerville and Blue Ridge Summit. The forest encompasses the broad South Mountain range, characterized by rounded, relatively gentle knobs, with maximum elevations near 2,000 feet. The northern terminus for this chain of mountains is near White Rocks Ridge, south of Boiling Springs. The chain stretches south and continues into Maryland. South Mountain is the northern end of one of the predominant ridge systems in the Appalachian Mountains, paralleling the other ridge systems all the way to Georgia, though South Mountain is unusual for its abrupt end in southern Pennsylvania.

The state forest features many miles of gated trails and old woods roads for hiking. Numerous highways and an extensive system of forest roads make the entire area readily accessible to the public. About 36 miles of the Appalachian Trail (see the Long-Distance Trails chapter) pass through Michaux State Forest. Blue-blazed side trails off the AT lead to points of interest or road access points. Some of these side trails may be used in conjunction with the AT to form loop hikes. Within the state forest are three state parks—Caledonia, Mont Alto, and Pine Grove Furnace—and Kings Gap Environmental Education and Training Center. These parks feature their own trail systems, which lead to more trails on adjacent state forest lands.

Buck Ridge Trail (6.1 miles): This orange-blazed trail connects Kings Gap Environmental Education and Training Center with Pine Grove Furnace State Park. The Kings Gap trailhead is at the mansion parking lot on top of the mountain. The Pine Grove Furnace trailhead is across the road from the park office, just north on PA 233 on the right side of the road.

For a copy of the public-use map and information on hiking opportunities, contact Michaux State Forest, 10099 Lincoln Way East, Fayetteville, PA 17222, (717) 352-2211, www.dcnr.state.pa.us/forestry/stateforests/michaux.aspx. Three excellent maps by Potomac Appalachian Trail Club cover the entire state forest. Maps 2 and 3 (the AT from PA 94 to Caledonia State Park) and Map 4 (the AT from US 30 to the state line) show many adjacent hiking trails and roads in a multicolored, topographical format. PATC also publishes Jean Golightly's *Circuit Hikes in Virginia, West Virginia, Maryland, and Pennsylvania* (2004), which covers Michaux State Forest. You can order the maps and book from Potomac Appalachian Trail Club, 118 Park St. SE, Vienna, VA 22180, (703) 242-0693 or (703) 242-0965 for the activities tape, or visit patc.net.

33

Pine Grove Furnace State Park

This park was inspired by an iron furnace that manufactured cast-iron products for more than 120 years, starting in 1764. Pine Grove was then a prosperous iron company town. When cold-blast furnaces became obsolete, the company built recreational facilities. In 1913, the state purchased the land now occupied by the state park, and in 1977, the furnace was listed on the National Register of Historic Places. Pine Grove is situated in a beautiful setting along Mountain Creek in southern Cumberland County, between the convoluted ridge of South Mountain and the narrower ridge of Piney Mountain.

Hiking trails abound in the park and the adjoining sections of Michaux State Forest. Within the park are a few short loop trails and a designated hiker-biker trail. The park boasts the halfway point of the 2,174-mile Appalachian Trail (see the Long-Distance Trails chapter), which slices through the middle of the park past the iron furnace. Side trails of the AT lead to outstanding geologic features and grand views.

Creek Trail (.5 mile): This trail begins at the amphitheater and winds past vernal ponds and a stand of white pine along Mountain Creek, near the camping area.

Koppenhaver Trail (1 mile): This scenic, yellow-blazed loop trail begins at the far end of Fuller ball field. The footpath crosses Tom's Run and passes through stands of mature pines and hemlocks.

Mountain Creek Trail (1.4 miles): This trail links Fuller Lake (via the bicycle trail) and Laurel Lake (via Icehouse Road). It offers a pleasant walk to Laurel Lake Day Use Area, along scenic Mountain Creek and through forests and wetlands. You may see deer, herons, waterfowl, and beavers.

Pole Steeple Trail (.8 mile): This rugged and rocky blue-blazed trail starts on the south side of Laurel Lake at a parking area on Railroad Bed Road, .5 mile west of the intersection with Hunters Run Road. The trail enters state forest land and climbs very steeply toward the Pole Steeple outcropping of quartzite rock. There is an outstanding view of Mountain Creek Valley and the surrounding highlands of South Mountain. The trail traverses a treacherous area of loose scree rock just under the vista; use extra caution here. You can create loop hikes of varying lengths using this trail, the AT, Railroad Bed Road, and nearby dirt roads.

Swamp Trail (.3 mile): This trail begins and ends at the bicycle path and explores a small, forested swamp filled with interesting plants and animals.

To reach the state park from I-81, take Exit 37 to PA 233, and head south for 8 miles. For further information, contact Pine Grove Furnace State Park, 1100 Pine Grove Rd., Gardners, PA 17324, (717) 486-7174, www.dcnr.state.pa.us/stateparks/parks/pinegrovefurnace.aspx.

Dead Woman Hollow
and Michener Area Trails

Dead Woman Hollow and the Michener area are in Michaux State Forest, a few miles southwest of Pine Grove Furnace State Park. There are a number of roads and blazed trails in the area that you can use to form loop hikes. The Appalachian Trail parallels Ridge Road to the northwest.

Dead Woman Hollow Road is a gated snowmobile trail leading 2 miles down the mountain through the hollow to PA 233. Blue-blazed Dead Woman Hollow Trail is on your left, .6 mile down this road from the parking area. The trail goes .8 mile to Michener Cabin, operated by Potomac Appalachian Trail Club. Two other blue-blazed trails begin at the cabin. One goes north for .3 mile to the AT. Turning left (south) on the AT returns you to the parking area after .8 mile. The other blue-blazed trail, the 1.6-mile Blueberry Trail, leads east from the cabin. It crosses a small stream, ascends briefly to a lookout, and then descends steeply to Dead Woman Hollow. It terminates at the junction of Tumbling Run and a tributary of Mountain Creek. The Blueberry Trail is also accessible from PA 233, using a road pull-off at the Cumberland–Adams County line, 3.8 miles south of the intersection with Hunters Run Road at Pine Grove Furnace State Park. From the pull-off, take an old dirt road downhill to the stream junction, where the blue blazes begin. The bridge washed out years ago, so you will have to ford the stream.

This area is shown on the PATC maps for the Appalachian Trail (Maps 2 and 3). Tumbling Run Game Preserve, adjacent to this area to the east, is off-limits to hikers without permission, except for a short stretch of the AT in its northwest corner. From Pine Grove Furnace State Park, take PA 233 south for 6 miles; then turn west on Arendtsville-Shippensburg Road. Follow this road for about 2.5 miles, climbing to the top of Big Flat Ridge. Turn right (north) on Ridge Road shortly after the AT crossing. Follow Ridge Road for 1.2 miles to a parking area on the right, near Dead Woman Hollow Road. For more information, contact Potomac Appalachian Trail Club, 118 Park St. SE, Vienna, VA 22180, (703) 242-0693 or (703) 242-0965 for the activities tape, or visit patc.net.

Rocky Knob Trail
4.2 miles

Rocky Knob Trail, a pleasant loop trail in Michaux State Forest, is about 5 miles north of Caledonia State Park. The orange-blazed Rocky Knob Trail was constructed in 1976 by the Youth Conservation Corps. The trail follows a gentle path up to Sier Hill, where there are several good views to the southeast toward East Big Flat Ridge and also to the south toward Long Pine Reservoir. The trail descends Rocky Knob to an old roadbed started by the Civilian Conservation Corps in 1937; the railroad was never completed because of the rugged local geology. The trail follows this grade, paralleling Knob Run to end the loop.

From the intersection of US 30 and PA 233 at Caledonia State Park, take PA 233 north 1.6 miles to gravel Milesburn Road on the left. Follow Milesburn Road for 2.9 miles, bearing right at a fork in the road and continuing another 1.3 miles to Ridge Road. Turn right and drive 1.6 miles to a signed trailhead pull-off on the right. The area is shown on the PATC maps for the Appalachian Trail (Maps 2 and 3). A free pamphlet with map and guide is available from Michaux State Forest, 10099 Lincoln Way East, Fayetteville, PA 17222, (717) 352-2211, www.dcnr.state.pa.us/forestry/stateforests/michaux.aspx.

36
Caledonia State Park

The 1,125-acre Caledonia State Park, like Pine Grove Furnace State Park nearby, highlights a historic charcoal iron furnace, built in 1837 by the famed abolitionist and statesman Thaddeus Stevens. During the Civil War, the Confederates destroyed the furnace because of Stevens's antislavery views. In 1927, the Pennsylvania Alpine Club reconstructed the old furnace at a reduced scale. Caledonia is the second-oldest state park in Pennsylvania, and with its many recreational attractions, it is one of the most popular. A short section of the Appalachian Trail traverses the park, and you can enjoy more than 10 additional miles of hiking, historic, and nature trails. Park trails are yellow-blazed, except for the white-blazed AT and a couple of the AT's blue-blazed side trails. The park is also a hub for many trails in adjacent tracts of Michaux State Forest. For a beautiful figure-eight hike through varied terrain and many rhododendron, use the Ramble, Three Valley, Hosack Run, Locust Gap, and Appalachian Trails.

Charcoal Hearth Trail (2.7 miles): This trail, when combined with the Thaddeus Stevens Historic Trail, forms a 3-mile loop that ascends Piney Mountain and visits five different charcoal hearth sites. The trail climbs Graefenburg Hill, then descends the narrow ridge to the historic trail at the iron furnace replica.

Hosack Run Trail (1.2 miles): This blue-blazed trail leads through rhododendron in Dark Hollow. Its southern end meets the Locust Gap Trail .8 mile northwest of that trail's intersection with the Appalachian Trail. Beyond the hollow, the trail climbs steeply on switchbacks to meet the AT .7 mile north of the Quarry Gap Shelters.

Locust Gap Trail (3.8 miles): This blue-blazed trail is a gated woods road, also known as Locust Gap Road or Greenwood Furnace Road. It extends from

PA 997 in the west to Milesburg Road at Long Pine Run Reservoir in the east.

Three Valley Trail (.7 mile): This short blue-blazed trail ascends Ore Bank Hill through the state park, from the Ramble Trail to the AT.

Ramble Trail (2.2 miles): This yellow-blazed loop trail passes through scenic lowlands on both sides of Conococheague Creek.

Caledonia State Park is on South Mountain, along US 30 and PA 233 in Adams and Franklin Counties, 10 miles east of Chambersburg and 13 miles west of Gettysburg. It is also 12 miles southwest of Pine Grove Furnace State Park. Trail guides and maps are available at the park office. For further information, contact Caledonia State Park, 101 Pine Grove Rd., Fayetteville, PA 17222, (717) 352-2161, www.dcnr.state.pa.us/stateparks/parks/caledonia.aspx.

37
Chimney Rocks and Hermitage Cabin Area

The Chimney Rocks and Hermitage Cabin Area is located in the southern portion of Michaux State Forest east of Waynesboro and is accessed from Old Forge Road (Antietam Road on some maps). Park at the Old Forge Picnic Area on Old Forge Road approximately 5 miles north of its intersection with PA 16 (just west of Rouzerville). If the picnic area is closed, continue another .1 mile and turn right onto Rattlesnake Run Road to a small parking area to the left of the Appalachian Trail crossing. For more direct access to Hermitage Cabin, operated by Potomac Appalachian Trail Club, take Swift Run Road north from Old Forge Road, going about 1 mile to the point where the road turns sharply to the left. A blue-blazed access trail on the right leads to Shaffer Rocks (also called Monument Rocks) and the cabin.

You can use the Appalachian Trail, which runs east and north of Hermitage Cabin, and a couple of blue-blazed side trails to create loop hikes of varying lengths. A side trail leads east from the AT to the top of Buzzard Peak and Chimney Rocks. In addition to the cabin, two AT shelter sites are nearby: Tumbling Run, 1.2 miles south of the side trail to Chimney Rocks, and Antietam, .1 mile south of the Old Forge Picnic Area. This area is shown on the PATC map of the Appalachian Trail (Map 4). For more information, contact Potomac Appalachian Trail Club, 118 Park St. SE, Vienna, VA 22180, (703) 242-0693 or (703) 242-0965 for the activities tape, or visit patc.net.

38
Cowans Gap State Park

The 1,085-acre Cowans Gap State Park, located in a beautiful valley between the parallel ridges of Tuscarora and Cove Mountains, is surrounded by the large Allens Valley Area tract of Buchanan State Forest. The valley elevation at Cowans Gap Lake (1,217 feet) is considerably higher than that of Path Valley, just east of Tuscarora Mountain. Cowans Gap has 10 miles of hiking trails, with many more trails in the adjacent state forest. Some trails have steep terrain, especially sections of Cameron, Horseshoe, and Three Mile Trails, and are not for beginners. A 2.3-mile section of the Tuscarora Trail passes through the park, and the southern end of the Standing Stone Trail is just outside the park boundaries (see the Long-Distance Trails chapter). You can combine the Tuscarora Trail with other park trails to form a strenuous loop hike around the park, climbing and descending Tuscarora and Cove Mountains.

The park is located in northwestern Fulton County, between McConnellsburg and Fort Loudon. From the PA Turnpike, use Exit 180 (Fort Littleton), and then take US 522 north to Burnt Cabins, where signs lead to the park. From US 30, take PA 75 north from Fort Loudon to Richmond Furnace; then turn left on Richmond Road to the park. Information on trails and a park map are available from Cowans Gap State Park, 6235 Aughwick Rd., Fort Loudon, PA 17224, (717) 485-3948, www.dcnr.state.pa.us/stateparks/parks/cowansgap.aspx. For a map of trails in the nearby state forest tracts, contact Buchanan State Forest, 440 Buchanan Trail, McConnellsburg, PA 17233, (717) 485-3148, www.dcnr.state.pa.us/forestry/stateforests/buchanan.aspx.

REGION 3

Seven Mountains

Region Editor: Tom Thwaites

The Seven Mountains Region is dominated by the roughly parallel and arcing ridges that make up the northern and western portion of Pennsylvania's Ridge and Valley Province. The region is bounded on the south by the Maryland border; on the east by US 522 to Selinsgrove then US 15 to Williamsport; on the north by US 220 and I-80 to Milesburg; and on the west by old US 220 and I-99 to Maryland.

Just like the Blue Mountain region, the Seven Mountains Region consists of long, narrow valleys between steep, rocky ridges that are dozens or even hundreds of miles long and are only occasionally breached by rivers. The predominant ridges of the region include Evitts, Tussey, Sideling, Lock, Terrace, Jacks, Canoe, Bald Eagle, Nittany, and Brush Mountains. The ridges charge northbound out of Maryland in a roughly parallel pattern, with several becoming jumbled in the aptly named Seven Mountains area between State College and Lewistown. The ridges then untangle themselves and continue their journey on a more northeasterly track toward New Jersey. These steep ridges make up the western vanguard of the Appalachian range, before the landscape rises up the Allegheny Front escarpment and stays at a high elevation, forming the plateaus of the Laurel Highlands, Pennsylvania Wilds, and Endless Mountains Regions.

The Seven Mountains Region is well stocked with public lands, including four state forests, sixteen state parks, twenty-six state game lands, and Stone Valley and Raystown Lake Recreation Areas. There are four state forest wild areas and thirteen state forest natural areas, with Hook Natural Area in Centre County being the largest in the state. Areas of hiking interest are concentrated in Martins

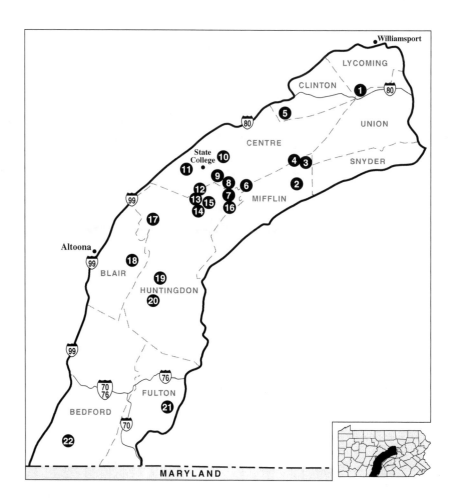

Hill Wild Area and Sweet Root Natural Area in the southern part of the region, the Raystown Lake–Terrace Mountain area, and the very large collection of public lands in Rothrock, Bald Eagle, and Tiadaghton State Forests in the northern part of the region.

Most of the hiking opportunities in the Seven Mountains Region involve the Mid State Trail System and its many side and spur trails. For a map and guidebook, contact Mid State Trail Association, P.O. Box 167, Boalsburg, PA 16827, www.hike-mst.org. Also use this contact information for any of the hikes in this chapter in which the MST or MSTA maps are mentioned. A few short hikes involving portions of this network are described in this chapter, but for complete information on the MST's hiking opportunities, guidebook, and map series, see the Long-Distance Trails chapter.

Also see that chapter for information on the region's other primary footpath, the Standing Stone Trail (formerly known as the Link Trail), which leads south from Greenwood Furnace State Park into the Blue Mountain Region. The Mid State Trail and the Standing Stone Trail are connected by the Greenwood Spur, which is described in this chapter.

Between Hook Natural Area in Centre County and Ravensburg State Park in Clinton County, hikers are advised to treat red-blazed trails with caution. These trails are part of the 118-mile Central Mountains Multi-Use Trail System (CMMUT), which has been built primarily for mountain bikers and horseback riders. This trail network can still be used by hikers, though some may not enjoy the encounters with bikes and horses. These multiuse trails are also poorly blazed and laid out, and they have disrupted the routes of existing hiking trails, particularly near Ravensburg State Park, causing confusion for hikers. Similar multiuse pressures have also affected the 30-mile Terrace Mountain Trail.

Regardless, some of Pennsylvania's most challenging and rewarding hikes are found in the Seven Mountains Region, with a preponderance of stunning vistas, rugged climbs, and rocky ridgetops. Because the ridges are so steep and rocky, developments have been largely confined to the narrow valleys. Though there are signs of past resource extraction and logging, the ridgetops offer hiking opportunities with a surprising amount of seclusion and solitude, not to mention great scenery and wildlife.

1
Merrill Linn Trail
1 mile

The Merrill Linn Trail is a side trail of the Mid State Trail System, found just north of the boundary between Bald Eagle and Tiadaghton State Forests and in the backcountry east of Ravensburg State Park. The trail is shown on MSTA Map 207. This blue-blazed circuit uses an old logging railroad grade plus new footpaths to circle several small ponds that are believed to be pingo scars, formed by giant frost heaves and melting ice during periods of glaciation. There is no direct road access to the Merrill Linn Trail; the best access is to use the MST a short distance to the southeast of the intersection of Mohn Mill and Pipeline Roads. From PA 880 just north of the I-80 underpass, take Mohn Mill Road east for about 5 miles.

2

Reeds Gap Spur

13.8 miles

Reeds Gap Spur is a major side trail in the Mid State Trail System. It connects Reeds Gap State Park with the Mid State Trail at Poe Paddy State Park, via Bear Gap Picnic Area. The Reeds Gap Spur uses existing trails on an as-is basis, meaning they have not been constructed to meet the standards of the main Mid State Trail. The route of the Reeds Gap Spur has been marked with blue blazes, but for the most part it has not been cleared, definitely making this a long pants and heavy boots trail. The Reeds Gap Spur is shown on MSTA Map 212 and is described in Section D of the Mid State Trail guide.

The High Top Trail, a portion of the Reeds Gap Spur on Thick Mountain, has been damaged by ice and snowstorms and is best avoided by using nearby Knob Ridge Road. The northern trailhead for the Reeds Gap Spur is at Poe Paddy State Park (see the John L. Snyder Trail entry for directions). The southern trailhead is at Reeds Gap State Park. From the Milroy exit of US 322, follow the signs to the state park, using a series of paved roads for a total of 7 miles. For more information, contact Reeds Gap State Park, 1405 New Lancaster Valley Rd., Milroy, PA 17063, (717) 667-3622, www.dcnr.state.pa.us/stateparks/parks/reedsgap.aspx.

3

White Mountain Ridge Trail

Probably the most isolated and remote trail in Bald Eagle State Forest, White Mountain Ridge Trail traverses the entire length of White Mountain Wild Area from Wesley Forest to the Long Path Trail, which is part of the Reeds Gap Spur. There is a trail sign at this junction. For many years, this trail was lost to gypsy moths and could not be followed, though it has since been reopened and blue-blazed as an Eagle Scout project involving three different troops. It is not maintained, however, and remains a challenge to follow. White Mountain Ridge Trail is shown in part on MSTA Maps 205, 206, and 212. White Mountain Ridge Trail can only be reached by following Reeds Gap Spur Trail south about two miles from Poe Paddy State Park. See the John L. Snyder Trail entry below for directions.

John L. Snyder Trail

.6 mile

This unblazed trail on private land follows Penns Creek from Poe Paddy State Park to Penns Creek Path (the old Penn Central Railroad grade). The John L. Snyder Trail provides a pleasant alternative to the Mid State Trail, which is on a forestry road in this area. One end is at the Penns Creek access in Poe Paddy, where there is a trail sign. Follow the obvious footway along the edge of Penns Creek, and climb a metal staircase to reach the railroad grade at the end of the bridge over the creek. The MST follows this sturdy bridge and then enters a tunnel through the next mountain. To reach Poe Paddy State Park, use US 322 between State College and Lewistown. About 1.5 miles south of Potters Mills, turn onto unpaved Sand Mountain Road, where there are signs pointing to Poe Valley and Poe Paddy State Parks. Follow the road for 13 miles to Poe Paddy, passing Poe Valley along the way. For more information, contact Poe Paddy State Park, c/o Reeds Gap, Milroy, PA 17063, (717) 667-3622, www.dcnr.state.pa .us/stateparks/parks/poepaddyalt.aspx.

Broad Mountain West Loop

3 miles

The blue-blazed Broad Mountain West Loop is just east of Penn-Roosevelt State Park in Rothrock State Forest and uses a portion of the Mid State Trail. The loop trail leaves the MST east of Penn-Roosevelt and proceeds up Sassafras Run on a rocky footway. It turns right on Tar Pit Trail and climbs steeply up Broad Mountain to a junction with the MST at TriCounty Point, where Centre, Huntington, and Mifflin Counties meet. The loop hike then turns right and returns to Penn-Roosevelt on the MST. This trail will be shown on the new 300 Series map for the Mid State Trail, covering the section from US 22 to Penns Creek. Reach Penn-Roosevelt via US 322 east of State College. South of Potters Mills, use either Crowfield Road or Stone Creek Road, which begins just below the runaway truck ramp. You cannot access Stone Creek Road from the westbound lanes on US 322. For more information, contact Penn-Roosevelt State Park, c/o Greenwood Furnace, Huntingdon, PA 16652, (814) 667-1800, www.dcnr.state.pa.us/stateparks/parks/pennroosevelt.aspx.

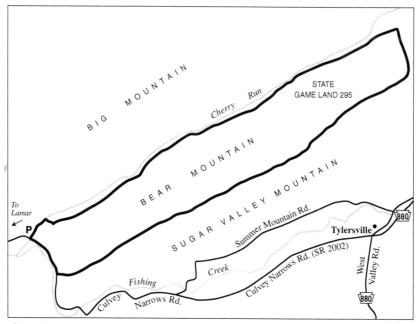

Cherry Run

6

Cherry Run
(State Game Land 295)

10 miles

Cherry Run is a 12,000-acre tract of heavily wooded mountains south of Lamar. The area came into public ownership thanks to the Western Pennsylvania Conservancy, which purchased all the shares of the lumber company that owned the land. The tract is divided by a paved road along Fishing Creek. You can reach the western portion either from the north on an old railroad grade along Fishing Creek or from PA 445. The eastern portion is larger and offers a 10-mile circuit hike, including some road walking, which is described in *50 Hikes in Central Pennsylvania* (2001), by Tom Thwaites. Cherry Run Valley has an abundance of evergreens that make the area particularly attractive in the winter for cross-country skiing. State Game Land 295 is shown on the Bald Eagle State Forest public-use map. To access the eastern tract from I-80, take Exit 173 and follow PA 64 south to just beyond Lamar. At a township park, turn left onto Washington Avenue, which later becomes Narrows Road. Proceed for 3.7 miles to the first of several sportsmen's parking lots.

7

Alan Seeger Natural Area
1.2 miles

At the junction of paved Stone Creek Road and unpaved Seeger Road in Rothrock State Forest is the small Alan Seeger Natural Area, named after an American poet killed in World War I. A short loop trail takes you through this beautiful area, past some of the oldest trees in the state. It is remarkable that these trees survived repeated threats from forest fires, charcoal production for nearby Greenwood Iron Furnace, a water-powered sawmill, and a logging railroad. A rhododendron jungle blooms in early July, and the towering trees are an incredible sight at any time of the year. The Greenwood Spur (see separate entry below) uses a portion of the loop trail through Alan Seeger. Reach the natural area via the narrow but paved Stone Creek Road, about halfway between US 322 and PA 26. For more information, visit www.dcnr.state.pa.us/forestry/old growth/alanseeger.aspx.

8

Bear Meadows Natural Area

The unique Bear Meadows Natural Area is a national natural landmark high in the hills behind Tussey Mountain Ski Area outside of State College. This unusually high and flat valley is a natural gathering place for water, but it is almost entirely surrounded by ridges, offering the water little chance to escape. The result is a bog and swamp ecosystem that is quite uncommon for this region of the United States, with plenty of unique wildlife present, especially bears and migratory birds.

Jean Aron Path (.5 mile): This blue-blazed trail runs from North Meadows Road just east of the Lonberger Path to Bear Meadows Road near the bridge over Sinking Creek, passing through an abandoned picnic area and some wild spruce along the edge of the bog.

John Wert Path (3.5 miles): This blue-blazed trail parallels Sinking Creek from Bear Meadows Road to Thickhead Mountain Road and incorporates the old Sinking Creek Trail. John Wert Path forms the boundary of Thickhead Mountain Wild Area and is particularly enjoyable in July when the rhododendron are in bloom.

Bear Meadows Loop (3 miles): This mostly blue-blazed route encircles Bear Meadows Natural Area. From the parking lot on Bear Meadows Road at the natural area monument, cross the bridge over Sinking Creek and turn right onto the trail. Soon you pass a side trail on the right that leads to an observation deck. Following the loop trail, you pass a signed junction with Gettis Trail. Continue through an unsigned junction where the Bear Meadows Trail turns left near Sand Spring. Emerge into a clearing and turn sharply right at a poorly marked turn. You will soon see that you are on an old road. Follow it along the edge of the bog to a junction with North Meadows Road, where you turn right. After a short distance on the road, turn right on Jean Aron Path to complete the loop.

Reach Bear Meadows Natural Area via Bear Meadows Road, about halfway between Tussey Mountain Ski Area and Stone Creek Road. This road starts at US 322 east of Boalsburg, one intersection east of the beginning of the bypass around State College. The trails are shown on MSTA Map 203. For more information on Bear Meadows Natural Area, visit www.dcnr.state.pa.us/FORESTRY/ oldgrowth/bearmeadows.aspx.

9

Shingletown Gap

Several new trails have been cut and blue-blazed in Rothrock State Forest between Galbraith and Shingletown Gaps, just southwest of Boalsburg in Centre County. Shingletown Gap is a linear notch in Tussey Mountain that has been protected by the water authorities in the State College region. The area is outstandingly tranquil and scenic, with babbling brooks and rock formations on the steep hillsides. The hiking trails are shown in an inset on the most recent edition of MSTA Map 201. Three of the trails—Deer Path, Tower Trail, and 1-2 Link— provide access to the Mid State Trail from Shingletown Gap. Laurel Run Road provides access from Galbraith Gap. This area is very popular with day hikers in the State College area, and parking is at a premium. Prepare to meet many other hikers, especially on weekends.

To reach Shingletown Gap and its hiking trails, from PA 45 in Shingletown, between Boalsburg and Pine Grove Mills, turn onto Mountain Road and proceed to a parking lot at a small water treatment facility.

10

Mount Nittany

There are two marked trails on Mount Nittany in Centre County. One of these is above Lemont and is the most heavily used trail in the Centre region. The other is east of Centre Hall and Pleasant Gap and is rarely used.

White Trail: This tourist-oriented trail was built by Penn State Outing Club in 1978 and named for Harold White, the club's faculty advisor since 1954. To reach the trailhead, travel to the village of Lemont outside of State College, and drive up Mount Nittany Road, bearing left near the top. Park your car as best you can where the road becomes a private driveway. Follow the strenuous white-blazed trail up the side of the mountain; do not use the old unblazed trail that cuts off the switchback. The White Trail was invaded by motorized devices in the early 1970s, starting an erosion process that continues today. At the top, the White Trail joins a system of circuit trails around the end of Nittany Mountain. To the right is the famed overlook of State College and Penn State University. A return route circles to the south edge of the mountain above Oak Hall, with another vista toward Boalsburg (avoid a posted tract of private land), and then returns along the northern edge. The entire circuit is about 1.8 miles. Do not use any of the old unblazed trails descending the end of the mountain above Lemont, because they lead either to posted land or to a shale pit where seedlings have been planted. A hike on Mount Nittany is described in *The Short Hiker* (1999), by Jean Aron. A map of the trails is sometimes available at the parking area.

James Cleveland Trail: This trail was built by Boy Scout troops from Centre Hall and Pleasant Gap. The south end is on PA 192 about 2 miles east of the junction with PA 144 in Centre Hall and is marked with a large sign. On the south side of the ridge, the trail is marked with occasional arrows fixed to trees. Nevertheless, it is easy to follow, particularly beyond the state forest boundary. Near the top is a view over Penns Valley. Just beyond this vista is the site where James Cleveland crashed his mail plane into the mountain in 1932. From here on, the trail is blazed with irregular white paint marks and is more difficult to follow. It leads down the first ridge of Nittany Mountain, crosses Little Fishing Creek, and ends at Greens Valley Road. You can reach this road from PA 144 at the top of Centre Hall Mountain.

11

The Barrens

The Barrens are a region of low shale ridges just southwest of State College. About 5,000 acres of the Barrens lie within the boundaries of State Game Land 176 and contain the ghost towns of Towhill and Scotia, as well as old iron ore pits and railroad grades. This wooded area with gently rolling hills is a climatic anomaly, with killing frosts every month of the year. It probably becomes the coldest spot in the country more frequently than even Havre, Montana, or International Falls, Minnesota. How this area can have a frigid, desertlike climate, with temperatures dramatically different than those in developed areas less than a mile away, is a mystery that is only partially understood.

The Barrens are primarily of interest to cross-country skiers because of the modest grades and excellent snow-holding qualities. The area has a total of 7

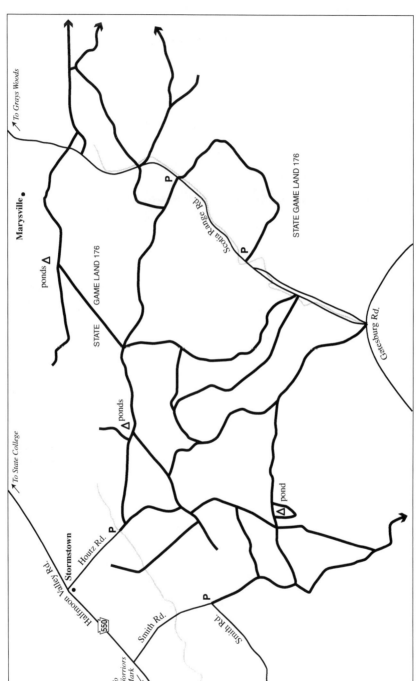

The Barrens. Please note that most trails in this area are unnamed.

miles of trails. Penn State Outing Club has identified at least twice this amount, but as of this writing, none of these trails are marked. Several hikes in the Barrens are described in *The Short Hiker* (1999), by Jean Aron.

You can reach the Barrens via Scotia Road from US 322 or Tadpole Road from Fairbrook. In winter, the area is most easily reached from Greenbriar Road near Circleville.

12
Jackson Trail
2.8 miles

The scenic Jackson Trail, offering incredible views of the State College area and the surrounding valleys and ridges, begins at Jo Hays Vista on PA 26, 2 miles south of Pine Grove Mills. The trail is a spur of the Mid State Trail on top of Tussey Ridge and provides a shortcut along the ridgetop if you don't want to follow the MST's camping loop down into Shavers Creek Valley. This trail is shown on MSTA Map 202 and is described in Section C of the guide to the Mid State Trail System.

13
Ironstone Loop
14.3 miles

The blue-blazed Ironstone Loop is a spur that leaves the Mid State Trail on top of Tussey Ridge, crosses Leading Ridge to Stone Valley Recreation Area, and then returns to the MST via Monroe Furnace and Beaver Pond. The loop is best hiked counterclockwise, starting from Jo Hays Vista on PA 26, 2 miles south of Pine Grove Mills. First hike southwest from PA 26 on the MST for 2.9 miles to the junction at the top of Indian Steps; then turn left on the Ironstone Loop. The Ironstone Loop and the intervening section of the MST constitute a very challenging loop hike. The Ironstone Loop is described in Section B of the guide to the Mid State Trail System and is shown on MSTA Map 202.

14

Lake Trail,
Stone Valley Recreation Area

Penn State University's Stone Valley Recreation Area has a trail network offering views of Tussey Ridge and Leading Ridge, with visits to Lake Perez and Shavers Creek Nature Center. Many of the park's most interesting features are reached via the 2.9-mile Lake Trail, which shares a portion of its path with the Ironstone Loop (see separate entry above). The Lake Trail is shown on MSTA Map 202. Multiple hikes at Stone Valley are described in *The Short Hiker* (1999), by Jean Aron. You can reach the recreation area by car from PA 26 between Pine Grove Mills and McAlevys Fort, via Charter Oak Road. For more information, visit www.psu.edu/Stone Valley or call (814) 863-1164.

15

Whipple Lake Trail
3 miles

An earlier trail at Whipple Lake State Park was destroyed by Hurricane Ivan in 2004. A new trail was built in 2005–06 by Eagle Scouts and a crew from Rockview Prison. From the beach area, the yellow-blazed Whipple Lake Trail proceeds upstream between Laurel Run and Laurel Run Road, crosses the run on an impressive new 40-foot bridge, and turns left on Beidler Road. Take the second turn to the left and climb Beidler Ridge on an old road. There are occasional views of Greenlee Ridge across the valley. The trail returns briefly to Beidler Road before descending steeply to the picnic area in the park. Follow the road across the dam to return to the beach area and your car. Reach the state park via PA 26 in northern Huntingdon County, 12 miles south of State College. At the signs for the state park, turn east onto Whipple Dam Road and proceed about half a mile to the beach parking area. For more information, contact Whipple Dam State Park, c/o Greenwood Furnace, Huntingdon, PA 16652-9006, (814) 667-1800, www.dcnr.state.pa.us/stateparks/parks/whippledam.aspx.

Greenwood Spur
6.7 miles

The blue-blazed Greenwood Spur was the first major side trail in the Mid State Trail System. It leads north from Greenwood Furnace State Park on PA 305, via Greenwood Fire Tower and Alan Seeger Natural Area (see separate entry above), to a junction with the main Mid State Trail in Detweiler Valley. The Greenwood Spur is shown on MSTA Map 203 and is described in Section A of the MST guidebook. At Greenwood Furnace State Park, it joins the Standing Stone Trail (see the Long-Distance Trails chapter), which leads 71 miles to the Tuscarora Trail near Cowans Gap State Park. A hiker can travel from the Mid State Trail in Centre County to the Appalachian Trail in northern Virginia by using the Greenwood Spur, the Standing Stone Trail, and the Tuscarora Trail. Greenwood Furnace State Park is on PA 305, 4 miles east of McAlevys Fort and 10 miles west of Belleville. For more information, contact Greenwood Furnace State Park, 15795 Greenwood Rd., Huntingdon, PA 16652, (814) 667-1800, www.dcnr.state.pa.us/stateparks/parks/greenwoodfurnace.aspx.

Yellow Arrow Trail
1.3 miles

This blue-blazed trail was the former route of the Mid State Trail to Colerain, before the MST was extended south to US 22. The Yellow Arrow Trail starts at Colerain Picnic Area, 5 miles northeast of Spruce Creek on PA 45. The trail climbs steeply to an outstanding vista at Indian Overlook, where you must watch your footing very carefully, then leads to the Mid State Trail on top of Tussey Ridge. You can create a loop by returning on Colerain Road. This trail and road are found on MSTA Map 201.

Lower Trail
11.1 miles

The Lower (rhymes with "flower") Trail is a rail-trail on the abandoned Petersburg branch of the Penn Central Railroad. It follows the Frankstown Branch of the Juniata River from Williamsburg to Alfarata. In March 1991, Rails to Trails of Central Pennsylvania purchased the entire abandoned right-of-way, thanks to a generous donation from T. Dean Lower of Hollidaysburg in memory of his wife, Jane, and son Roger. Before this route was a railroad, it was part of the Pennsylvania Canal. Ruins of the canal, including a lock, are visible along the Lower Trail.

In 2004, portions of the Lower Trail were severely damaged by flooding from Hurricane Ivan. The trail was swiftly repaired, thanks largely to materials and labor donated by Grannas Brothers construction company of Williamsburg. Shortly thereafter, an extension from Williamsburg to near Canoe Creek State Park was opened. Like most rail-trails, the Lower Trail is multiuse, but it has unique grade separation. Hikers follow a grassy strip on the east side, bikers follow a crushed stone path in the middle, and horseback riders follow a grassy path on the west. Trailhead parking is available in downtown Williamsburg just off PA 866, or in Alfarata on US 22 just east of the PA 453 intersection. For a free map of the Lower Trail, contact Rails to Trails of Central Pennsylvania, P.O. Box 592, Hollidaysburg, PA 16648, (814) 832-2400, www.rttcpa.org. At the time of this writing, the Lower Trail is carrying the southern extension of the Mid State Trail, though a relocation for the MST has been planned through a state game land nearby.

Old Loggers Trail
6.2 miles

Do not confuse this trail with the Old Loggers Path, a long-distance backpacking trail in Loyalsock State Forest (see the Endless Mountains Region chapter). The Old Loggers Trail is located on U.S. Army Corps of Engineers land along Raystown Lake. From PA 26 south of Huntington, follow the road to the Seven Points Recreation Area. Just after passing the entrance station, look for a small parking area on your right. The Old Loggers Trail begins on the other side of the road at a large interpretive sign and consists of an entrance trail that leads to a loop. Old Loggers Trail is described in *50 Hikes in Central Pennsylvania* (2001), by Tom Thwaites. To learn more about hiking opportunities in the Raystown Lake area, including the long-distance Terrace Mountain Trail, visit raystown.nab.usace.army.mil/Activities/hiking.htm.

20
Trough Creek State Park

In this beautiful state park, Trough Creek cuts through Terrace Mountain to Raystown Lake. Trough Creek Gorge and the surrounding ridges provide the setting for outstanding hikes to waterfalls, vistas, and features of geologic interest ranging from immense rock formations to an ice mine. There are also historic features, including an old iron furnace, a forge, and a CCC camp. A circuit hike on much of the trail network in the park is described in *50 Hikes in Central Pennsylvania* (2001), by Tom Thwaites. The park is 16 miles south of Huntington via PA 994 and a park entrance road, about 5 miles east of PA 26. For a park map and more information, contact Trough Creek State Park, RR1, Box 211, James Creek, PA 16657, (814) 568-3847, www.dcnr.state.pa.us/stateparks/parks/trough creek.aspx.

21
Meadow Grounds Lake

Meadow Grounds Lake, in State Game Land 53, is perched in a hanging valley just to the west of McConnellsburg. Two trails in the area, the Bear Trail and the Fish Trail, allow a hike on the west side of the lake and then to a couple of waterfalls on Roaring Run. This in-and-out hike is described in *50 Hikes in Central Pennsylvania* (2001), by Tom Thwaites. From McConnellsburg, take PA 16 west away from downtown. Just before the US 30 bypass, turn left onto Back Run Road. A little more than 1 mile up this road, turn right on Meadow Grounds Road and proceed to a parking area at the entrance to the state game land.

22
Martin Hill Wild Area

Martin Hill Wild Area in Buchanan State Forest, on the southernmost rampart of Tussey Ridge in Bedford County, offers various circuit hikes of different lengths. The trailhead is at the parking area at the junction of Beans Cove Road and Martin Hill Road. Cross Beans Cave Road, walk around the vehicle gate, and head south on Tussey Mountain Road (which here carries the Mid State Trail). Various side trails plunge down the ridge to the left, and loop hikes return on Gap Trail, which parallels the MST partway down the east flank of Tussey Ridge. For a short hike, cut across on Fetters Trail, or for a longer hike, cut over on the Johnson

Trail. For a real boot-buster, cut over via the Carnes Trail. In all cases, follow the Gap Trail north to Beans Cove Road. Turn left on the road and climb back up Tussey Ridge. These trails are shown on the Buchanan State Forest public-use map and MSTA Map 213. To reach the trailhead, take US 30 2 miles east of Bedford, and turn south on PA 326. Follow PA 326 into southern Bedford County to a picnic area at Beans Cove. Here, bear right onto Black Valley Road; then after .75 mile, turn right on Park View Road. This road becomes Beans Cove Road and climbs Tussey Mountain. The parking area is at the crest of the ridge, at the corner of Martin Hill Road. For more information on Martin Hill Wild Area, visit www.dcnr.state.pa.us/forestry/stateforests/buchananwild.aspx.

REGION 4

Laurel Highlands

Region Editor: Mike Lipay

The Laurel Highlands Region consists of south-central Pennsylvania between the Pittsburgh metro area to the west and the Appalachian Mountains to the east. This region is bounded on the south by the Mason-Dixon line; on the east by US 220 and I-99 from Maryland to Port Matilda; on the north by US 322 from Port Matilda to near Dubois; and on the west by US 119.

This region is dominated by Laurel Mountain, the long and broad ridge that comes up out of Maryland and West Virginia and is breached spectacularly by the Youghiogheny and Conemaugh Rivers; and by the high plateau lands above the Allegheny Front, an abrupt rise in the landscape to the west of the Appalachian Mountains.

The area's first settlers did little to change the environment, and as you hike the Allegheny Plateau today, you may well be following trails first laid out by the Lenni-Lenape, known to the settlers as the Delaware Indians. This section of Pennsylvania was crossed by many important Indian paths, most notably the Kittanning and Frankstown Paths, which led to the great Frankstown village near what is now Altoona; the Turkeyfoot Path, in southern Fayette and Somerset Counties; and the Conemaugh Path, between what are now Johnstown and Bedford. Modern US 40 follows the old Braddock's Road, which in turn followed the Nemacolin Path, used by the Indians.

Geographically, the Laurel Highlands make up the western and southern escarpment of Pennsylvania's Allegheny Plateau, with high elevations that reach 3,213 feet at Mount Davis in Somerset County, the highest point in Pennsylvania. There is a high degree of variability in the weather from the lowlands to the

Laurel Highlands and the Allegheny Plateau. Winters are more severe in the higher elevations, and you should be prepared for rapidly changing conditions.

The Laurel Highlands of Somerset, Fayette, and Westmoreland Counties are a popular recreation area. Hiking opportunities are provided in the area's many state forests, state game lands, and state parks. The long-distance Laurel Highlands Hiking Trail is managed by two parks: the southern section by Laurel Ridge State Park, and the northern section by Linn Run State Park. Gallitzin and Forbes State Forests feature three natural areas—Charles F. Lewis, Roaring Run, and Mount Davis—and two wild areas, Clear Shade Creek and Quebec Run.

Of special recreational interest are a ski slope at Laurel Mountain State Park and premier whitewater rafting on the Youghiogheny River at Ohiopyle State Park. The latter park is also a hub for the Great Allegheny Passage (see the Long-Distance Trails chapter) and the Laurel Highlands Hiking Trail. The Laurel Highlands are home to a number of private and commercial caves, including Laurel Caverns, purportedly the largest cave system in Pennsylvania and featuring many undeveloped passages that visitors may explore at their own risk, allowing perhaps the only significant underground hike in the commonwealth.

1

Clearfield to Grampian Trail
13.1 miles

The Clearfield to Grampian Trail is a multiuse rail-trail that runs between these two towns in Clearfield County. The trail features a crushed limestone surface and follows the West Branch of the Susquehanna River from Clearfield to Curwensville through lightly developed areas. The segment from Curwensville to Grampian is more densely forested and rises to the top of a ridge. See map on page 88.

To reach the Clearfield end of the trail, take Exit 120 off I-80. Go about 3 miles south on PA 879 and turn right on Spruce Street. Then take the first left onto Chester Street, proceed 200 yards, and turn left before the True Value Hardware Store. The trail and parking area are ahead on the left. The Grampian end of the trail is reached via PA 729, one block south of that road's interchange with US 219 and PA 879 in the center of town. You can find intermediate parking along the route at St. Timothy Church, except when services are in session, and at Stronach parking area. For more information, contact Clearfield County Rails to Trails Association, 310 E. Cherry St., Clearfield, PA 16833, (814) 765-1701.

2

Ghost Town Trail
30 miles

In 1991, Kovalchick Salvage Company donated 12 miles of the former Blacklick and Ebensburg Railroad to the Indiana County parks system. Connecting sections have been donated in the years since. The railroad corridor has been transformed into the popular multiuse Ghost Town Trail, reaching 30 miles from Dilltown to Ebensburg, including a side trail called the Rexis Branch, which leads north to White Mill Crossing. At the time of this writing, there are plans for a 6-mile spur to connect the Ghost Town Trail at Black Lick to the Hoodlebug Trail near Homer City, as well as an extension of the West Penn Trail to the west (see the Three Rivers Region chapter) that would connect that trail to the Hoodlebug and Ghost Town Trails, thus creating an extensive rail-trail network of great historical interest.

The eastern half of the main trail, from Nanty Glo to Ebensburg, climbs gradually to the top of a mountain, creating a challenge for bikers and extra exercise for walkers, while the rest of the system is quite flat. The Ghost Town Trail derives its name from several mining and lumbering towns that once stood along the railroad line. Wehrum, the largest of the towns, once boasted 230 homes, a hotel, company store, jail, and bank. The town was developed by Warren Delano, uncle

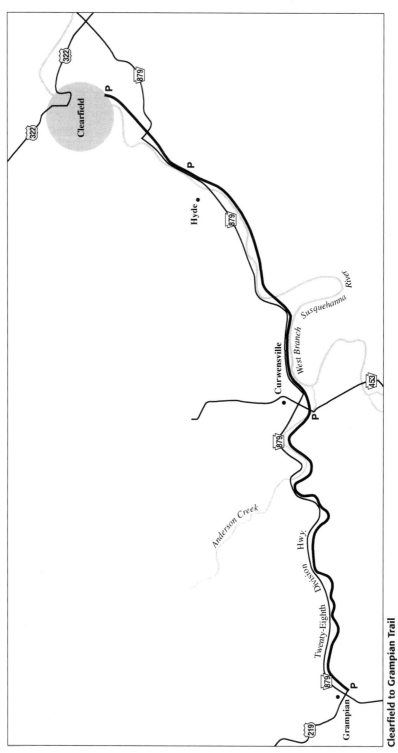

Clearfield to Grampian Trail

of President Franklin D. Roosevelt. This and several other towns have since disappeared, and historical markers along the trail describe the Blacklick Valley's intriguing history. A portion of the trail passes through state game lands, and one highlight is Eliza Iron Furnace, a well-preserved national historic site.

There are six easily reached access areas: Dilltown, Wehrum, and Rexis in Indiana County; and Twin Rocks, Nanty Glo, and Ebensburg in Cambria County. You can reach the Ghost Town Trail via US 22, PA 403, US 422, or PA 271 to any of these towns. Each access area offers parking and restroom facilities. The trail's midpoint at Eliza Station in Vintondale includes a picnic area with a large pavilion. For more information on the Indiana County section, contact Indiana County Parks and Trails, 1128 Blue Spruce Rd., Indiana, PA 15701, (724) 463-8636, www.indianacountyparks.org/parks/gtt/gtt.html. For more information on the Cambria County section, contact Cambria County Conservation and Recreation Authority, 401 Candlelight Dr., Suite 234, Ebensburg, PA 15931, (814) 472-2110, ctcnet.net/cccra.

3

Blue Knob State Park

The 5,298-acre Blue Knob State Park was previously one of several National Park Service demonstration areas in Pennsylvania that later became state parks after World War II. Blue Knob is located in the extreme northern tip of Bedford County, just west of US 220, and is accessible from numerous points on that highway between Bedford and Duncansville. The peak of Blue Knob, at 3,146 feet, is the second-highest point in Pennsylvania. In winter, this site provides an active ski slope. Excellent hiking trails with many overlooks extend throughout the park area. The extensive trail system is well blazed in a variety of colors, and the northeastern terminus of the Lost Turkey Trail is located here (see separate entry below). For further information, contact Blue Knob State Park, 124 Park Rd., Imler, PA 16655, (814) 276-3576, www.dcnr.state.pa.us/stateparks/parks/blueknob.aspx.

Chappell's Field Trail (2.5 miles): Marked by orange V blazes, this is a gently sloping multiuse trail with little gradient change, ideal for family hiking and cross-country skiing. It follows the back end of Chappell's Field through wildlife management areas, crosses Blue Knob Fork Road, continues to the bottom loop of the campground, and returns through forest to the starting point. Park at the upper end of Chappell's Field.

Crist Ridge Trail (1.9 miles): This orange-blazed trail starts at an intersection with Chappell's Field Trail and extends to near the park pool. This is an easy downhill hike for the entire family. Park at the picnic area just south of the pool or up the road at the crossing of Chappell's Field Trail.

Homestead Trail (1.8 miles): This easy orange-blazed trail starts at the second major switchback on Whysong Road and leads to Willow Springs Picnic Area, winding through old homestead sites in a rolling valley area. This is a wide, gentle trail with some mild uphill walking and is suitable for the whole family. The old fields offer opportunities for bird watching.

Three Springs Trail (2 miles): This orange-blazed multiuse trail is wide and gentle, traversing the mountain on service roads and waterlines. It starts at the electrical substation near the ski resort and is intertwined with Mountain View Trail, which you can use to reach Willow Springs Picnic Area. Three Springs Trail leads through mountain forests, with views of lowlands 2,000 feet below.

Mountain View Trail (5 miles): This challenging multiuse trail is marked with double red blazes and leads into a wilderness area, intertwining with the Three Springs Trail. The loop trail begins and ends at Willow Springs Picnic Area and includes a short spur trail to the ski resort, where there is alternate parking next to the electrical substation. The trail heads north from the picnic area along an old waterline to Deep Hollow Run, then climbs the mountain to a junction with Three Springs Trail. Mountain View Trail then turns south to an outstanding vista before looping back to another junction with Three Springs Trail. Descend along Beaverdam Creek and then skirt the edge of the mountain to return to the picnic area. The section of this trail to the vista is suitable for the whole family, but the rest of the trail is for experienced hikers with proper footwear. You can access the vista via a section of Three Springs Trail. Do not attempt to hike this trail during inclement weather, because the mountaintop is prone to thick fog.

Sawmill Trail (3 miles): This moderately challenging trail is marked with yellow blazes and uses pipelines and service roads. The trail begins on the main park road at Chappell's Field across from the campground, heads south through Group Camping Area #1 to Willow Springs Picnic Area, then goes to Queen Road near the park's southern boundary.

Rock n' Ridge Trail (2.8 miles): This moderately challenging trail is marked with blue T blazes. The multiuse trail starts at the picnic pavilion above the park pool, then follows a homestead road that weaves through the center of the park along a mountain brook. A steady uphill climb reaches almost to the peak of the mountain, and then the trail returns along the high ground connecting the ridge to the pool complex. Park at Mowry Hollow Picnic Area.

4

Lost Turkey Trail
26.3 miles

The long-distance Lost Turkey Trail was built by the Youth Conservation Corps in 1976 and playfully named in tribute of the original trailblazers. This challenging trail provides a quiet passageway through the forest west of the Allegheny Front, before plunging down off the Front and then climbing steeply up to the second-highest point in Pennsylvania. The trail winds through parts of Somerset, Cambria, and Bedford Counties, cutting through Gallitzin State Forest, state game lands, and Blue Knob State Park. Backpack camping along the trail is permitted only in the state forest, creating a challenge in mapping out backpacking routes. Fee campgrounds are available at the state park, but these are near the trail's northeastern terminus, near the ski area. The southwestern terminus of Lost Turkey Trail is at a parking lot on PA 56, across the road from Babcock Picnic Area, about 10 miles southeast of Johnstown.

From its southwestern terminus, Lost Turkey Trail leads for about 14 miles through easy to moderately challenging terrain along Pot Ridge. It then meets Little Break Hollow in the crest of the Allegheny Front, and the hiking becomes very challenging for the remainder of the route. The trail descends to Burnt House Picnic Area, crosses PA 869, and follows the edge of Forks Ridge above an impressive canyon. It then descends to beautiful Bobs Creek, climbs steeply up and down Hogback Ridge, and at mile 24 reaches a monument to two pioneer children who got lost in the area and died mysteriously in 1856, after which it begins a challenging climb to the top of Blue Knob.

Lost Turkey Trail was constructed on existing trails with the addition of some new connectors. It is marked with 2-by-6-inch red blazes. In the state forest section, part of the trail shares a pathway with an existing snowmobile trail, and in this area the red blazes share space with orange diamond-shaped blazes. Another part of the trail passes through private land; permission has been secured, but the landowners have requested the prohibition of fires, motorized vehicles, and littering. This creates another challenge for the planning of backpacking trips. Day hikes on Lost Turkey Trail are certainly possible, but the limited access points usually necessitate car shuttling.

An excellent map produced by Gallitzin State Forest prominently features Lost Turkey Trail and the nearby John P. Saylor Memorial Trail (see separate entry below). To obtain this map, and for further information, contact Gallitzin State Forest, P.O. Box 506, Ebensburg, PA 15931, (814) 472-1862, www.dcnr.state.pa.us/forestry/stateforests/gallitzin.aspx.

John P. Saylor Memorial Trail

17.3 miles

The double-loop John P. Saylor Memorial Trail traverses predominantly flat landscapes to the west of the rugged rise of the Allegheny Front, through Gallitzin State Forest and Clear Shade Wild Area. An easy but lengthy 12.3-mile main loop leads to a more challenging 5-mile side loop. You can hike either loop separately, though the second is more difficult to reach by car. Both loops can be combined to create a figure-eight hike of 17.3 miles, which would make for a relatively easy overnight trip for beginning backpackers, though camping is not permitted in the wild area. The trail is a memorial to John P. Saylor, a longtime western Pennsylvania congressman and conservationist who is best known for helping pass the 1964 Federal Wilderness Act and the 1968 National Scenic Trails Act. Saylor died in 1973.

The orange-blazed trail rolls gently through terrain between 2,180 and 2,580 feet in elevation, taking you to unique high-altitude meadows, an old splash dam, the visible remains of railroad trestles, a swinging bridge over Clear Shade Creek (the beginning of the second loop), the relics of old work camps, and scenic but heavily vandalized formations at Wolf Rocks. The forest is mainly of the northern hardwoods type, containing sizable amounts of black cherry, American beech, red maple, sweet birch, and some scattered hemlock. A hike on the 12.3-mile main loop is featured in *50 Hikes in Central Pennsylvania* (2001), by Tom Thwaites.

John P. Saylor Memorial Trail begins at Babcock Picnic Area on the south side of PA 56, about 10 miles southeast of Johnstown. The map for this trail is combined with that for Lost Turkey Trail. Contact Gallitzin State Forest, P.O. Box 506, Ebensburg, PA 15931, (814) 472-1862, www.dcnr.state.pa.us/forestry/stateforests/gallitzin.aspx.

Bog and Boulder Trail

2 miles

The Bog and Boulder Trail was established by Gallitzin State Forest and is marked with yellow blazes. It intersects both sides of the John P. Saylor Memorial Trail loop (see separate entry above) and is shown on that trail's map. The Bog and Boulder Trail traverses a number of interesting ecological habitats, including a large, open bog supporting wetland species such as sphagnum moss, sundews, sedges, and rushes. An area dominated by native shrubs and a boulder field, an extension of the Wolf Rocks area, is also located along the trail. For the trail map and additional information, contact Gallitzin State Forest, P.O. Box 506, Ebensburg, PA 15931, (814) 472-1862, www.dcnr.state.pa.us/forestry/state forests/gallitzin.aspx.

7

Charles F. Lewis Natural Area

The unique and scenic 384-acre Charles F. Lewis Natural Area was named after Dr. Charles F. Lewis, a noted western Pennsylvania newspaperman and conservationist. The natural area features a spectacular grove with several scenic waterfalls and rock formations.

Clark Run Trail (1.6 miles): At the trailhead parking lot, a natural gap in the mountain from which Clark Run flows will draw your attention. A log archway marks the start of the yellow-blazed Clark Run Trail. The trail winds its way up the steep, rocky hillside, crosses Clark Run, then loops back to the stream at the first waterfall. The rise in elevation from the parking lot to the top of this very steep trail is 1,000 feet over a distance of only half a mile. Accordingly, the stream flows rapidly, passing over several small, scenic waterfalls. A short walk up the south side of the trail gives an excellent view of the beauty and unique character of this little gorge. Along the ridge, approximately .5 mile from the terminus, is an extensive outcropping of rock towering 30 feet into the air. This ledge extends for 150 yards parallel to the ridge. Huge boulders are strewn at the foot of this outcropping, adding difficulty to the hike. This area is not recommended for young children or persons not in good physical condition. The Clark Run Trail is steep and rough and requires proper hiking boots.

Rager Mountain Trail (3 miles): This orange-blazed trail was built by the Youth Conservation Corps. The Rager Mountain Trail leaves the Clark Run Trail where it meets an old woods road. It then proceeds almost to the top of Rager Mountain, where it loops and returns to the Clark Run Trail on the old woods road. At the top of the loop, the trail crosses an old toll road that ran between Johnstown and Cramer; at this intersection, you can still see the remains of the Harvey Stahley homestead. About 100 yards beyond is an old charcoal hearth, a flat, circular area about 30 feet in diameter. Farther down the trail is a similar but somewhat larger area. Hearths in this area produced 6 million bushels of charcoal for the iron and steel industries between 1898 and 1906.

A loop hike incorporating both trails is included in *50 Hikes in Western Pennsylvania* (2000), by Tom Thwaites.

Reach the natural area via PA 403, approximately 7 miles northwest of Johnstown. Park in the boulder-lined gravel lot near the natural area sign. For a map and further information, contact Gallitzin State Forest, P.O. Box 506, Ebensburg, PA 15931, (814) 472-1862, www.dcnr.state.pa.us/forestry/stateforests/gallitzin.aspx.

8

Laurel Highlands Hiking Trail

70.1 miles

The Laurel Highlands Hiking Trail (LHHT) is one of the finest natural trails in Pennsylvania. In winter, the trail supports cross-country skiing and snowshoeing, both of which can be combined with winter backpacking. Some portions of the trail, especially near the southern end, are quite rugged, and provisions have been made to keep the trail as primitive as possible. Hikers are also encouraged to create in-and-out day hikes on the trail, given its diverse character and scenery. In particular, wildflowers are widespread in the spring, and the views off the mountain are enhanced in the winter. The ridge provides several natural vistas overlooking the nearby valleys and a huge expanse of uninterrupted forest.

The Laurel Highlands Hiking Trail extends for 70.1 miles from Conemaugh Gorge near Johnstown to the rugged and picturesque Youghiogheny River Gorge at Ohiopyle State Park. The northern terminus is a few miles east of Seward off PA 56, and the southern terminus now connects with the Great Allegheny Passage (see the Long-Distance Trails chapter) at Ohiopyle. Most of the trail is on Laurel Mountain, with a high average elevation, topping out above 2,700 feet, but there are some sections where it drops 1,000 feet or so to the valley floor (usually to avoid private land) or winds across the plateau of Fayette and Somerset Counties at a slightly lower average elevation. A short distance northwest of Somerset, the trail crosses the Pennsylvania Turnpike on a footbridge over the expressway.

There are eight overnight shelter areas along the trail, situated 8 to 10 miles apart. Each contains five shelters with tent pads, two comfort stations, a fireplace, and water sources. These overnight areas are not directly on the trail, but are set back somewhat to retain a wilderness atmosphere. The shelters are of the Adirondack type, constructed of lumber to blend in with the environment, and each can accommodate six people. These shelter areas can be reached only on foot, and overnight camping is by mandatory reservation with a required fee. Overnight stays are limited to one night at each shelter area. Call Laurel Ridge State Park at (412) 455-3744 prior to your trip for reservations.

The Laurel Highlands Hiking Trail has 2-by-5-inch yellow blazes. Large signs indicate access points, and markers appear at every mile. When using the trail, abide by the governing rules and regulations posted at parking lots and camping areas. The regulations are also available at the headquarters of Laurel Ridge State Park. The trail passes through that mostly undeveloped park, which was conceived and designed with the day hiker and backpacker in mind. In the winter, the park houses a major cross-country ski center with rentals, food, and lessons available.

The Allegheny Group of Sierra Club has published the *Hikers Guide to the Laurel Highlands Trail.* The guide includes trail descriptions; information on the local geology, flora, and fauna; topographic maps and elevation profiles; advice on planning hikes and backpacking trips; and a list of hiking organizations in the area. For ordering information, visit www.alleghenysc.org/publications.

A color trail brochure, with descriptions of trailhead parking areas, an elevation chart, and a trail map in a durable paper folder, is available from the state park. For more information, contact Laurel Ridge State Park, 1117 Jim Mountain Rd., Rockwood, PA 15557, (412) 455-3744, www.dcnr.state.pa.us/stateparks/parks/laurelridge.aspx.

9

PWS Ski Trail System
34 miles

The interconnected PWS Ski Trail System uses a combination of paved and unpaved roads and an original railroad bed. The trails are marked for snowmobiling and cross-county skiing, and they provide easy hiking during the off-season. Most of the trails in the PWS System can be accessed from the main trailhead at Laurel Mountain State Park. Cross-country ski parking is located on Laurel Mountain Road south of Laurel Mountain Village. For more information, contact Laurel Mountain State Park, c/o Linn Run, P.O. Box 50, Rector, PA 15677, (724) 238-6623, www.dcnr.state.pa.us/stateparks/parks/laurelmountain.aspx.

10

Linn Run State Park
and the Laurel Mountain Division
of Forbes State Forest

In 1909, the Linn Run watershed was the first tract of land in the Ohio River basin acquired by the commonwealth of Pennsylvania for forestry purposes. This was after the area was completely denuded of forest, but the flora and fauna have since been successfully reestablished. The area now consists of the Laurel Mountain Division of Forbes State Forest and Linn Run State Park. Several marked and unmarked trails lead to the park's points of interest, including the remains of the Pittsburgh, Westmoreland, and Somerset (PW&S) Railroad and various scenic viewpoints. Some of the major hiking trails are described here.

Grove Run Trail (3.8 miles): This blue-blazed trail can be accessed from Grove Run Picnic Area off Linn Run Road in the state park. The trail forms a circuit that climbs counterclockwise up the mountain along Grove Run and crosses over the height of land after a climb of more that 800 feet. It then descends Boot

Hollow, crosses Quarry Trail (a snowmobile trail), and shortly reaches a junction where the Fish Run Trail diverges to the right. The Grove Run Trail bears left at this junction, crosses the Quarry Trail again, and turns left to parallel Linn Run Road before returning to the picnic area. Please sign in at the trail register on the west side of the summit. For alternate access to this trail, use the Quarry Trail from Linn Run Road.

Fish Run Trail (2.5 miles): This easy trail begins at the upper end of the parking area just above the metal bridge, about 1.5 miles above the park office. It uses or parallels the route of the PW&S Railroad. The first section of trail follows an old tram railroad bed, and the middle section is on the original PW&S grade. Watch for the old stone bridges where the stream crosses under the trail. The upper trail section parallels Linn Run Road. The grade climbs to the top of the mountain, and the trail terminates at Laurel Summit State Park.

Wolf Rocks Trail (4.5 miles): This trail starts at the far left corner of Laurel Summit Picnic Area at the trail sign. Blue blazes mark the hiking portion of the trail, and red blazes mark the section that was relocated for cross-country skiing. The trail crosses a pipeline and a stand of rhododendron that blooms in July. When you come to a sign at the junction of Wolf Rocks Loop and Wolf Rocks Trail, follow Wolf Rocks Trail. Shortly, the trail becomes very rocky and leads to a nice overlook from which you can see down Linn Run Valley and across to Chestnut Ridge in the west. Retrace your steps to the junction sign, and this time follow Wolf Rocks Loop. When you reach a T in the trail, bear left, following the red blazes. This trail leads back to Wolf Rocks Trail, which takes you back to the picnic area.

Spruce Flats Bog (.5 to 1.5 miles): This 28-acre bog is only a two-minute walk northeast from Laurel Summit Picnic Area. A sign directs you to the path of the PW&S Railroad, which traveled across the bog early in the twentieth century. Dress appropriately, because you can't help but get wet. A small observation deck has been built for those who wish to keep their feet dry. The bog features scenery that closely resembles the bogs of eastern Canada. Because it is on the crest of Laurel Mountain at an elevation of 2,660 feet, this unusual site supports wetland plant and bird species more commonly found at lower elevations hundreds of miles to the north. In the bog, you can find interesting plants such as the large cranberry, pitcher plant, sundew, and cotton grass. Birds are also in abundance here.

The area is accessible from Linn Run Road, 3 miles from Rector, which is on PA 381 about 4 miles south of US 30. For brochures featuring maps of the trails, contact Forbes State Forest, P.O. Box 519, Laughlintown, PA 15655, (724) 238-1200, www.dcnr.state.pa.us/forestry/stateforests/forbes.aspx; or Linn Run State Park, P.O. Box 50, Rector, PA 15677, (724) 238-6623, www.dcnr.state.pa.us/stateparks/parks/linnrun.aspx.

11
Roaring Run Natural Area

Located on the west slope of Laurel Mountain in Westmoreland County, the 3,593-acre Roaring Run Natural Area protects a complete mountain stream and its watershed. The area is mostly wooded and includes old fields and pastures now reclaimed by the forest. There are several trails throughout the area, including a section of the Laurel Highlands Hiking Trail. Nine maintained and blazed hiking trails constitute an interconnected system of about 20 miles, from which several linear or loop hikes can be devised. The trails are marked with 2-by-6-inch blue blazes. Red blazes indicate those portions of the hiking trails used for ski touring.

Roaring Run Trail (4 miles): Located in the heart of natural area, this trail follows Roaring Run for most of its length down the mountainside. A portion of the trail is on an old logging railroad grade. Because the trail crosses the stream twenty-eight times in 3 miles, you are advised to carry extra shoes and socks. Three landmarks divide the hike into roughly equal parts. About 1 mile into the hike, the trail passes the steep-walled mouth of an unnamed tributary on the right. A larger tributary, draining a slightly wider hollow, enters Roaring Run from the left near the 2-mile point, and at the 3-mile mark, rhododendron thickets line the stream banks. The trail runs from Fire Tower Road west to Painter Rock Trail; turn left on that trail and head to County Line Road. This hike is best done with two cars, one parked at Fire Tower Road and one at County Line Road.

Painter Rock Trail (1.8 miles): Leaving from and returning to the Roaring Run Trail, this trail goes up Painter Rock Hill to a scenic vista over Roaring Run Valley. You will see abandoned fields reverting to forest.

South Loop Trail (3.7 miles): This trail forms a loop starting from and returning to the Roaring Run Trail. The South Loop travels above the Roaring Run drainage and connects to other side trails leading to County Line Road. It uses old logging roads and skid trails.

North Loop Trail (3.7 miles): This loop starts from and returns to Painter Rock Trail.

To reach Roaring Run Natural Area, take PA 31 east from Donegal, and turn right onto Fire Tower Road near the top of Laurel Ridge. This road is the eastern boundary of the natural area. You can also reach the area from Jones Mills by going south on PA 711/PA 381 and turning left on County Line Road, which is the southern boundary. The Laurel Highlands Hiking Trail also crosses Fire Tower Road .2 mile east of the beginning of the Roaring Run Trail. Parking is available on County Line Road, Fire Tower Road, and at Nedrow Cemetery (on County Road 301). The Roaring Run Natural Area map shows additional parking areas. A map and further information about hiking in Roaring Run Natural Area can be obtained from Forbes State Forest, P.O. Box 519, Laughlintown, PA 15655, (724) 238-1200, www.dcnr.state.pa.us/forestry/stateforests/forbes.aspx. The area is also featured in *50 Hikes in Western Pennsylvania* (2000), by Tom Thwaites.

12
Bear Run Nature Reserve

The 5,000-acre Bear Run Nature Reserve is owned by the Western Pennsylvania Conservancy. The natural area lies along the west slope of Laurel Mountain, facing the Youghiogheny River gorge, with more than 20 miles of marked trails through an area of great natural diversity. The reserve is open to the public year-round for hiking, ski touring, nature study, photography, and backpacking. Pets are prohibited.

A trail map is available at the Bear Run Nature Reserve parking lot. The map contains a short description of each trail with its length and approximate walking times between points. The trails are well marked with signposts at each intersection. A loop hike incorporating many of the reserve's most interesting trails is featured in *50 Hikes in Western Pennsylvania* (2000), by Tom Thwaites. Nearby is Fallingwater, Frank Lloyd Wright's most famous house. You can tour the house and the grounds for a fee.

Bear Run Nature Reserve is located 3.5 miles north of Ohiopyle on PA 381. For more information on the reserve, contact Western Pennsylvania Conservancy, 209 Fourth Ave., Pittsburgh, PA 15222, (412) 288-2777, www.paconserve.org. To learn more about Wright's house, contact Fallingwater, P.O. Box R, Mill Run, PA 15464, (724) 329-8501.

13
Ohiopyle State Park

Ohiophyle State Park encompasses 19,052 acres of rugged natural beauty. The park's focal point is more than 14 miles of the Youghiogheny River gorge, with spectacular scenery and some of the best whitewater in the eastern United States. In addition to serving as the southern terminus of the Laurel Highlands Trail, the park contains 41 miles of hiking trails and an extensive bicycle trail that has now been incorporated into the Great Allegheny Passage (see the Long-Distance Trails chapter).

The area has many points of interest for the hiking enthusiast, including spectacular rock formations, waterfalls, vistas, and Ferncliff Natural Area, with numerous botanical treasures on a system of easy walking trails. Multiple hikes to the best of the park's scenic offerings are featured in *50 Hikes in Western Pennsylvania* (2000), by Tom Thwaites. The park is located at the PA 381 crossing of the Youghiogheny River. For more information and a park trail map, contact Ohiopyle State Park, P.O. Box 105, Ohiopyle, PA 15470, (724) 329-8591, www.dcnr.state.pa.us/stateparks/parks/ohiopyle.aspx.

14
Quebec Run Wild Area

Quebec Run Wild Area is a heavily forested section of land along the eastern slope of Chestnut Ridge in Fayette County. A short distance north of the Pennsylvania–West Virginia border, the area consists of 7,441 acres that encompass almost all of the Quebec Run and Tebolt Run watersheds. The area contains six maintained hiking trails, totaling 23.2 miles and marked with 2-by-6-inch blue blazes, as well as many unmarked logging roads and trails for those wishing to get off the beaten path.

For a 4.5-mile circuit hike to some of the most interesting parts of the wild area, follow Mud Pike for 1.4 miles, and park in the hard-surfaced parking lot on the right side of the road. The trailhead sign displays a map of Quebec Run Wild Area and its trails. Begin by taking Miller Trail on the east side of the parking lot (on the left as you face the sign and gate across Quebec Road), and follow the blue blazes. After .5 mile, you can tell you are hiking along a ridge between two stream valleys. As the trail descends, it becomes narrower and steeper. On the floodplain of Mill Run, a number of trails intersect. Here, turn right onto Mill Run Trail, which goes along the bank of the stream. Shortly, you pass some downed trees all lying in the same direction. Look carefully for a blue T on a tree at a trail intersection (unless the sign has been replaced by the time of your visit). Turn right onto Rankin Trail, which crosses Quebec Run twice and proceeds to Quebec Road. Cross the road and make a sharp jog to the right; watch the blazes carefully. Rankin Trail follows the hillside again until it joins an old logging road. Turn left onto the logging road, and continue past some large boulders to a sign for Hess Trail to the left. Continue on Rankin Trail; then turn at the second sign for Hess Trail, which leads uphill to your right (north). This section of Hess Trail begins with a strenuous climb out of the valley, then proceeds northeast across the top of the ridge. The trail dips down to cross a tributary of Mill Run, and from this point it is a short walk back to the parking lot. A longer loop hike incorporating more of the wild area's most interesting trails is featured in *50 Hikes in Western Pennsylvania* (2000), by Tom Thwaites.

To reach Quebec Run Wild Area, take US 40 to the top of Chestnut Ridge east of Uniontown. Just to the east of the Mount Summit Inn, turn south on Skyline Drive. Proceed for 6.5 miles, past the entrance to Laurel Caverns to the junction with Quebec Road. From this junction, Skyline Drive to the south (via Mud Pike) and Quebec Road to the east form the boundaries of the wild area, and both lead to trailheads. Developed parking areas are shown on the wild area map. These and other area roads, some of which are closed to motor vehicles, provide access and allow for day hikes and loop hikes of various lengths. For a map of the Quebec Run Wild Area trail system, contact Forbes State Forest, P.O. Box 519, Laughlintown, PA 15655, (724) 238-1200, www.dcnr.state.pa.us/forestry/stateforests/forbes.aspx.

15

Mount Davis Natural Area

The 581-acre Mount Davis Natural Area surrounds the highest point in Pennsylvania, at 3,213 feet above sea level. Despite its name, Mount Davis is not a self-contained mountain, but a high point on an otherwise unobtrusive ridge. It was named for John N. Davis, an early settler and former owner of the site. The natural area is surrounded by a 5,685-acre section of Forbes State Forest. Several short trails form a small hiking system through the natural area and the surrounding territory. These include High Point Trail (.8 mile), Mount Davis Trail (.3 mile), Shelter Rock Trail (1.1 miles), and Tub Mill Run Trail (2.8 miles). There are several more trails to the south of the natural area, including Livengood Trail (1.1 miles), Wolf Rock Trail (.8 mile), and Laurel Run Trail (1.9 miles). To reach Mount Davis Natural Area, take US 219 to Meyersdale in southern Somerset County. Turn west on SR 2004 (Broadway Street) and proceed 9.2 miles to the natural area. You can combine trails to form several interesting loop hikes. A loop hike is also featured in *50 Hikes in Western Pennsylvania* (2000), by Tom Thwaites.

The Bureau of Forestry has published an educational guide containing a map, selected trail descriptions, and recommended hikes, as well as material of geologic and historical interest. Contact Forbes State Forest, P.O. Box 519, Laughlintown, PA 15655, (724) 238-1200, www.dcnr.state.pa.us/forestry/stateforests/forbes.aspx.

REGION 5

Three Rivers

Region Editor: Ben Cramer

Contributor: Jerry Hoffman

The Three Rivers Region consists of the Pittsburgh metro area and the south-western corner of Pennsylvania. This region is bounded on the south by the Maryland and West Virginia borders; on the east by US 119 from Maryland to I-80; on the north by I-80 from Dubois to the Ohio border; and on the west by the Ohio and West Virginia borders.

This region lies on the rolling Appalachian Plateau as it descends westward from the Laurel Highlands toward the plains of Ohio. This area is in the physio-graphic region known as the Low Pittsburgh Plateau, a raised area with steep slopes through which waterways have cut deep canyons. The Pittsburgh area has been heavily populated since Colonial times, and the region is extensively indus-trialized, with a large amount of infrastructure but a relatively small amount of public land. Nevertheless, the city and county park system offers great urban hik-ing opportunities, and the area features many small nature reserves. The rest of southwestern Pennsylvania is still heavily wooded, with small areas resembling the pre-Colonial wilderness.

Although there are many good hiking opportunities, long-distance backpack-ing routes through remote wilderness are largely absent from this region. Instead, many trails emphasize places of historical interest, from the pre-Colonial period through the industrial revolution to the present. Other trails pass through rural farm environments or emphasize small surviving natural areas that provide a delightful and illuminating contrast to their surroundings. Meanwhile, many of the railroads that helped build the region as an industrial powerhouse, but were later abandoned, have been converted to multiuse trails that provide both histor-

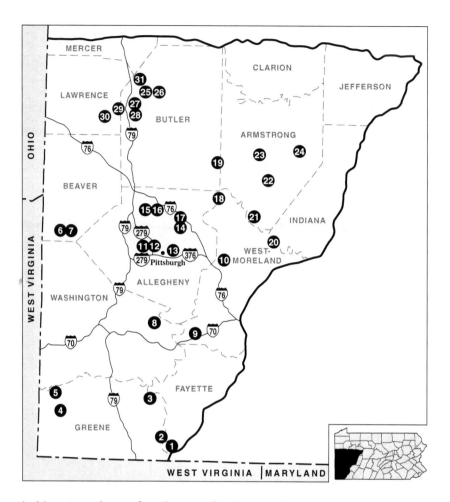

ical interest and a newfound respect for the region's natural offerings. After the era of heavy timbering and mining, much of the rural terrain has been naturally reforested, and there are many reclaimed and rehabilitated areas such as Moraine State Park that are well on the way to becoming wild once again.

1

Friendship Hill
National Historic Site

Friendship Hill National Historic Site, the historic home of pioneer, diplomat, scholar, and early Secretary of the Treasury Albert Gallatin, is on a bluff overlooking the Monongahela River in Fayette County. Gallatin's stately home, built "deep in the western wilderness" of the eighteenth century, has been restored by the National Park Service. The 661-acre estate features 10 miles of trails. The most popular trail begins along the bluff and visits specimens of 200- to 300-year-old oak, pine, and beech trees, giving you a glimpse of the Appalachian Plateau as it was in Colonial times. The trail then descends gradually to parallel the Monongahela River for 1 mile before returning to the homestead. The property's rich woods and meadows make this hike a rewarding experience for bird watchers and botany enthusiasts. There are several other shorter trails on the estate's grounds that can be combined into a variety of day hikes.

Reach Friendship Hill via PA 166 just south of New Geneva, about 3 miles north of US 119 at Point Marion and about 5 miles south of PA 21 at Masontown. Watch for signs for the national historic site. For more information about the indoor and outdoor activities available at the estate, contact Friendship Hill National Historic Site, 223 New Geneva Rd., Point Marion, PA 15474, (724) 725-9190, www.nps.gov/frhi.

2

Warrior Trail
45 miles in Pennsylvania

Warrior Trail predates the European settlement of Pennsylvania by several millennia. It follows a path used for 5,000 years by Native Americans going to Flint Ridge, Ohio, for trading and conferencing. The route was first studied by professors at Waynesburg College in the 1930s. The path now carries Warrior Trail, offering a hike of great historical interest, as well as pastoral farm scenery and stunning rural vistas. This is not a wilderness trail and is not suitable for primitive backpacking, but it is unique for Pennsylvania, reminiscent more of a European countryside path than an eastern American forest trail.

Warrior Trail reaches from the Monongahela River at Greensboro to the Ohio River south of Moundsville, West Virginia. The total distance is 67 miles, with 45 miles in Pennsylvania. Marked with yellow blazes and red mileposts, the trail mostly follows an east-west course 5 to 6 miles north of the Pennsylvania–West Virginia border, along the ridges that form a divide between watersheds. Interestingly, there are no streams to ford along the trail's entire length. Three Adirondack-type shelters are spaced relatively evenly along the trail's distance in Pennsylvania. Warrior Trail is entirely on private property, and volunteers have worked very hard to maintain the cooperation of landowners. Please allow this advantageous situation to continue by respecting private property.

Warrior Trail Association has published a trail guide. To obtain a guide or for further information, contact Warrior Trail Association, P.O. Box 103, Waynesburg, PA 15370.

3
Catawba Trail
30 miles

The Catawba Trail is a primitive and undeveloped trail in Greene County, extending from Rices Landing on the Monongahela River south-southwest to Mason-Dixon Historical Park near Mount Morris. The trail merges briefly with Warrior Trail at a road crossing over I-79. The trail was developed by Warrior Trail Association. There are Adirondack-style shelters at each trailhead, and the trail is marked with aluminum arrows.

For further information, contact Warrior Trail Association, P.O. Box 103, Waynesburg, PA 15370.

4
Ryerson Station State Park

Ryerson Station State Park in Greene County features 11 miles of trails around a 62-acre lake. Popular trails include the Feather Nature Trail, Lazear Trail, and Pine Box Trail. You can create an enjoyable figure-eight hike of 5.3 miles by hiking the Lazear and Pine Box loops, with Iron Bridge Trail as a connector.

Ryerson Station State Park is off PA 21, 3 miles southwest of Wind Ridge. For a park brochure and map, contact Ryerson Station State Park, 361 Bristoria Rd., Wind Ridge, PA 15380, (724) 428-4254, www.dcnr.state.pa.us/stateparks/parks/ryersonstation.aspx.

5
Enlow Fork Natural Area

The remote Enlow Fork Natural Area encompasses the Enlow Fork of Wheeling Creek in Greene County. Through the efforts of the Western Pennsylvania Conservancy, this area has been permanently protected within State Game Land 302. An easy and scenic trail follows a closed dirt road with two iron bridges along the stream through a delightful forest ecosystem, with special interest for bird watchers and wildflower enthusiasts. The typical hike through the area is an in-and-out trek of about 6.5 miles, turning around at a flood-control dam near a gate in the road.

To reach the trailhead, use I-70 to Exit 6 at Claysville. Follow US 40 east into town; then turn south on PA 231. Proceed 3.5 miles, and then bear right on

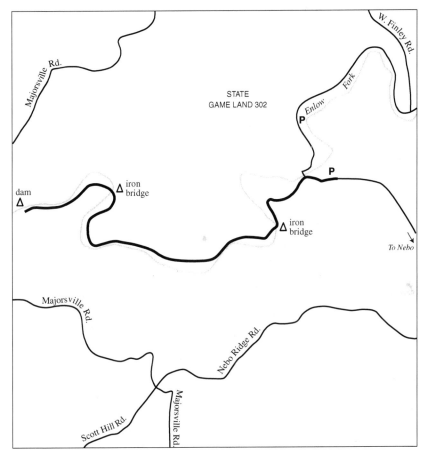

Enlow Fork Natural Area

Burnsville Ridge Road (SR 3029). Follow this road for 7.9 miles to a junction in West Finley, where you turn left onto West Finley Road (SR 3037). Follow this road for 2.4 miles; then just after an iron bridge, turn onto unpaved Walker Hill Road. Follow this road uphill for 1.7 miles, and then turn very sharply right onto unpaved Smoky Row Lane, at a sign for the state game land. Follow this road for 1.2 miles downhill, and park in a field on the left just before a gate at the bottom of the road. The hike into the natural area follows this road beyond the gate.

6

Raccoon Creek State Park

The 7,572-acre Raccoon Creek State Park is in Beaver County, about 3 miles west of Pittsburgh International Airport. It originated as a mini national park set up for demonstration and public-works purposes during the Great Depression, one of five such parks in the commonwealth. The lands were later transferred to the state park system, which developed the lake, campground, and trail network.

Raccoon Creek State Park features 44 miles of trails, from which you can create a variety of day hikes. For a 19.5-mile backpacking loop, follow the green blazes along the Heritage, Forest, and Appaloosa Trails and a portion of Lakeside Lodge Road. Backpack camping is allowed in four areas along this loop, but a permit is required in advance. There are several multiuse trails of variable length and difficulty for hiking, biking, and horseback riding. Of special interest is the 1.9-mile Lake Trail, which follows Traverse Creek to Raccoon Lake and leads to an elaborate two-story springhouse dating from 1846.

The park also has more than a dozen hiking-only trails, consisting of one-way routes of varying lengths, and some short connector trails that can be used to form loop hikes through a variety of landscapes. Of historical interest is the 1.2-mile Mineral Springs Loop Trail, which leads to springs and a small waterfall that were once thought to possess healing powers, alongside the remains of the nineteenth-century Frankfurt Mineral Springs Resort. A substantial loop hike of 8.3 miles in the remote western section of the park is described in *50 Hikes in Western Pennsylvania* (2000), by Tom Thwaites.

PA 18 passes through the center of the park and is used as the main access route, and US 30 passes through the eastern corner of the park. The small portion of the park east of US 30 is known as the Wildflower Reserve (see separate entry below). For a detailed park map and descriptions of the many trails, contact Raccoon Creek State Park, 3000 State Route 18, Hookstown, PA 15050, (724) 899-2200, www.dcnr.state.pa.us/stateparks/parks/raccooncreek.aspx.

7

Wildflower Reserve

The eastern corner of Raccoon Creek State Park, a small parcel of 314 acres that is cut off from the rest of the large park by US 30, is called the Wildflower Reserve. This is the only portion of the state park that actually borders on Raccoon Creek, and it features one of the most diverse stands of wildflowers in western Pennsylvania. From late March through October, more than 500 species of flowers bloom here; peak blooms occur from late April through mid-May and

August through October. A network of easy hiking trails leads through the best wildflower viewing areas in season and provides enjoyable hiking at any time of year. This is a series of intertwining short trails totaling about 4.5 miles, and at no time are you more than 1 mile from the trailhead. To protect the wildflowers, dogs are not allowed in the reserve and activities are restricted to hiking on the designated trails. The reserve also features an interpretive center where maps and information on the wildflower trails are available.

Access this portion of the state park via US 30, 3 miles northwest of Clinton. For more information, contact Raccoon Creek State Park, 3000 State Route 18, Hookstown, PA 15050, (724) 899-2200, www.dcnr.state.pa.us/stateparks/parks/raccooncreek.aspx.

8
Mingo Creek Park

The 2,600-acre Mingo Creek Park in Washington County offers a large network of multiuse trails, with 15 miles of bridle trails that you can use to form a variety of day hikes. There are also designated routes for hikers, which include the 1-mile Hemlock Trail, an interpretive nature path.

The park is on PA 136 about 12 miles east of Washington. For more information, contact Washington County Parks and Recreation, Courthouse Square, 100 W. Beau St., Suite 604, Washington, PA 15301, (724) 228-6867.

9
Cedar Creek Gorge Trail

Cedar Creek Gorge, in Westmoreland County near West Newton, features beautiful forested slopes, waterfalls, and shale steps. A 1.4-mile loop hike combines the park trails with a portion of the Youghiogheny River Trail, and Cedar Creek Park is now a major access point for the Great Allegheny Passage multiuse trail (see the Long-Distance Trails chapter). From the park, the Cedar Creek Gorge Trail starts at the bottom of the parking lot near the boat launch. This broad trail follows the stream up the gorge and across two suspension bridges. After the second bridge, the trail splits, with the main path switching back up the hill and then staying above the gorge, while the other continues to follow the creek. Kids can play in the creek and look for crayfish. From the high trail, you may see unmanned aircraft operated from the nearby MonValley Radio Control Airfield.

To reach Cedar Creek Park, take I-70 to the PA 51 North (Pittsburgh) exit. Follow PA 51 for a quarter mile; then turn right onto the park access road. For more information, contact Westmoreland County Bureau of Parks and Recreation, 194 Donohoe Rd., Greensburg, PA 15601, (724) 830-3950, www.fay-west.com/westmoreland/cedar_creek/guide.

10
Duff Park

The 148-acre Duff Park is a municipal park in Murrysville, east of Pittsburgh, but it is situated in a natural area with hilly and wooded terrain. Numerous hiking trails offer the opportunity for hikes of various lengths and levels of difficulty. Funk Trail runs along a bucolic creek, and Round Top Trail is a strenuous climb to the top of a hill. The park features an abundance of wildflowers in the spring, and you can reach viewing areas via the aptly named Hepatica, Columbine, and Trillium Trails.

Reach Duff Park via US 22 in Murrysville. It is about 1,000 feet south of US 22 via School House Road. For more information and a park map, contact Municipality of Murrysville, 4100 Sardis Rd., Murrysville, PA 15668, (724) 327-2100, www.murrysville.com/muni_parks.html.

11
Three Rivers Heritage Trail

Three Rivers Heritage Trail is a pedestrian trail and greenway that runs throughout the city of Pittsburgh and its suburbs for 37 miles on both sides of the Allegheny, Monongahela, and Ohio Rivers. The trail network is used by hikers, runners, bikers, and in some areas rollerbladers. At the time of this writing, the network was nearly complete, and the trail provides not just exercise and recreational opportunities, but also connections between many of Pittsburgh's most important parks and public areas. The trail route features dozens of large interpretive signs denoting points of natural or historical interest. A portion of the Three Rivers Heritage Trail is incorporated into the Great Allegheny Passage from Pittsburgh to Maryland (see the Long-Distance Trails chapter).

There are numerous access points to the trail throughout the metro area. For more information and a very detailed map, contact Friends of the Riverfront, 33 Terminal Way, Pittsburgh, PA 15219, (412) 488-0212, www.friendsoftheriverfront.org/new_pages/heritage.htm.

12
Pittsburgh Trail

The Pittsburgh metro area's many patches of undeveloped forests and hillsides have been linked by the Pittsburgh Trail, a 50-mile circuit route that is entirely within city limits. The trail route gives you a look at the city's rich natural geography and takes you through many of its urban neighborhoods. It makes liberal use of pedestrian-oriented architecture, including the many stairways, overpasses, and walkways that were built to overcome natural obstacles such as steep hills, ravines, and rivers, not to mention man-made obstacles like multilane highways and railroad tracks. Side streets are incorporated into the network to create a grand tour of the Pittsburgh environment.

There are numerous access points and parking areas for the trail throughout the city. For more information and a series of small sectional maps, visit www .geocities.com/pittsburghtrail.

13
Frick Park

With more than 600 acres, Frick Park is the largest public park within the Pittsburgh city limits. The park lies along Beechwood Boulevard near the Squirrel Hill section of the city, in a spot that is surprisingly wild for a heavily urban area. A network of challenging trails leads through the park's wooded slopes and steep valleys. Many miles of trails are squeezed into a small area, making possible loop hikes ranging from easy to difficult.

From downtown Pittsburgh, follow Forbes Avenue east to Squirrel Hill, and turn onto Beechwood Boulevard, which takes you to the Frick Environmental Center near the park entrance. For a detailed trail map and a description of all the park's offerings, contact Pittsburgh Parks Conservancy, 2000 Technology Dr., Suite 300 Pittsburgh, PA 15219, (412) 682-7275, www.pittsburghparks.org/Frick17.

14
Beechwood Farms
Nature Reserve

Beechwood Farms Nature Reserve, operated by the Audubon Society of Western Pennsylvania, is a 134-acre estate in the Fox Chapel section of Pittsburgh, on the site of a former dairy farm that is being allowed to return to its natural state.

Included in the reserve are a 40-acre native plant sanctuary and an educational center. The reserve also features a network of scenic trails with many possibilities for loop hikes. A loop hike through the reserve's most interesting areas is described in *50 Hikes in Western Pennsylvania* (2000), by Tom Thwaites.

From downtown Pittsburgh, take PA 28 northeast to the exit for PA 8 North. At the first light, turn right onto Kittanning Road, which becomes Dorseyville Road. Beechwood Farms is on the left after 4.5 miles. For further information and a trail map, contact Beechwood Farms Nature Reserve, 614 Dorseyville Rd., Pittsburgh, PA 15238, (412) 963-6100, www.aswp.org/beechwood.

15

Rachel Carson Trail
35.7 miles

The long-distance Rachel Carson Trail travels through mostly private land in northern Allegheny County, through suburban districts to the north and northeast of Pittsburgh. It was built by the Pittsburgh Council of American Youth Hostels in 1972–73. The trail passes near the birthplace of influential environmentalist Rachel Carson and is named in her honor. The route follows a salvaged portion of Baker Trail (see the Long-Distance Trails chapter), which originally started in Pittsburgh and went north to Allegheny National Forest in northwestern Pennsylvania. Part of that original trail in the northern Pittsburgh metro area was cut off by development and then added to the route of the Rachel Carson Trail. This trail has since suffered significant development pressures of its own, resulting in several recent trail relocations. At the time of this writing, the entire route is open.

The yellow-blazed Rachel Carson Trail leads you through a green suburban landscape skirting residential areas and farms, crossing several streams (without footbridges), traversing open fields and woods, and occasionally following steep bluffs. Some areas are surprisingly rugged for the suburban setting. The southwestern end of the trail is at North Park, the northeastern end is at Harrison Hills Park, and the trail traverses several other county parks in between. Spur trails lead to Hartwood Acres (see separate entry below) and the Rachel Carson Homestead. There are no shelters or feasible camping areas along the trail, and it is meant to be day-hiked in sections.

Rachel Carson Trails Conservancy has published a hikers guide to the trail, and it is strongly recommended that anyone planning to hike the trail have a copy because of special instructions for parking and crossing private land. For more information, contact Rachel Carson Trails Conservancy, P.O. Box 35, Warrendale, PA 15086, www.rachelcarsontrails.org. The page dedicated to the Rachel Carson Trail is at www.rachelcarsontrails.org/rct.

16
North Park

North Park is a large park in Allegheny County, on the northern end of the Pittsburgh metro area. It features a lake and nature center and serves as the southwestern terminus for the Rachel Carson Trail. North Park offers a 4.6-mile multiuse trail around the lake and a new hiking trail near the nature center.

Reach the park via Wildwood Road (the Yellow Belt) between US 19 and PA 8 in the McCandless area. For more information and a park map, contact North Park, Pearce Mill Rd., Allison Park, PA 15101, (724) 935-1766, www.county .allegheny.pa.us/parks/npfac.aspx.

17
Hartwood Acres

Hartwood Acres is a 629-acre estate of historical and recreational interest, featuring a mansion, stables, an outdoor performing-arts area, and scenic gardens. Part of the 2006 major motion picture *10th & Wolf,* starring James Marsden and Giovanni Ribisi, was filmed at Hartwood. The site was chosen for its stately country estate style mansion and dining room. On the estate grounds are 5.7 miles of trails that are suitable for hiking, horseback riding, and cross-country skiing, and you can easily create loops of various lengths.

The main entrance to the Hartwood estate is off Saxonburg Boulevard, north of Etna. For more information and a park map, contact Hartwood, 200 Hartwood Acres, Pittsburgh, PA 15238, (412) 767-9200, www.county.allegheny .pa.us/parks/hwfac.aspx.

18
Harrison Hills Park

The 500-acre Harrison Hills Park, in Allegheny County near PA 28, features several miles of hiking and multiuse trails, plus a spectacular overlook of the Allegheny River. Surprisingly for its suburban setting, the park contains a beaver pond and steep cliffs that rise 250 feet above the Allegheny. It serves as the northeastern terminus for the Rachel Carson Trail, which traverses the park on a salvaged section of the original Baker Trail that had been cut off by development. The Baker Trail now starts below here on the other side of the river near Freeport (see the Long-Distance Trails chapter). From the main parking area, a

2.5-mile in-and-out hike on the Rachel Carson Trail takes you along the edge of the cliffs rising above the river. You can use a variety of other paths to form loops.

Reach Harrison Hills Park via PA 28. Take Exit 16, turn east, and travel .6 mile to Freeport Road. Turn right on Freeport Road, continue for .9 mile, and turn left into the park. For more information and a park map, contact Harrison Hills Park, 5200 Freeport Rd., Natrona Heights, PA 15065, (724) 295-3570, www.county.allegheny.pa.us/parks/hhfac.aspx.

19

Todd Nature Reserve

Todd Nature Reserve is a 162-acre wildlife sanctuary in the southeast corner of Butler County that is owned by the Audubon Society of Western Pennsylvania. It is open for public use, with several short hiking trails that you can use to form a great variety of scenic and educational loops. The sanctuary features varying habitats that provide many opportunities for viewing wildflowers and birds. It is particularly suitable for kids because of the many chances to see and discover.

Reach Todd Sanctuary via PA 28 northeast of Pittsburgh. Take the exit for PA 356, and go north toward Sarver for .8 mile. At the first traffic light, turn right onto Monroe Road. Follow this road for 1.2 miles to a fork near Buffalo Golf Course, and bear right onto Kepple Road. Continue for 1.8 miles to the sign on the right for the reserve. For more information and a trail map, contact Audubon Society of Western Pennsylvania, Beechwood Farms Nature Reserve, 614 Dorseyville Rd., Pittsburgh, PA 15238, (412) 963-6100, www.aswp.org/todd.html.

20

West Penn Trail

17 miles

West Penn Trail is a multiuse rail-trail following the former Pennsylvania Railroad route (built on the route of the old Main Line Canal) from Saltsburg to near Blairsville in Indiana County. The trail is a component of the proposed Pittsburgh-to-Harrisburg Main Line Canal Greenway, a projected 320-mile corridor linking sites of historical and natural interest. A short spur trail follows the Kiskiminetas River near Saltsburg, and the main trail follows the Conemaugh River upstream from just west of Saltsburg to a Westinghouse plant near Blairsville. At the time of this writing, an extension into Blairsville is planned, including the construction of a 580-foot bridge over the Conemaugh. This will link the West Penn Trail to the Hoodlebug and Ghost Town Trails to the east (see the Laurel Highlands chapter), forming an extensive rail-trail network. The western portion of the West Penn Trail can be accessed at North Park and Canal Park in downtown Saltsburg. Intermediate access points can be found at Conemaugh Dam and Livermore. The east end of the trail is currently near the Westinghouse Plant just west of Blairsville; the extension to the trail will include access in downtown Blairsville.

For more information and a trail map, contact Conemaugh Valley Conservancy, P.O. Box 502, Hollsopple, PA 15935, www.conemaughvalleyconservancy .org/recreation/recreation.html.

21
Roaring Run Trail

The gently meandering Roaring Run Trail takes you along the scenic Kiskiminetas River, near Apollo in Armstrong County, then up bucolic Roaring Run. From a parking lot at the end of Canal Road at the south end of Apollo, use a portion of the old Pennsylvania Main Line Canal route to a footbridge over Roaring Run just before that stream enters the river. This section of the canal route has been developed as a multiuse trail that will be incorporated in the proposed Pittsburgh-to-Harrisburg Main Line Canal Greenway (see the West Penn Trail entry above). Here the Rock Furnace Trail turns up the scenic hollow of Roaring Run, reaching Brownstown Road at about 3 miles. The main trail also continues along the Kiskiminetas River beyond Roaring Run.

For more information and a trail map, contact Roaring Run Watershed Association, Box 333, Apollo, PA 15613, (724) 478-3366, www.roaringrun.org/trail.html.

22
Crooked Creek Lake
Recreation Area

Crooked Creek Lake Recreation Area is an extensive recreational park around a flood-control reservoir in Armstrong County. Both are managed by the U.S. Army Corps of Engineers. The park contains about 6 miles of the Baker Trail (see the Long-Distance Trails chapter) plus many other hiking trails that you can use to form loops of varying lengths and levels of difficulty. Several interpretive trails are dedicated to plants, animals, songbirds, and outdoor education for kids.

Reach the recreation area via PA 66 between Ford City and Vandergrift. For more information and a recreation area map, contact U.S. Army Corps of Engineers, Crooked Creek Lake, 114 Park Main Rd., Ford City, PA 16226, (724) 763-3161, www.lrp.usace.army.mil/rec/lakes/crookedc.htm.

23

Armstrong Trail
52.5 miles

Armstrong Trail is a multiuse rail-trail that mostly follows the Allegheny River from Schenley in Armstrong County to East Brady in Clarion County. The trail follows the route of the former Allegheny River Railroad, which originally hauled coal and was later used to transport oil from the fields of northwestern Pennsylvania to Pittsburgh. At the time of this writing, most of the trail is unimproved, with the original bed of ballast and cinders, though a section in Ford City and another from Manorville to Kittanning have been improved. In 2006, a 1-mile spur was added along Cowanshannock Creek to Buttermilk Falls.

For more information and a trail map, contact Armstrong Rails-to-Trails Association, Kittanning Visitors Center, Market and Water Sts., P.O. Box 777, Kittanning, PA 16201, (724) 543-4478, www.armstrongtrail.org.

24

Great Shamokin Path
4 miles

This hiking and biking trail in Armstrong County is named after the Great Shamokin Path, the trail network used by Native Americans from the Allegheny River at modern-day Kittanning to the Susquehanna River in central Pennsylvania. The present, mostly grass-covered, hiking and biking trail runs between Numine and Rose Valley, parallel to Cowanshannock Creek. It follows the route of the former Rural Valley Railroad, past Devil's Washbasin, an artificial lake that supplied railroad steam engines—leading to an eerily steamy setting during the railroad era. At the time of this writing, a 7.5-mile extension to be called the Kavolchick Trail has been proposed.

The trailheads for Great Shamokin Path are on PA 85 near Yatesboro and in Numine near White Lake Picnic Area. For more information, contact Cowanshannock Creek Watershed Association, P.O. Box 307, Rural Valley, PA 16249, (724) 783-6692, www.cowanshannock.org.

25

Miller Esker Natural Area

Miller Esker Natural Area, a 32-acre mound of sand and gravel, is one of the most unusual geologic formations in western Pennsylvania. The Natural Area encompasses the most accessible portion of this geologic feature. Nearly 3 miles long, 360 feet wide, and 40 feet high, the esker is composed of gravel carried south from Canada by glaciers thousands of years ago. An easy hike takes you over and around the esker. Part of the esker is forested, and part is covered by a grassland mowed by the Western Pennsylvania Conservancy.

Reach the natural area via PA 528 in Butler County north of Moraine State Park. From PA 528, turn onto West Liberty Road, and travel 2 miles to a T intersection. Turn right and proceed .2 mile into West Liberty; then turn left at the four-way intersection. Follow this road over a small bridge and then bear right, still following West Liberty Road. Continue for 1.6 miles to the esker, and park at a revealing road cut across from a farm. The fields are privately owned, so park on the right side of the road. Access the esker by walking through the woods along the eastern edge of the fields, and then go up the esker. For more information, contact Western Pennsylvania Conservancy, 209 Fourth Ave., Pittsburgh, PA 15222, (412) 288-2777, www.paconserve.org/conservation/naturalresource/wpcowned/milleresker.htm.

26
Jennings Environmental Education Center

Jennings Environmental Educational Center was established in the late 1950s by the Western Pennsylvania Conservancy to preserve the blazing star, a beautiful and rare prairie flower. This small area, in the midst of the eastern deciduous forest, is one of Pennsylvania's few remaining tracts of the true prairie that once stretched from the Appalachians to the Rockies. The center is now administered by the Bureau of State Parks, and the educational focus makes it ideal for kids. A number of short trails have been cleared through the grounds of the center, with a special emphasis on visiting areas populated by wildflowers and other unique prairie flora. The trails also lead into wooded areas surrounding the prairie tract, where the work of beavers is often visible. A 2.2-mile loop hike through many noteworthy natural features is described in *50 Hikes in Western Pennsylvania* (2000), by Tom Thwaites.

The center is in Butler County on PA 528, just a few hundred yards southwest of the intersection with PA 8 and PA 173. For more information, contact Jennings Environmental Education Center, 2951 Prospect Rd., Slippery Rock, PA 16057, (724) 794-6011, www.dcnr.state.pa.us/stateParks/parks/jennings.aspx.

27
Glacier Ridge Trail
14 miles

The long-distance Glacier Ridge Trail connects Jennings Environmental Education Center with Moraine State Park. Except for the segment through the
grounds of the center, the trail is almost entirely within the expansive boundaries
of the state park, passing through some surprisingly remote areas of the park's
backcountry in addition to developed recreational areas. Glacier Ridge Trail has
been named a component of the proposed route of the North Country National
Scenic Trail (see the Long-Distance Trails chapter), though at the time of this
writing, this segment is not yet connected with the completed sections of the
NCNST to the northeast at Cook Forest State Park. A connector is under construction to the next NCNST section to the west at McConnells Mill State Park.

The blue-blazed Glacier Ridge Trail, as the name implies, follows a ridge and
other geologic features formed by glaciers during the ice ages. There are some
yellow-blazed side trails that you can use to form loops. At the time of this writing, the most easily available map depicting the Glacier Ridge Trail is the official
map for Moraine State Park, which also includes Jennings Environmental Education Center. Contact Moraine State Park, 225 Pleasant Valley Rd., Portersville,
PA 16051, (724) 368-8811, www.dcnr.state.pa.us/stateparks/parks/moraine.aspx.

28
Moraine State Park

This large 16,275-acre state park, along US 422 west of Butler and just east of
I-79, highlights many glacial features of great geologic interest. The general area
was once covered by the immense Lakes Arthur and Edmund, which contained
vast amounts of meltwater in basins carved out by retreating glaciers. Today a
dam at Moraine State Park creates a smaller descendant of Lake Arthur. At the
time the state park was founded, the region had been severely damaged by coal
mining and oil and gas extraction; these areas have since been rehabilitated with
great effort. The park grounds include many recreational opportunities around
the lake, plus a large and remote backcountry. The park contains 28.6 miles of
hiking trails, including most of the Glacier Ridge Trail (see separate entry above).
You can use a variety of shorter trails to form loop hikes of varying distances and
degrees of difficulty. There are also several multiuse trails. For more information
and a park map, contact Moraine State Park, 225 Pleasant Valley Rd., Portersville,
PA 16051, (724) 368-8811, www.dcnr.state.pa.us/stateparks/parks/moraine.aspx.

29

McConnells Mill State Park

This 2,546-acre park in Lawrence County encompasses a portion of the spectacular Slippery Rock Creek Gorge. Most of the developed recreational areas of the park are at the north end of the gorge near US 422; the southern portions of the park lands protect the deepest and most remote portions of the gorge. McConnells Mill (a restored gristmill) and a covered bridge add historical interest to the state park.

Slippery Rock Creek Gorge is a national natural landmark featuring rocky cliffs, hanging valleys, huge boulders, and waterfalls. It formed as glacial lakes to the north drained away rapidly down the course of Slippery Rock Creek, abruptly carving a steep-sided gorge with many large boulders left behind in the creekbed, some of which had been transported from as far away as Canada. The gorge was named after an actual slippery rock noted by Native Americans at a spot where they frequently crossed the creek. The rock was near a natural oil seep that has since been cut off by modern drilling operations.

The park contains several scenic and challenging hiking trails. Alpha Pass Trail leads steeply from an overlook to the creek and then to the mill; you can create a loop by walking back on park roads. Kildoo Trail is a moderately difficult 2-mile loop along Slippery Rock Creek from the covered bridge to Eckert Bridge, crossing both bridges and leading you along both banks of the creek. A short and easy trail at Hell Hollow in the southwestern portion of the park follows Hell Run to a lime kiln and a waterfall; exercise caution in slippery areas. The undeveloped areas of the park contain the route of the outstanding Slippery Rock Gorge Trail (see separate entry below).

All these trails feature spectacular scenery, especially during spring wildflower season and in the autumn. Even more hiking challenges are available for those willing to bushwhack through the gorge's numerous scenic side hollows. McConnells Mill State Park has been named a component of the proposed route of the North Country National Scenic Trail (see the Long-Distance Trails chapter).

Reach the park via US 422 just to the west of I-79. The southwestern portion of the park can be accessed only via a succession of rural roads between PA 65 and PA 488. For more information and a park map, contact McConnells Mill State Park, RR 2, Box 16, Portersville, PA 16051, (724) 368-8091, www.dcnr .state.pa.us/stateparks/parks/mcconnellsmill.aspx.

30

Slippery Rock Gorge Trail

6.1 miles

The spectacularly scenic and very challenging Slippery Rock Gorge Trail follows its namesake gorge through the undeveloped areas of McConnells Mill State Park (see separate entry above). This blue-blazed, one-way trail leading from Eckert Bridge to Hell Hollow was opened in 1994 after an arduous construction process led by Shenango Outing Club with the assistance of Keystone Trails Association. The trail features a lot of climbing in and out of steep areas of the gorge, and the footway is often narrow along precipitous ledges. If you have stamina and wear the proper footwear, you will experience one of the most rewarding hikes in western Pennsylvania. The trail follows Slippery Rock Creek and its gorge for about 4 miles, then leads up picturesque Hell Hollow, which contains a waterfall, cave, and three natural bridges, one of which the trail crosses.

Slippery Rock Gorge Trail can be accessed only via the trailheads at Eckert Bridge and Hells Hollow. The Eckert Bridge trailhead can be reached on foot via the trails leading south from McConnells Mill State Park. By car, follow Kennedy Road south away from the park's main parking areas. At the end of the road, turn right on Cheeseman Road and proceed downhill to a gate at Eckert Bridge over Slippery Rock Creek. The bridge is closed and parking is limited.

To reach the Hell Hollow trailhead, use Exit 96 off I-79 (PA 488) and go west 4.3 miles. Turn right on Heinz Camp Road and continue 4.7 miles. Turn right on Shaeffer Road and drive just .1 mile to the Hell Hollow Falls parking lot. For more information, contact McConnells Mill State Park, RR 2, Box 16, Portersville, PA 16051, (724) 368-8091, www.dcnr.state.pa.us/stateparks/parks/mcconnellsmill.aspx.

31

Wolf Creek Narrows Natural Area

1.5 miles

Wolf Creek Narrows Natural Area is operated as a 125-acre wildflower preserve by the Western Pennsylvania Conservancy (WPC). A loop trail with an entrance trail, adding up to a hike of 1.5 miles, leads into the best wildflower-viewing spots in the natural area. The trail is picturesque and pleasant at any time of the year, but especially in late April and early May, when the wildflowers are in bloom. WPC owns another tract of land on the opposite side of Wolf Creek; there are no marked trails, but adventurous hikers can reach the area by fording the creek.

Wolf Creek Narrows Natural Area is just outside Slippery Rock in Butler County, on West Water Street 1.7 miles west of PA 258 in the center of town. For more information, contact Western Pennsylvania Conservancy, 209 Fourth Ave., Pittsburgh, PA 15222, (412) 288-2777, www.paconserve.org.

REGION 6

Northwest and Allegheny National Forest

Region Editor: Jim Ritchie

The Northwest and Allegheny National Forest Region consists of the northwestern corner of Pennsylvania. For clarity, this chapter has two sections. The first section concentrates exclusively on the hiking opportunities in Allegheny National Forest; the second covers the plateau and plain areas that make up the rest of the region. The Northwest and Allegheny National Forest Region is bounded on the north by the New York state line and Lake Erie; on the west by the Ohio state line; on the south by I-80; and on the east by US 219 to McKean County and then US 6, PA 46, and PA 446 to the New York state line.

Northwestern Pennsylvania is made up of two physiographic regions: the Allegheny Plateau and the Lake Plain. The region's scenic and geologic diversity is due to the glaciers that smoothed out the plain along Lake Erie into a series of wide terraces that rise step by step to the plateau. Both the plain and the plateau are covered with wetlands, lakes, ponds, and bogs. The higher areas of plateau are heavily forested and have largely resisted urban and agricultural development, but not the resource extraction industries that covet the area's vast timber, oil, and gas resources.

The Lake Plain is known for the diverse wildflowers that grace both its deep woods and open wetlands. Songbirds with cheery voices cover this area each spring, and migrating waterfowl flocks pass through the wetland areas every spring and fall. It is not unusual to see dozens of species on any outing. The moderately wooded plains gradually rise to the heavily forested plateau, where

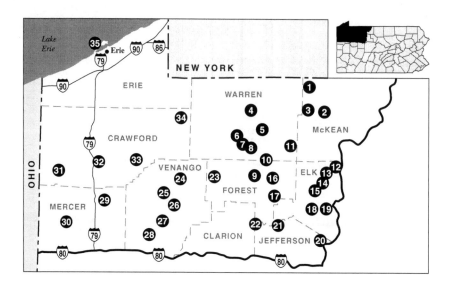

the mixed-hardwood forest provides a varied canopy and a stunning palette of colors in the autumn. Long stretches of open woods and fields on gently rolling terrain allow for beautiful and exploratory hiking. This region is also the snowiest area of Pennsylvania by a wide margin, leading to hardship for winter hikers and euphoria for cross-country skiers.

The Northwest and Allegheny National Forest Region does not feature major vistas and long, steep climbs, but hiking on the plains offers relaxation and historical interest, and the forests create a feeling of vastness and solitude. If you enjoy more subtle and laid-back hiking with a sense of exploration and natural appreciation, this region is for you.

Allegheny National Forest Section

Allegheny National Forest (ANF) consists of more than 500,000 acres of federally managed forest lands. It is full of old logging roads, abandoned railroad grades, and utility rights-of-way that have become excellent hiking trails. The forest features several stands of mature or virgin timber that attract large numbers of visitors, most notably at Hearts Content and Tionesta Scenic Areas.

An extensive system of trails has been developed in the national forest, nearly 200 miles of which are specifically designated for hiking. An extensive system of forestry roads provides access to the trails and allows for a variety of day-hiking opportunities. Camping is permitted almost everywhere, with the exception of Hearts Content Scenic Area, Tionesta Research Area, Tionesta Scenic Area, and within 1,500 feet of the Allegheny Reservoir or the Longhouse Scenic Highway. Hiking cross-country using topographic maps is not difficult in the national forest. Most stream valleys have old logging railroad grades, and there are many old logging roads and pipelines. Unfortunately, some areas also have many new logging and oil and gas development roads.

A guide to hiking in Allegheny National Forest can be obtained from Sierra Club's Allegheny Group. For ordering information, visit www.alleghenysc.org/publications. *Hiking the Allegheny National Forest: Exploring the Wilderness of Northwestern Pennsylvania* (2007), by Jeff Mitchell, describes a variety of family-friendly day hikes and a few extended backpacking trips. For information on forest policies and access, a large-scale map of the forest region, and maps and descriptions of many different individual hiking trails, visit the US Forest Service website at www.fs.fed.us/r9/forests/allegheny. Most of the trails in this section have their own pages on the ANF website, with downloadable maps featuring the particular trail and often other nearby trails. For specific information on forest and trail conditions, contact one of these three offices: Allegheny National Forest, 227 Liberty St., Box 847, Warren, PA 16365, (814) 723-5150; Bradford Ranger District, 29 US Forest Service Drive, Bradford, PA 16701, (814) 362-4613; or Marienville Ranger District, Star Route 2, Box 130, Marienville, PA 16239, (814) 927-6628. The two ranger stations are especially useful for obtaining localized weather information. Conditions in the ANF can be quite unpredictable, and storms frequently cause trail damage.

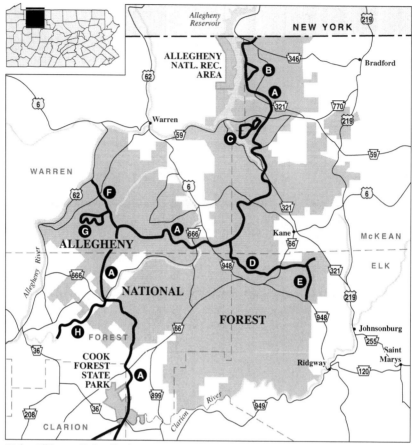

Major Hiking Trails in Allegheny National Forest

- **A** North Country National Scenic Trail
- **B** Tracy Ridge Hiking System
- **C** Morrison Trail
- **D** Twin Lakes Trail
- **E** Mill Creek Trail
- **F** Tanbark Trail
- **G** Hickory Creek Wilderness Trail
- **H** Kellettville to Nebraska Trace

1

Tracy Ridge Hiking System

8.7 miles

The Tracy Ridge Hiking System is a loop hike in the far northern reaches of Allegheny National Forest that makes use of a section of the North Country National Scenic Trail (NCNST; see the Long-Distance Trails chapter) along the east shore of Allegheny Reservoir, plus the 2.3-mile Johnnycake Trail and the 4-mile Tracy Ridge Trail. The white-blazed Tracy Ridge Trail begins at PA 321, just north of the driveway to Tracy Ridge Campground, and heads west toward the reservoir along a wooded ridge. Near the campground, pass the junction with Johnnycake Trail, on which this loop hike returns. Tracy Ridge Trail ends at the NCNST. Turn left and follow the NCNST 2.3 miles to a junction with the white-blazed Johnnycake Trail. Turn left and follow this trail 2.3 miles back to the campground, where it ends at Tracy Ridge Trail. Turn right for a .1-mile walk back to the trailhead. This is just one possible hike in the Tracy Ridge area, where many different trails offer a plethora of hiking opportunities.

Timberdoodle Flats
Wildlife Interpretive Trail
1.4 miles

The Timberlake Flats Wildlife Interpretive Trail is a double loop trail named for the American woodcock, also known as the timberdoodle, a bird common in the ANF region. The trail is blazed with off-white diamonds and features self-guided interpretive markers and a hardened surface for accessibility. The trail is located on PA 59 a quarter mile east of the intersection with PA 321 North, near the Warehouse Restaurant and just west of Marshburg.

Morrison Trail
14.7 miles

The highly scenic and challenging Morrison Trail system consists of a .5-mile entrance trail and two loops—the 8.1-mile Rimrock Trail Loop and the 5.5-mile Morrison Trail Loop—that share a 1.3-mile connector trail. For an enjoyable 14.7-mile day hike or short backpacking trip, complete both loops in a figure eight, which necessitates using the cutoff and entrance trails twice. Access is from PA 59, 3 miles east of the bridge over the reservoir.

After you follow the access trail to the loop junction, to your left the Morrison Trail (the east loop) leads along the plateau parallel to PA 59, then turns sharply to the southwest and descends the upper branch of Morrison Run. If you turn right from the entrance trail and follow Rimrock Trail (the west loop) counterclockwise, you can complete the steepest part of the system in the downhill direction. Later the views along Morrison Run improve as you follow it upstream. The trail is on the high plateau, with fine stands of mountain laurel. To the south, the Rimrock Loop descends to the Allegheny Reservoir, with a great view from a large boulder 100 feet from the trail on the downhill side. The trail leads to the Morrison boat-in campground, reachable only by boaters and hikers, and then ascends scenic Morrison Run to the cutoff trail. The cutoff trail climbs alongside a scenic tributary of Morrison Run, with many waterfalls and rock jumbles.

Buckaloons Recreation Area
1 mile

The Seneca Interpretive Trail is an educational loop trail leading around the picnic area and campground at Buckaloons Recreation Area, meandering along the Allegheny River and Irvine Run. Buckaloons is on the site of an old Indian village on the banks of the river. To reach the recreation area, take the US 62 South exit (to Tionesta) off the US 6/US 62 expressway near Irvine. Just before the bridge over the Allegheny, turn right into the recreation area. The Seneca Interpretive Trail is not blazed, but you can follow numbered markers to points of interest.

Chapman State Park

The 805-acre Chapman State Park, west of Clarendon, is surrounded by Allegheny National Forest. It includes a 68-acre lake on the West Branch of Tionesta Creek and seven trails that are excellent for day hikes. You also can use the park campground and parking facilities as a base for backpacking on the adjacent national forest lands; sign in at the park office for multiday trips. The hiking trails within the park include Hunters Ridge Trail (2.5 miles), Nature Loops (1.7 miles), Adams Run Trail (2.9 miles), Game Lands Trail (2.2 miles), Lowlands Trail (.2 mile), Penny Run Trail (1.4 miles), and Lumber Trail (.4 mile). A loop hike through the most interesting features of the state park is described in *50 Hikes in Western Pennsylvania* (2000), by Tom Thwaites. Reach Chapman State Park via a 5.1 mile paved road leading from Clarendon, on US 6 southeast of Warren. For more information, contact Chapman State Park, RR 2, Box 1610, Clarendon, PA 16313, (814) 723-0250, www.dcnr.state.pa.us/stateparks/parks/chapman.aspx.

Hickory Creek Wilderness Trail
11.1 miles

This remote loop trail travels through Hickory Creek Wilderness, one of only two federally designated wilderness areas in Pennsylvania as of 2007. The other is also in the ANF, at Allegheny River Islands. Hickory Creek Wilderness Trail starts at a trailhead parking lot .5 mile north of Hearts Content Scenic Area, on Hearts Content Road (see separate entry below for directions). At the time of this writing, the trail is marked with yellow blazes, but they are very infrequent and are also in the process of being phased out (allowed to fade) in accordance with federal wilderness guidelines. Those guidelines also dictate that future trail obstructions will not be removed if doing so will cause environmental damage. This will also be the case after storms. These regulations will enhance the remote and unspoiled wilderness character of the area but will make the trail difficult to follow. Hiking should be attempted only by experienced hikers who are adept at using forestry maps and even GPS devices.

From Hearts Content, an entrance trail for the Hickory Creek Wilderness Trail leads about a quarter mile to the loop. Clockwise on the loop, the trail proceeds southbound for about 2 miles, and then turns west until it reaches Jacks Run. The trail then turns to the north and about a mile later turns back to the east, following the top of the plateau between East Hickory and Middle Hickory Creeks back to the entrance trail.

The wilderness area's topography is varied, ranging in elevation from 1,400 to 1,900 feet. There are few steep areas, making the trail comfortable for hiking and excellent for cross-country skiing. For a backpacking trip, you can camp in beautiful clearings along the southern portion of the loop or along Middle Hickory Creek off the trail to the south. The Hickory Creek Wilderness Area also offers great opportunities for bird watchers. History buffs will note the long-abandoned remains of logging camps and old railroad grades.

7
Hearts Content Scenic Trail
1.3 miles

Hearts Content Scenic Area, 15 miles southwest of Warren, features a 122-acre remnant of old-growth forest with immense white pine and beech trees, representing the type of wild and rugged virgin environment the early pioneers encountered when they first settled northwestern Pennsylvania. Hearts Content Scenic Trail is a loop that meanders through the best of the old-growth, beginning and ending on the east side of the picnic ground. From the Mohawk exit off the US 6 expressway in Warren, turn onto Pleasant Drive (later Pleasant Road) and travel south for 11 miles. At a hard curve, bear left onto the gravel section of Hearts Content Road, and continue 4 miles to the scenic area.

Tanbark Trail

8.8 miles

The white-blazed Tanbark Trail branches off the North Country National Scenic Trail near Hearts Content Scenic Area, then leads northwest through the scenic area to a trailhead on US 62 along the Allegheny River. The trail passes through some of the most primitive woodland on the Allegheny Plateau. To reach the Tanbark Trail, use the trailhead parking area on PA 62, 8.9 miles north of Tidioute and 6.7 miles south of US 6, or at Hearts Content Scenic Area (see separate entry above for directions). The southern end of the trail, at the NCNST, is at Dunham Siding, just to the southeast of Hearts Content.

Kellettville to Nebraska Trace

12 miles

The Kellettville to Nebraska Trace is an outstandingly remote and scenic trail that is primitive and unimproved, starting in Kellettville campground on PA 666 and ending at the boat launch at Nebraska Bridge on Tionesta Lake. Parking is available at both sites. The trail follows Tionesta Creek on a grass and dirt surface, with lots of great scenery and fishing and four bridgeless crossings of side streams. The primitive pathway is for hiking only. At the time of this writing, this trail was closed because of a shortage of funds and volunteers needed to fix storm-related damage suffered in 2003–04. Kellettville to Nebraska Trace is not referenced on the ANF website, but more information about the trail can be found on the websites for several regional recreational and historical associations. No trail map has been produced as yet, so skills at pathfinding and reading topo maps are required.

Minister Creek Trail

6.6 miles

Minister Creek Trail is a loop trail traversing the extraordinarily scenic Minister Creek Recreation Area along PA 666, offering one of the most interesting day hikes in Allegheny National Forest. The trail, marked with white, diamond-shaped blazes, is very popular and often crowded, and for good reason: It climbs the valley alongside picturesque Minister Creek to the plateau where it meets and briefly follows the North Country National Scenic Trail (see the Long-Distance Trails chapter). The loop hike then returns down the other side of the valley. Parts of the trail follow old railroad grades. The loop passes a variety of immense rock outcroppings, with an outstanding view on the west side. The recreation area also features a campground, with toilets and water pump; and six small campsites along the creek, each with a picnic table, fire ring, and tent pad. At the northern end of the loop along the NCNST, Triple Forks Camp, at the confluence of three branches of the creek, has been designated specifically for backpackers. To reach the recreation area parking lot, follow PA 666 southwest from Sheffield for 14.7 miles.

11
Tionesta Scenic Area Interpretive Trail
1.4 miles

Tionesta Scenic Area Interpretive Trail is within the 2,018-acre scenic area, and immediately adjacent is the 2,113-acre Tionesta Natural Area. Together, these two areas represent a remnant of the original forest that once covered 6 million acres of the Allegheny Plateau. The tornadoes that roared across northwestern Pennsylvania in 1985 caused a great amount of damage to Tionesta Scenic Area, the effects of which can be seen from this interpretive trail. The trail also leads to several features that illustrate the natural uniqueness of the area, including many old-growth trees. To reach the trail, take US 6 to Ludlow, between Sheffield and Kane. Watch for signs to Tionesta Scenic Area, and turn south onto South Hillside Street. In one block, turn left on Water Street, then right on Scenic Drive, which later becomes FR 133. Follow this road for 5.8 miles away from US 6; then turn right on an access road (FR 133E) and continue 1.2 miles to the trailhead and a scenic area marker. Signs along FR 133 direct you to the site.

12
Black Cherry National Recreation Interpretive Trail
1.4 miles

Black Cherry National Recreation Interpretive Trail leads from Twin Lakes Recreation Area's parking lot to the long-distance Twin Lakes Trail (see separate entry below) and can be used with that trail to create hikes of various lengths. This educational and interpretive trail is blazed with off-white diamonds. To reach the trailhead at Twin Lakes Recreation Area, use PA 321 between Kane and Wilcox to the area's entrance road. The trailhead parking lot is just prior to entering the recreation area, and the trail is shown on the Twin Lakes Trail map.

Twin Lakes Trail
15.8 miles

After the North Country National Scenic Trail (see the Long-Distance Trails chapter), this is the second-longest trail in Allegheny National Forest. The white-blazed Twin Lakes Trail starts at the recreation area of the same name near Wilcox and leads west over the plateau and into the headwaters of Wolf Run. After crossing PA 66, the trail continues down Wolf Run to its confluence with the south branch of Tionesta Creek. After crossing that creek and Crane Run, Twin Lakes Trail swings northwest and north toward Tionesta Natural Area, finally ending at the NCNST within Tionesta Scenic Area. The trail travels through some of the more heavily developed areas of the ANF; oil and gas extraction activities are evident. To reach the trailhead at Twin Lakes Recreation Area, use PA 321 between Kane and Wilcox to the area's entrance road. The Twin Lakes Trail does not quite reach the recreation area parking lot, so you must use a portion of the Black Cherry Interpretive Trail (see separate entry above) as access.

Mill Creek Trail
5.6 miles

Mill Creek Trail, marked with off-white diamonds, serves as a connector between Twin Lakes Recreation Area, off PA 321 near Wilcox, and Brush Hollow Hiking and Cross-Country Ski Area, on PA 948 north of Ridgway (see separate entries in this section). At the northern terminus, 1.2 miles west of Twin Lakes, Mill Creek Trail leaves Twin Lakes Trail and heads south, passing Kane Experimental Forest and proceeding through a pleasant variety of landscapes along Big Mill Creek. The last mile of the trail on the southern end follows an old railroad grade before hopping across the creek and ending at the Brush Hollow entrance trail, just north of that system's parking lot. Parking is available at Twin Lakes Recreation Area (see the entry above); at the junction of Twin Lakes and Mill Creek Trails, at a crossing of FR 138 about 1 mile west of the recreation area; or at Brush Hollow (see separate entry below).

15
Brush Hollow Hiking
and Cross-Country Ski Area

A network of three interconnected trails at Brush Hollow Hiking and Cross-Country Ski Area can be used for hiking, mountain biking, or cross-country skiing. The three separate loops can be hiked individually or in several combinations to make hikes of various lengths. A hike around the outer edges of the loop system is 7.7 miles in length. The trails are blazed with blue, diamond-shaped markers nailed to trees. The parking area is on PA 948, 10 miles north of Ridgway. A brochure with map is usually available at the parking lot.

16
Beaver Meadows
Hiking Trail System

The wetland-intensive Beaver Meadows Recreational Area near Marienville features five interconnected trails: Beaver Meadows Loop Trail, Seldom Seen Trail, Salmon Creek Loop Trail, Penoke Path, and Lakeside Loop Trail. The total length of the trails is 7.1 miles, and a variety of loops can be created. All the trails are blazed with blue diamonds, except Beaver Meadows Loop Trail, which is blazed with off-white diamonds. The network winds through wetland areas along Beaver Meadows Lake and into the surrounding forested hills. To reach Beaver Meadows Recreation Area, turn north onto North Fourth Street at the main interchange in Marienville. This street becomes Beaver Meadows Road. At 4 miles from Marienville, turn right onto FR 282 at a sign for the recreation area, and drive to a parking lot near the dam.

17
Buzzard Swamp
Wildlife Viewing Area

The unique Buzzard Swamp Wildlife Viewing Area lies on a flat and open plateau near Marienville, with many swamps, wetlands, and ponds. Here, 9.6 miles of hiking trails meander through a special management area that emphasizes wildlife habitat and visitor recreation. Migratory birds are particularly fond of the area, and the fifteen man-made ponds contain many species of gamefish that are favorites of fishermen. The flat plateau landscape offers little protection from sun and wind, so be prepared. Most of the area's trails are not marked, but signs provide some information; follow the area hiking map carefully. Mountain biking and cross-country skiing are also permitted on the trails. To reach the southern trailhead, follow Loleta Road 1 mile south from Marienville; then turn left on FR 157 into the wildlife viewing area. To reach the northern side of the area, where there are two trailheads, travel east from Marienville on Lamonaville Road (which becomes FR 130) for about 2 miles, to the north boundary of the wildlife viewing area.

18

Little Drummer Historical Pathway

4.4 miles

The Little Drummer Historical Pathway consists of two loops of 1.3 miles and 3.1 miles, which can be easily hiked in a figure eight of 4.4 miles. The trail name derives from the grouse that live locally, known for their drumlike sounds, and from the extensive number of historic railroads, pipelines, and camps in the area. Located within Owl's Nest Ecosystem Management Demonstration Area, managed to provide wildlife habitat, the trail offers opportunities to view both upland and riparian species. Cole Run Pond is located next to the trail. The two loops are blazed with off-white, diamond-shaped markers on trees. The parking area is 8 miles west of Ridgway on TR 307, also known as Laurel Mill Road or Spring Creek Road, and west of Laurel Mill Hiking Trail (see separate entry below).

19

Laurel Mill Hiking Trail

The Laurel Mill network of hiking and cross-country ski trails consists of six different loops blazed with diamond-shaped markers on trees. The loops can be hiked individually or in several combinations to make hikes of various lengths. The area is maintained for cross-country skiing; mountain bikes are prohibited, though hikers are welcome in the off-season. To reach the trailhead, travel about 3 miles west from downtown Ridgway on West Main Street, which becomes Laurel Mill Road and then TR 307, also known locally as Spring Creek Road. The trailhead offers brochures, restrooms, and a warming hut.

Northwest Plateau and Plains Section

20

Clarion–Little Toby Creek Trail
18 miles

The Clarion–Little Toby Creek rail-trail, at the time of this writing, runs 18 miles from Brockway to Ridgway, but a southern extension from Brockway to Brookville has been proposed. The current route of the trail follows Little Toby Creek along its southern half and the Clarion River along the northern half. The trail is on an easy, flat grade with spectacular scenery, and since most of the route is within State Game Land 44, you see pristine forest for almost the entire distance. The southern half of the trail features numerous ghost towns, quarry ruins, the remains of a collapsed earthen dam, and the site of a train wreck. A swinging bridge at the junction of a spur grade offers a great side excursion over Little Toby Creek. For more information, contact TriCounty Rails to Trails Association, P.O. Box 115, Ridgway, PA 15853, pavisnet.com/tcrtt. See map on page 132.

21

Clear Creek State Park
and Clear Creek State Forest

The 1,836-acre Clear Creek State Park is in Jefferson County along Clear Creek and the Clarion River just to the west of PA 949. To the east across PA 949 is a large section of Clear Creek (formerly Kittanning) State Forest. Camping in the park is allowed only at designated campsites or rustic cabins. The park also contains about 15 miles of marked trails. The Jefferson County units of Clear Creek State Forest comprise 9,089 acres, including the Beartown Rocks recreational area, with rock formations and impressive views of the plateau reaching far into Allegheny National Forest.

The orange-blazed Beartown Rocks Trail starts on PA 949 across from the state park and forms a loop that passes through Beartown Rocks. Several side trails and many access roads allow for a good variety of hiking possibilities in this area of the state forest. Beautiful stands of mountain laurel bloom in mid to late June. Backpacking, with some restrictions, is permitted on the state forest lands. The book *50 Hikes in Western Pennsylvania* (2000), by Tom Thwaites, features two loop hikes in this area: one within the state park and one through the state forest tract to Beartown Rocks.

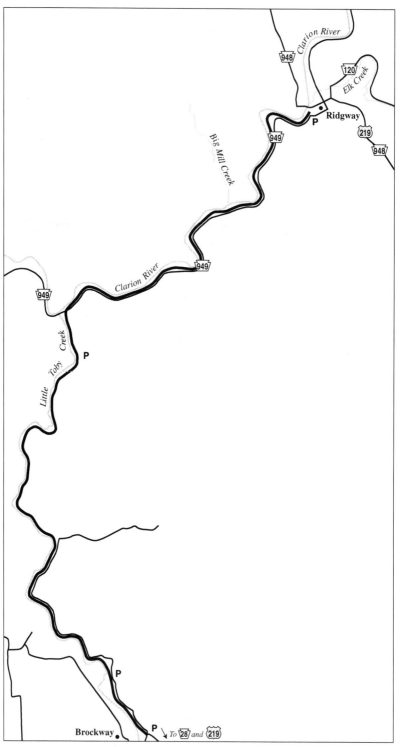

Clarion–Little Toby Creek Trail

For a park map and more information on the state forest trails, contact Clear Creek State Park, 38 Clear Creek State Park Rd., Sigel, PA 15860, (814) 752-2368, www.dcnr.state.pa.us/stateparks/parks/clearcreek.aspx.

22

Cook Forest State Park

The 7,132-acre Cook Forest State Park, on the Clarion River just to the south of the ANF, contains a significant stand of virgin white pine and hemlock that has been designated a national natural landmark. The park has a 29-mile trail network with sixteen marked trails. The terrain is rolling hills and cool valley streams, with vistas and rock formations in the high areas and the scenic Clarion River meandering below the hills. The 141-mile Baker Trail passes through the park on its way from the ANF to the Pittsburgh area, sharing its path here with the North Country National Scenic Trail (see the Long-Distance Trails chapter). Many different hikes can be planned on the trail network. To obtain a recreational guide and trail information, contact Cook Forest State Park, P.O. Box 120, Cooksburg, PA 16217, (814) 744-8407, www.dcnr.state.pa.us/stateparks/parks/cookforest.aspx.

23

Cornplanter State Forest

Cornplanter State Forest is a demonstration forest used by the Pennsylvania Bureau of Forestry for environmental education and wildlife management, particularly for the woodcock. The interpretive area features 1.5 miles of self-guided nature trails and 7 miles of cross-country ski trails for the winter enthusiast. The major ski trails are Hunter Run Trail and LaSure Trail System, which can also be used by hikers off-season. Reach Cornplanter State Forest via PA 36, west of the Allegheny River and 4 miles north of Tionesta. For more information, contact Cornplanter State Forest, Bureau of Forestry, Forest District #14, 323 N. State St., Warren, PA 16365, (814) 723-0262, www.dcnr.state.pa.us/forestry/stateforests/cornplanter.aspx.

24
Oil Creek State Park

The 7,244-acre Oil Creek State Park is in Crawford and Venango Counties; the southern end of the park is 4 miles north of Oil City. The park adjoins Drake Well Museum to the north, and the entire area is rich with the history of the early petroleum industry. There are more than 73 miles of hiking trails, many of which explain and interpret the historical and industrial artifacts and points of interest.

The park's longest trail is Gerard Trail (formerly Oil Creek Hiking Trail), which forms a 36-mile circuit paralleling both sides of Oil Creek. This hiking trail is mainly the work of Ray Gerard of Titusville. He has recruited enough volunteers to keep the trail in good shape, in an excellent example of how volunteers can work with a state agency and conservancy to build, maintain, and expand a hiking resource. The main trail is blazed with yellow rectangles. Five cross-connector trails, blazed in white, allow for loop hikes of varying lengths. Adirondack-type shelters and tent sites are located in two areas along Gerard Trail; each group has six shelters, vault toilets, a fire ring, and water. A nominal fee is charged to use the shelters, and advance reservations from the park office are required. Camping is permitted in the shelter areas only. Oil Creek State Park also features a 9.5-mile paved bike path, and a 15-mile cross-country ski network is available in winter.

The main park entrance is located on PA 8, 1 mile north of Rouseville; turn right onto the first road after the bridge over Oil Creek. For more information and a recreational guide, contact Oil Creek State Park, 305 State Park Rd., Oil City, PA 16301, (814) 676-5915, www.dcnr.state.pa.us/stateparks/parks/oilcreek.aspx#recreation.

25
Two Mile Run County Park

Two Mile Run County Park is located off PA 417 and PA 428 between Franklin, Oil City, and Titusville in Venango County. The park boasts a total of 26 miles of trails, with various paths shared by hikers, mountain bikers, horseback riders, cross-country skiers, and in some cases snowmobilers. This area of the county suffered a "microburst"—a sudden storm with highly concentrated downward winds—in 2003, and at the time of this writing, more than a million board feet of timber is lying on the ground over a 600-acre area. In one spot, 15 acres were leveled. Some trails have been reopened, but more than half of the 26 miles of trails remain closed because of salvaging operations. It is recommended that you check with the park in advance for trail conditions. Contact Two Mile Run County Park, 471 Beach Rd., Franklin, PA 16323, (814) 676-6116.

Allegheny River Trail
and Samuel Justus Trail
31 miles open, additional miles proposed

The Allegheny River Trail and Samuel Justus Trail are two multiuse recreational trails that together form a continuous 31-mile strand of flat and smooth asphalt on an abandoned railroad grade, following the Allegheny River from Oil City to Emlenton, except for a .5-mile gap at Sunny Slope, 14 miles south of Franklin, which is bypassed via a private dirt road. This stretch of the Allegheny is included in the National Scenic Rivers System. The Samuel Justus Trail currently makes up the northern half of the network from Oil City to US 322, and the Allegheny River Trail continues as the southern half. At the time of this writing, the trail is rough and unimproved south of Emlenton, though it can be mountain biked. Proposals have been made to extend the improved trail to the south.

Approximately 9 miles south of Franklin is Indian God Rock, on which are more than fifty rock carvings dating from the years 1200 to 1750. This large rock sits at the edge of the river and is on the National Register of Historic Places. You can access the rock from the trail. There are also two railroad tunnels on the Allegheny River Trail: the 3,350-foot Kennerdell Tunnel, 15 miles south of Franklin, and the 2,868-foot Rockland Tunnel, 21 miles south of Franklin. The trail is paved through the tunnels, with rows of reflectors along the edges and center. The tunnels are very dark, so take along a light.

You can reach this trail system from Oil City, Franklin, Brandon, Rockland Station, or Emlenton. For trail maps and a brochure describing points of interest, contact Allegheny River Trails Association, P.O. Box 264, Franklin, PA 16323, www.avta-trails.org/allegheny-samuel-trails.

Sandy Creek Trail
8 miles

This multiuse trail on an abandoned railroad grade features seven pedestrian-safe bridges and a reconstructed railroad tunnel. The trail winds along East Sandy Creek through some of western Pennsylvania's most spectacular hills, valleys, and forests. It runs east-to-west, crossing over the Allegheny River and the Allegheny River Trail (see separate entry above) 5 miles south of Franklin. Belmar Bridge is 1,385 feet long, with a wooden deck and railings, and provides a great view of the river valley. The area is almost entirely undeveloped, remote, and of great natural beauty.

The western trailhead is in Belmar, on the west bank of the river. From Franklin, take PA 8 south for 3 miles. Turn left on Pone Lane, pass Franklin High School; then turn right on Belmar Drive. Follow this road down the hill to the parking area, with the river and bridge in sight. The east trailhead is in Van on US 322. From Van, turn south onto Tarklin Hill Road and go .5 mile to the parking area. The trail may also be accessed from Rockland Road near Cranberry Mall. From the mall, travel south on PA 257 for 3 miles to the trail crossing, just before the bridge over Sandy Creek. Turn right onto an access road. For more information, contact Allegheny River Trails Association, P.O. Box 264, Franklin, PA 16323, www.avta-trails.org/allegheny-samuel-trails.

28
Clear Creek State Forest: Kennerdell Tract

The Bureau of Forestry, in conjunction with Grove City Outing Club, has constructed a network of trails within this 3,200-acre tract of state forest land along the Allegheny River, across from Kennerdell in southern Venango County. The area is locally known as the Allegheny Gorge. There are 27 miles of hiking trails within the tract. The trails to the south of Dennison Run, including the Goat and Ho-Ya-Neh Trails and the midsection of the River Trail, are restricted to hiking only for protection of the watershed. All the other trails in the area are also open to mountain biking, horseback riding, and cross-country skiing. Along the trails are the remains of an old iron furnace and iron ore pits. They offer a nice vista of the Allegheny River and Kennerdell, as well as bucolic deep-woods scenery with small runs leading to the river. A trail leads down to the river, where a large "bench" in the hillside serves as a primitive campsite for canoeists and backpackers. The site has a composting toilet and fire rings. If you wish to stay more than one night, you must obtain a permit from the state forest office in Clarion (see below).

To reach the area from the PA 8 expressway, take the exit for PA 308 and drive the short distance into Pearl. Turn right (north) on old PA 8, and after .4 mile, turn right on Dennison Run Road (T368). Go 1.7 miles, and then turn right on DeWoody Road (T371). Continue 1.1 miles to the parking lot for State Game Land 39. The hiking network passes through this game land before reaching the state forest. For more information and a trail map, contact Clear Creek State Forest, 158 S. Second Ave., Clarion, PA 16214, (814) 226-1901, www.dcnr.state.pa.us/forestry/stateforests/kittanning.aspx.

29
M. K. Goddard State Park

The 2,856-acre M. K. Goddard State Park in northeastern Mercer County was named for Maurice K. Goddard, the influential state official who inaugurated forty-five state parks during his twenty-four years of service. More than half of the park's acreage is taken up by man-made Lake Wilhelm. No overnight camping is allowed in the park. A robust trail network leads through woods and meadows around the lake. The main trail is a multiuse route for hikers and bikers that circumnavigates the lake for 12.3 miles. A variety of shorter hikes are possible with car shuttles. Using the Goddard-McKeever Trail, you can also explore the educational and interpretive trails at McKeever Environmental Education Center. For a recreation guide and map, contact M. K. Goddard State Park, 684 Lake Wilhelm Rd., Sandy Lake, PA 16145, (724) 253-4833, www.dcnr.state.pa.us/stateparks/parks/mauricekgoddard.aspx.

30
Shenango Trail
7.5 miles

The white-blazed Shenango Trail follows the route of the historic Erie Extension Canal along the Shenango River in Mercer County. The trail is on publicly owned lands around Shenango River Lake, managed by the U.S. Army Corps of Engineers. The trail mostly follows the towpath of the canal, just upriver from the modern reservoir. The canal operated from 1841 to 1871 and used mules to pull the boats. Both the towpath and canal channel are amazingly well preserved, with historic locks, loading bays, and buildings. Kidd's Mill Covered Bridge, built in 1868, is at the northern end of the trail.

The trail is easy and suitable for all ages. In addition to its historical interest, the area is rich in wildflowers, birds, and other wildlife. The southern portion is subject to flooding when the pool elevation of the artificial Shenango River Lake exceeds 900 feet. Up-to-the-minute elevation information is available from the Corps of Engineers Resource Manager's Office in Sharpsville, (412) 962-4384. Because of its location, vegetation along the trail, including poison ivy, can become quite dense during the summer; consider this if you plan to hike in June through September.

Parking is available at both ends of the trail. The northwestern trailhead is at Kidds Mill Covered Bridge, on Kidds Mill Road just east of PA 18 outside of Reynolds Heights. The eastern trailhead is at Big Bend Access Area on the reservoir, accessed via PA 258 east of Clark.

Intermediate access is available at the trail's midway point in New Hamburg, at the Hamburg Road crossing of the Shenango River about two miles southwest

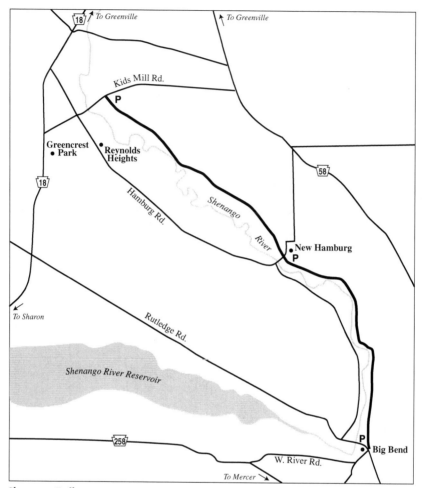

Shenango Trail

of PA 58. For more information, contact Shenango Outing Club, P.O. Box 244, Greenville, PA 16125, (724) 836-0843. The trail is also maintained by Shenango Conservancy, 747 Greenville Rd., Mercer, PA 16137, (724) 662-2242.

31
Erie Extension Canal Towpath
3 miles

The Erie Extension Canal Towpath is a delightful one-way hike through Pymatuning Swamp in State Game Land 214. This game land is adjacent to Pymatuning State Park to the north. The towpath for the former Erie Extension Canal is still intact, allowing an easy ramble through a wetland and swamp ecosystem. You can access the trail at Hartstown via US 322. Just east of PA 18, turn left on an access road and drive to the game land parking area. Other access points are on US 6 just to the west of Sharmansville, at the crossing of a former railroad grade (outside the game land and state park), and on PA 285 at the eastern boundary of the state park.

32
Ernst Bike Trail
5 miles, 5 additional miles in development

The Ernst Bike Trail is a crushed stone trail following the abandoned Bessemer and Lake Erie Railroad line in Crawford County. In the first quarter mile, the trail reaches a beautiful wooden covered bridge, the only one in Crawford County. The trail follows French Creek, which boasts sixty-six species of fish and twenty-seven species of mollusks. The section from the creek to US 19 is pastoral, passing through meadows, marshes, hardwood, and hemlock. At the time of this writing, the Ernst Trail Committee plans to extend the trail from US 19 west to Conneaut Lake. This proposed extension would parallel Conneaut Marsh and make use of an existing undeveloped trail with exciting views of the marshland, home to amphibians, bald eagles, and migrating waterfowl.

The trail begins just west of Meadville on US 6/US 19/US 322, with parking available at Beans Auto. For more information, contact French Creek Recreational Trails, 747 Terrace St., Meadville, PA 16335, (814) 333-7063, www.ernsttrail.org.

33
Erie National Wildlife Refuge

The Erie National Wildlife Refuge, located in Crawford County 35 miles south of Lake Erie, is named for the Erie Indians, a tribe that once resided in the area and lent its name to the great lake and several cities and counties around it. The refuge consists of two separate parcels. The 5,025-acre Sugar Lake Division lies 10 miles east of Meadville, on the outskirts of the village of Guys Mills. The 3,594-acre Seneca Division is located 10 miles to the north, 4 miles southeast of Cambridge Springs. The refuge's diverse habitats attract 236 different species of birds, and 112 species nest here.

There are five separate hiking trails—three in the Sugar Lake Division and two in the Seneca Division. Four of the trails are easy to walk but can be wet in spring. The other is a challenging primitive trail that requires dexterity to use rope pulls across short ravines. The combined length of the trails is 6.6 miles. For more information, contact Erie National Wildlife Refuge, 11296 Wood Duck Lane, Guys Mills, PA 16327, (814) 789-3585, www.fws.gov/northeast/erie.

34
East Branch Trail
7.5 miles, 11 additional miles proposed

The East Branch Trail, sometimes known as the Clear Lake Trail, is a rail-trail along the east branch of Oil Creek from Titusville north to Spartansburg. At the time of this writing, the trail surface is "improved gravel." The trail is used by walkers, bikers, hunters, snowmobilers, and Amish horse-drawn wagons. In 1988, the Clear Lake Authority purchased the 15.4-mile abandoned railroad corridor from Conrail, in order to create a route accessing 280-acre man-made Clear Lake. The original railroad right-of-way runs from Hydetown (just north of Titusville) to Spartansburg. The East Branch Trail passes wooded hillsides, Amish home-steads, farms, fields, and wetlands. You can access the trail at the Clear Lake park-ing area off PA 77 near Spartansburg or at Glynden on Glynden Road. For more information, contact Clear Lake Authority, P.O. Box 222, Spartansburg, PA 16434, (814) 654-7361.

35
Presque Isle State Park

Presque Isle was once an island but is now a peninsula, thanks to shifting currents in Lake Erie. This naturally formed sand spit extends into the lake away from the city of Erie. The state park features 11 miles of easy hiking trails, as well as a mul-tipurpose trail for joggers, bicyclists, skaters, and wheelchair users. The multipur-pose trail and its extension form a 13.5-mile circuit that reaches most of the park's natural and historic points of interest. Presque Isle is a jumping-off spot for spring migrating birds, and as many as 200 different species can be observed in May. The park also offers the only naturally occurring sandy beaches in Pennsylvania.

The longest designated hiking trail in the park is the Dead Pond Trail, a 2-mile walk over sand dunes that line a former shoreline that has since shifted westward. The 1.5-mile Gull Point Trail begins at the east end of Budny Beach (Beach #10) and loops through Gull Point, passing a shorebird observation platform. The 1.3-mile Sidewalk Trail was originally constructed by the U.S. Lighthouse Service as a path from the lighthouse to the service boathouse on Botany Bay.

There are no overnight accommodations in the park, but the Erie area offers a wide variety of motels and campgrounds. Reach Presque Isle State Park from the west side of the Erie metro area via PA 832 (Peninsula Drive), which leads north onto the peninsula. For a map and recreational guide, contact Presque Isle State Park, 301 Peninsula Dr., Suite 1, Erie, PA 16505, (814) 833-7424, www.dcnr .state.pa.us/stateparks/parks/presqueisle.aspx.

REGION 7

Pennsylvania Wilds

Region Editor: Ralph Seeley

Contributors: Ben Cramer, Ted Ligenza,
Jeanne Wambaugh, Bob Webber

The Pennsylvania Wilds Region consists of north-central Pennsylvania, easily the wildest and most remote area of the state. The region is bordered on the north by the New York state line; on the east by US 15 to Williamsport; on the south by US 220 to Port Matilda and then US 322 to the Dubois area; and on the west by US 219 to McKean County and then US 6, PA 46, and PA 446 to the New York state line. Because of the vastness of the region and its huge amount of hiking opportunities, this chapter is divided into three sections. The Moshannon and Elk Section reaches from the area around I-80 to the north and west toward the Sinnemahoning Creek watershed along PA 120 and PA 555. The Sproul Section covers the central district of the region toward New York and includes the majority of the region's state forest lands. The Northeast Section stretches toward Pine Creek Gorge and the eastern boundary of the region.

This region corresponds roughly with the Pennsylvania Wilds program, initiated by the commonwealth in 2004 to promote tourism and conservation in the vast and sparsely populated north-central forest areas. The region offers extensive uninhabited areas, breathtaking scenery, and a feeling of natural vastness and remoteness that comes as a surprise in the industrialized American northeast. A considerable percentage of Pennsylvania's public lands—state forests, parks, and game lands—are in this region, and about half of the region, nearly 1.5 million acres, is owned by the commonwealth. Though the public lands are in large and small noncontiguous blocks, the total acreage rivals that of Yellowstone National Park.

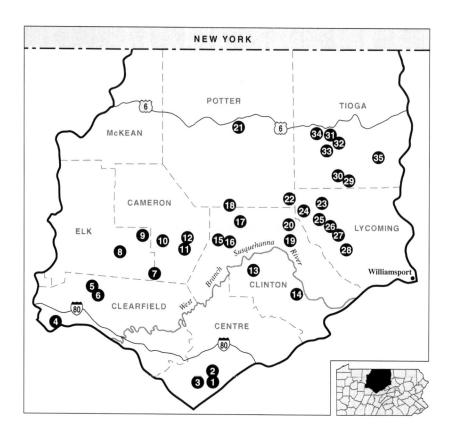

Thanks to these extensive forested areas, many of Pennsylvania's premier long-distance trails are in this region. Several different trails, already dozens of miles long, are now coming together via short connectors to form an extensive backpacking network that reaches to all corners of the region almost entirely on footpaths. This network ties together the Chuck Keiper, Quehanna, Bucktail Path, Donut Hole, Susquehannock, Black Forest, West Rim, and Mid State Trails into a hiking system with considerably more mileage than Pennsylvania's sections of the Appalachian and North Country National Scenic Trails. Many hikers would say that this network is considerably more beautiful and secluded too.

Except for the Mid State Trail (MST), which is covered in the Long-Distance Trails chapter, all of the above long-distance trails and the completed or proposed connectors are described in this chapter. Some shorter hikes in this region use parts of the MST, which are described here accordingly. The traditional northern terminus of the MST is at the West Rim Trail in Pine Creek Gorge. At the time of this writing, a northern extension of the MST has been partially completed, leading from Blackwell to the New York border, where it will connect with that state's Finger Lakes Trail, extending the Pennsylvania long-distance backpacking network still further.

The Pennsylvania Wilds Region sits almost entirely on the high Allegheny Plateau, which rises above the Allegheny Front. Unlike the Ridge and Valley Province to the southeast, which has the steep elevation changes, the plateau stays high in elevation, with rolling hills and significant river gorges. Watercourses are an important feature of this region, as the plateau sits astride an unusual triple divide that nurtures the sources of three major river systems. The tributaries of the Allegheny flow to the southwest, those of the Susquehanna flow to the southeast via the mighty West Branch, and the Genesee system flows north toward the Great Lakes basin.

The extensive forests of north-central Pennsylvania were almost completely logged throughout the nineteenth and early twentieth centuries. Early loggers constructed splash dams on the rivers and creeks to create man-made flash floods that carried valuable white pine logs downstream. The industry then progressed to narrow-gauge railroads and steam locomotives, which reached further and further into hills, almost completely denuding the area of trees by the end of the period. The forests have since recovered nicely, though almost all the trees are second- or third-growth, and the altered forest ecosystems resulted in serious changes to the resident flora and fauna. Fortunately, the sense of wilderness and remoteness has been restored, and the old road and railroad network has evolved into a great many hiking trails. For more hiking opportunities in the Pennsylvania Wilds region, see *Greate Buffaloe Swamp* (2001), by Ralph Seeley, and *Short Hikes in God's Country* (1995) and *Short Hikes in Pennsylvania's Grand Canyon* (2006), by Chuck Dillon.

On a map of the United States, if you draw a line west from New York City, along that line between the Atlantic Ocean and the Rocky Mountains, the most spectacular scenery and secluded wilderness are found in north-central Pennsylvania. The Pennsylvania Wilds Region offers vast expanses of scenic beauty, natural solitude, and the ultimate hiking experience, both for expert backpackers and for beginners who wish to learn about the state's natural and recreational opportunities. You can lose yourself here without losing your appreciation for what Pennsylvania hiking is all about.

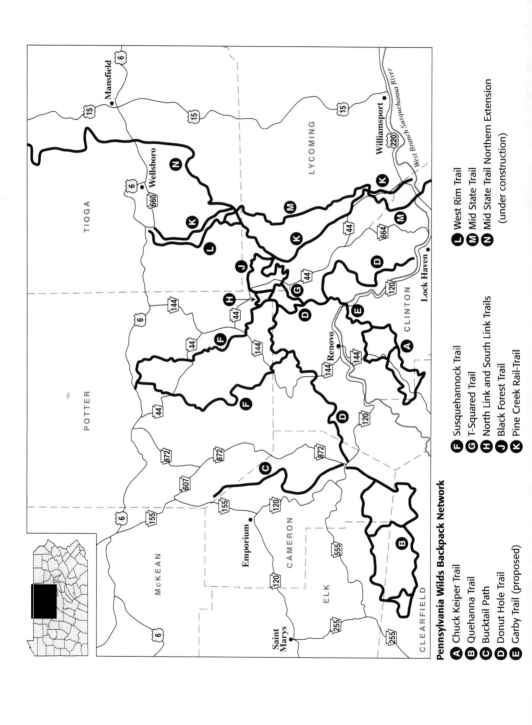

Pennsylvania Wilds Backpack Network

A Chuck Keiper Trail
B Quehanna Trail
C Bucktail Path
D Donut Hole Trail
E Garby Trail (proposed)

F Susquehannock Trail
G T-Squared Trail
H North Link and South Link Trails
J Black Forest Trail
K Pine Creek Rail-Trail

L West Rim Trail
M Mid State Trail
N Mid State Trail Northern Extension
    (under construction)

Moshannon and Elk Section

1

Allegheny Front Trail
41.8 miles

The Allegheny Front Trail, a relatively new trail in western Centre County, was built collaboratively in the late 1990s by Penn State Outing Club, Ridge & Valley Outing Club, Quehanna Area Trails Club, and Keystone Trails Association, the umbrella group for trail maintainers. The trail provides a wide variety of forest environments, including views over valleys to the east, trout streams, and marshlands. The orange-blazed trail surrounds Black Moshannon State Park and crosses PA 504 twice, though there is almost no road walking. Since its inception, the Allegheny Front Trail has changed very little, except for the addition of bog bridges through Black Moshannon Swamp upstream from Shirk Road.

Scattered along the trail are six trout streams; an acid-polluted stream of interest to activists, known as "Red" Moshannon Creek; and various small brooks. The trail includes about 3 miles on the edge of the Allegheny Front, with six identified vistas and some areas of nearly continuous views; extensive portions of the Ridge and Valley Province to the southeast are visible. Hiking is very rocky and steep along this portion of the trail, though you are rewarded with some of the finest overlooks in all of Pennsylvania.

You can easily find water on most of the Allegheny Front Trail even during droughts, but there is one 6-mile-long dry section from Smays Run to the headwaters of Benner Run. The works of beavers are easily seen on the southwest and northeast sections. Shorter loop hikes of 26 miles (on the eastern portion) and 20 miles (on the western portion) are possible by walking through Black Moshannon State Park via the blue-blazed Shingle Mill Trail along Black Moshannon Creek, and then the park's orange-blazed Moss Hanne Trail. In the state park, camping is permitted only at the official campground.

The Allegheny Front Trail was first measured by Ben Cramer in 2006; at the time of this writing, a detailed trail guide is being developed. *Greate Buffaloe Swamp* (2001), by Ralph Seeley, combines a trail guide with a historical narrative for the Black Moshannon area. This book is available from Quehanna Area Trails Club, 882 Rolling Stone Rd., Morrisdale PA 16858, www.westbranch.org/community%20pages/quehanna%20trail/quehanna%20trail.htm. You can also discuss trail conditions with Ralph Seeley or George Lockey via the contact information on the website.

The Allegheny Front Trail is accessed via PA 504 to the east and west of Black Moshannon State Park, with intermediate access points on several nearby back roads. For more information and an official map, contact Black Moshannon State Park, 4216 Beaver Road, Philipsburg, PA 16866, (814) 342-5960, www.dcnr

.state.pa.us/stateparks/parks/blackmoshannon.aspx; or Moshannon State Forest, 3372 State Park Rd., Penfield, PA 15849, (814) 765-0821, www.dcnr.state.pa .us/forestry/stateforests/moshannon.aspx. A trail maintainer also has created a website at alleghenyfronttrail.info providing a downloadable map and other useful information.

2

Rock Run Trails System
13 miles

The Rock Run Trails System was built in the early 1980s by the Penn State Outing Club for cross-country skiing and hiking. The network is in an isolated tract of Moshannon State Forest. The starting elevation is 2,370 feet, and the trail network gradually descends into a basin around Rock Run and its tributaries. Rock Run is a wild trout stream, with the trout coming up from Black Moshannon Creek to spawn in October. In recent years much of Rock Run has been altered by beavers that have constructed many ponds of considerable size.

The trail system consists of a two-way entrance trail leading north from PA 504 and a double loop with a short connector trail that forms a figure eight. The entrance trail plus both loops makes for a 13-mile round-trip hike; using only the southern loop and the entrance trail reduces the distance to 8 miles. The Rock Run Trails are blue-blazed. In the late 1990s, the Allegheny Front Trail (see separate entry above) reached the area and was added to the Rock Run entrance trail and part of the western side of the loop. These areas feature both the blue blazes of the Rock Run Trails and the orange blazes of the Allegheny Front Trail. Skiing here ranges from beginner to intermediate in difficulty, and there are ski bridges at stream crossings. During the off-season for skiers, the Rock Run Trails also offer excellent hiking with numerous options for backpack camping; camping permits from the state forest office are required for the area.

In the winter, the most feasible access to the trail system is via PA 504. In the summer, intermediate points can be reached from Governors Road (Snow Shoe Road on some maps). The primary access point is the parking lot shared with the Allegheny Front Trail, on PA 504 at the corner of unpaved Tram Road, 4.5 miles east of the bridge at Black Moshannon State Park and 7.2 miles west of Business US 220 at Unionville. Governors Road, which is not recommended for winter use even with four-wheel drive, intersects PA 504 about .8 mile east of the parking lot. During periods of very heavy snow, PA 504 can be a lonely road that is barely kept open by the plows.

For more information, a free map, and camping permits, contact Moshannon State Forest, 3372 State Park Rd., Penfield, PA 15849, (814) 765-0821, www.dcnr.state.pa.us/forestry/stateforests/moshannon.aspx. The Rock Run Trail System is also described in detail in *Greate Buffaloe Swamp* (2001), by Ralph Seeley, available from Quehanna Area Trails Club, 882 Rolling Stone Rd., Morris-dale, PA 16858, www.westbranch.org/community%20pages/quehanna%20trail/quehanna%20trail.htm. You can discuss trail conditions with Ralph Seeley or George Lockey via the contact information given on the website.

Black Moshannon State Park

Black Moshannon State Park is a short distance to the west of the Allegheny Front in Centre County and is traversed by PA 504 between Philipsburg and Unionville. The park is also known for its unique high-altitude bog and swamp ecosystem. Migrating whistling swans and ospreys may be seen on occasion. Both rustic and modern cabins are available on a reservation system, and there are two tenting areas for family and group camping.

The area features many premier cross-country skiing trails, which can also be used off-season for pleasant and easy hiking. One particularly noteworthy trail is found on PA 504, 2 miles east of the bridge over Black Moshannon Lake. On the north side of the road, a gate marks access to a large pipeline swath running parallel to the highway, plus a perpendicular feeder line. These rather narrow pipelines reduce the effects of sun and wind; the pipeline corridors are not blazed.

Black Moshannon State Park is the hub for the long-distance Allegheny Front Trail (see separate entry above), and there are also other well-marked trails inside the park. The 6-mile orange-blazed Moss Hanne Trail, which connects the main park area with the southern portion of the Allegheny Front Trail, passes on boardwalks through Black Moshannon Bog Natural Area, a reconstructed northern bog, and proceeds through several red pine plantations around the western side of the lake. The blue-blazed Shingle Mill Trail leads 3.7 miles from the park's dam to the northern section of the Allegheny Front Trail, following the very picturesque Black Moshannon Creek. For further information, contact Black Moshannon State Park, 4216 Beaver Rd., Philipsburg, PA 16866, (814) 342-5960, www.dcnr.state.pa.us/stateparks/parks/blackmoshannon.aspx.

Rockton Mountain Trails
16 miles

Rockton Mountain Trails is a ski trail system in Moshannon State Forest that was built in the mid-1990s, mostly by volunteers from the Curwensville area in cooperation with the Bureau of Forestry. The trailhead is on US 322 about 4 miles west of its intersection with PA 153, west of Clearfield. At the intersection with the unpaved and unplowed Pine Township Road, on the south side of the highway, is a parking lot with a map box. The trail system is on both sides of US 322 and features several loop trails mixing beginner and intermediate skill levels. Hikers are welcome during the off-season.

For more information, contact the Quehanna Area Trails Club. Contact information can be found in the entries for the Allegheny Front Trail and the Rock Run Trails System.

Parker Dam State Park

The 968-acre Parker Dam State Park is a walker's paradise, with a number of interpretive trails. Beaver Dam Trail along Mud Run traverses an area set aside as beaver habitat. The Trail of New Giants goes through the swath of the powerful 1985 tornado and shows how the forest is regenerating. Other trails follow some of the old logging railroad grades and slides. Parker Dam State Park also serves as a base for hiking the Quehanna Trail (see separate entry below), with a trail register outside park headquarters. To obtain a recreational guide and map, contact Parker Dam State Park, 28 Fairview Rd., Penfield, PA 15849, (814) 765-0630, www.dcnr.state.pa.us/stateparks/parks/parkerdam.aspx.

Quehanna Trail
76.2 miles

The Quehanna Trail (QT) is a long-distance loop trail in Moshannon and Elk State Forests. Blue-blazed connector trails in the western and eastern sections of the main loop allow shorter but still extensive backpacking loops. (Camping permits are required.) A number of blue-blazed cross-country ski trails in Quehanna Wild Area (see Quehanna Plateau Ski Trails entry below) intersect the eastern part of the QT loop and also can be used to fashion shorter circuit hikes. A spur trail called Old Sinnemahoning Road, a gated jeep road, connects the QT to the Donut Hole Trail and Bucktail Path near Sinnemahoning. Six parking lots are available for trail users: at Parker Dam State Park, forest foreman headquarters on Deible Road near Quehanna Highway, the Game Commission parking lot at the junction of Ardell and Merrill Roads, Marion Brooks Natural Area, the former forestry barn location on Wykoff Run Road, and on Quehanna Highway about a mile north of Piper.

The southern part of the Quehanna Plateau is a mostly oak-laurel ecosystem; the northern part is characterized by northern hardwoods mixed with hemlock and pine. Several of the QT connecting trails pass through State Game Land 34, featuring ponds that attract waterfowl. Feed plots and viewing platforms have been constructed throughout the whole Quehanna Plateau area, in order to satisfy public interest in viewing elk that have wandered south from their traditional stomping grounds north of Sinnemahoning Creek. The elk now can be found throughout the Quehanna area, but at such a low density that you are only occasionally rewarded with a sighting. The elk move easily through the forest, and a rare sighting is certainly a thrilling experience.

Part of the Quehanna Trail passes through the 50,000-acre Quehanna Wild Area. This is the largest wild area in the state, though it is traversed by two paved and several unpaved roads. The wild area is known for its beautiful streams and unusual open savannas with occasional black cherry trees that were apparently left when the area's vast hemlock forest was logged in the nineteenth century. Two natural areas feature stands of paper birch, near the southernmost limit of that tree's range.

Quehanna Wild Area was designated after the termination of industrial activities in the 1950s and 1960s in the southeast corner of the area, near Piper. In an ill-advised attempt to increase area employment, the state brought in a technology firm to conduct military research and devlopement in the wilderness. This enterprise failed, as did later private industrial activities. One side effect was industrial and low-level nuclear contamination at numerous dump sites in what is now the wild area. These sites all have been examined by the Pennsylvania Department of Environmental Protection and judged harmless to outdoor recreation enthusiasts. More recently, the former industrial complex at Piper became home to a PennDOT training facility and a low-security prison boot camp. The Quehanna Trail was rerouted to give the boot camp a wide berth.

Updates: There have been many recent developments on the Quehanna Trail and the other trails on the Quehanna Plateau. Numerous relocations and bridges, including major bridges on the main trail over Mosquito Creek and Medix Run, have been constructed collaboratively by Keystone Trails Association, Ridge & Valley Outing Club, Penn State Outing Club, and Quehanna Area Trails Club, with the continuing cooperation of the Bureau of Forestry. Volunteer maintainers in all of Moshannon State Forest are coordinated by Quehanna Area Trails Club. The following updates for the Quehanna Trail are based on mileage from the trailhead at Parker Dam State Park, proceeding counterclockwise around the loop.

At mile 6.5, cross the bridge at Trout Run, constructed in 2007. At mile 9, a 30-foot aluminum bridge at Roberts Run was constructed in 2002. East of Knobs Road, about 12 miles from Parker Dam State Park, the trail has been relocated to pass through the remains of a CCC camp near a recently rediscovered spring. Nearby, another relocation will lead to a less risky all-season crossing of Deer Creek.

In 2004, Hurricane Ivan destroyed the 60-foot swinging bridge over Mosquito Creek at Corporation Dam (mile 24), making much of the QT southern loop inaccessible without a considerable fording of the creek. Hikers resorted to crossing the stream on a large horizontal tree trunk that was also brought down by Ivan. At the time of this writing, the slow process of obtaining grant money for the costly bridge replacement is bearing fruit. A 72-foot fiberglass bridge has been installed with the assistance of National Guard helicopters.

At mile 32, a new timber bridge designed by Gert Aron was constructed over Upper Three Runs by a prison crew in 2005. At mile 40, another new bridge designed by Aron was installed at Wykoff Run. At mile 47 in Sanders Draft, KTA crews recently relocated the trail for a closer approach to several waterfalls. At Marion Brooks Natural Area (miles 50 to 53), in 2006 the Quehanna Trail was relocated away from the natural area boundary, resulting in both greater ecosystem protection and a better hiking experience on the trail. At mile 63, a 48-foot bridge was constructed over Medix Run in 1994, though this bridge was damaged by an ice flood in 1996. The main pier has been righted, and diversion structures have been constructed slightly upstream, though because of continuous undermining, the bridge remains slightly tilted and a solution to this engineering challenge has not yet been found.

On the Quehanna Trail Eastern Cross Connector, the bridge over Beaver Run about a mile south of the lake of the same name has had a complicated history. First, beaver dams inundated the valley and trail, isolating the original bridge in the middle of a pond. A 60-foot bridge was then constructed to reach the original bridge, but that structure was eliminated in 2004 by Hurricane Ivan. In 2007, a new bridge was constructed by boot camp crews and the trail was relocated around the beaver meadows.

A seven-day backpacking trip on the entire QT main loop is described in *50 Hikes in Central Pennsylvania* (2001), by Tom Thwaites. *Greate Buffaloe Swamp* (2001), by Ralph Seeley, combines a detailed trail guide with a historical narrative for the Quehanna Plateau. This book is available from Quehanna Area Trails Club, 882 Rolling Stone Rd., Morrisdale, PA, 16858, www.westbranch.org/ community%20pages/quehanna%20trail/quehanna%20trail.htm. Use the above trail updates in conjunction with the information in these publications. You also can discuss trail conditions with Ralph Seeley or George Lockey via the contact information given on the website. For maps of the Quehanna Trail, also featuring the two Cross Connector trails and many blue-blazed spur trails, and for the required camping permits, contact Moshannon State Forest, 3372 State Park Rd., Penfield, PA 15849, (814) 765-0821, www.dcnr.state.pa.us/forestry/stateforests/ moshannon.aspx.

7
Quehanna Plateau
Ski Trails

The skiable portions of the Quehanna Trail (see separate entry above), plus the blue-blazed trails in Quehanna Wild Area, create a 64-mile network for skiers and for hikers during the off-season. The elevation of the wild area ranges from 2,000 to 2,300 feet, and the area sometimes gets lake-effect snow from northwestern Pennsylvania. In late winter, the depth of the snowpack has reached 4 feet (recorded in March 1993 and March 1994), adding difficulty at stream crossings, both for existing bridges that were too low or narrow and at bridgeless crossings. More bridges have been built in recent years to counter this challenge.

Also during times of heavy snow, you may not find plowed parking areas, because the Bureau of Forestry does not have the necessary heavy equipment. It is wise to carry shovels to make your own slot along a plowed road; also carry tire chains, even if you have four-wheel drive. Quehanna Highway is kept open by PennDOT. Caledonia Pike is kept open pretty well from its east end to the Lawrence Township line, but from that point west and northwest, the township rarely maintains the road. The various unpaved forest roads are almost never plowed. For information on road conditions, contact the district forest office at (814) 765-0821 during business hours on weekdays or the Deible Road forest foreman station at (814) 787-8836 (this number typically is answered only during lunch hour on weekdays).

In the winter, access these trails at your own risk. In an emergency situation, call 911 and ask for Clearfield County Control. Identify the location of the emergency and where you can be contacted. Cell phones generally do not work on the high and rugged Quehanna Plateau. Some pay phones are available at the forestry offices and other facilities.

This large outdoor treasure awaits more skiers and snowshoers, and the area remains quiet because snowmobiles are not permitted in the wild area. Most of the trails are beginner level in difficulty, with a few approaching intermediate. During the nonskiing seasons, hikers are welcome to use the trails, because walking helps keep down the undergrowth. The ski trails are described in detail in *Greate Buffaloe Swamp* (2001), by Ralph Seeley. For more information on that book, and to obtain maps and other information, see the Quehanna Trail entry above.

Updates: The Crawford Vista Trail was recently extended. The trail no longer terminates at the vista but now continues east to Meeker Run, where it meets the QT Eastern Cross Connector Trail. The Bridge Trail has been abandoned because of little to no usage, though it is still shown on the 2003 Quehanna Trail map.

Elk Trail

15.8 miles

Elk Trail is a little-known long-distance backpacking trail through Elk State Forest, routed specifically to enhance viewing of the area's elk population. State Game Land 14, north of the trail, is also frequented by elk, as are some portions of the Quehanna Plateau to the south. Elk are also spotted frequently in and around Benezette at this trail's western end and at the nearby Winslow Hill viewing area. The orange-blazed Elk Trail is typical of those on the Allegheny Plateau, starting and ending in hollows and following old logging roads through meadows, hemlock groves, and open forest on top. There is only one steep climb, along the western portion of the trail north of Benezette.

Water sources are not too hard to find. Starting at the eastern trailhead, at 4.5 miles the trail crosses Shaffer Draft Road, then turns left onto a pipeline, with an undeveloped spring just after the turn. There is a good piped spring about 3 miles farther ahead at Bell Draft Road. After you leave Dents Run, there is no good water source for 3 miles. The last 4 miles of the trail pass several water sources and campsites as it winds through a number of elk feed plots. A camping permit may be required.

The eastern trailhead is on Dents Run Road, 2.2 miles northwest of Dents Run on PA 555. Dents Run is 7.9 miles east of Benezette and 11.7 miles west of Driftwood. The western trailhead is .4 mile north of PA 555, just outside Benezette. Turn north on Front Street, pass the Benezette Hotel, and continue to the end of the pavement. For an excellent written description of the Elk Trail, with accompanying map, and camping permits, contact Elk State Forest, 258 Sizerville Rd., Emporium, PA 15834, (814) 486-3353, www.dcnr.state.pa.us/forestry/stateforests/elk.aspx.

Pine Tree Trail

1.8 miles

Pine Tree Trail traverses Pine Tree Natural Area and is laid out and signed as a nature trail. The area was a settler's homestead more than 150 years ago, and the trail was developed in 1977–79 along the settler's access road by the Youth Conservation Corp. The trailhead is opposite Hicks Run Camping Area, which is just west of the split of Hicks Run Road into its East and West branches. Hicks Run Road turns off PA 555 about 1 mile east of Dents Run and 10 miles west of Driftwood. There is a forest ranger station about a mile up the road. If not present at the trailhead, a map and description can be obtained from Elk State Forest, 258 Sizerville

Rd., Emporium, PA 15834, (814) 486-3353, www.dcnr.state.pa.us/forestry/state forests/elk.aspx. This interpretive booklet is very well produced and will greatly enhance your hike, with information on natural and historic points of interest.

Fred Woods Trail
4.6 miles

Built by the Young Adult Conservation Corps, the Fred Woods Trail was named for a forest foreman who loved the area and was killed in the line of duty. A .8-mile entrance trail leads to a loop that takes you to outstanding views and rock formations. The Fred Woods Trail is nearly level, since it is on top of the Allegheny Plateau, though it overlooks a very rugged landscape. The southern portion of the loop leads to three excellent vistas (two reached via short side trails) over the Bennett Branch. The northern portion of the loop leads through and around many fascinating rock formations, with boulder piles to be climbed and labyrinthine rock slots to be explored.

The trailhead is on Mason Hill Road (Castle Garden Road on some older maps), which meets PA 555 a mile west of Driftwood. As it climbs away from the Bennett Branch of Sinnemahoning Creek, this road is very narrow, with no passing room. It has had a reputation for danger but has been improved. The trailhead is 3.9 miles up Mason Hill Road from PA 555, on the left across from a small parking area. To obtain either a state forest public-use map or a map specifically for the Fred Woods Trail, contact Elk State Forest, 258 Sizerville Rd., Emporium, PA 15834, (814) 486-3353, www.dcnr.state.pa.us/forestry/state forests/elk.aspx.

Bucktail Path
34.1 miles

The long-distance Bucktail Path is an isolated and demanding trail, maintained by Elk State Forest with occasional visits by the KTA trail care team. Do not expect to see anyone else when you hike. The trail is a rewarding experience for seasoned hikers seeking a challenge, because it offers extra loneliness and solitude, even for wild Pennsylvania. The Bucktail Path is not recommended for beginners, because much of the trail is very far from civilization, and there are several steep climbs and dozens of wet stream crossings. Some of the crossings require wading, though except in periods of unusually high runoff, you can easily manage the wider crossings with waterproof boots or hardened stream slippers.

There are three easy road approaches to the Bucktail Path. The southern terminus is at Sinnemahoning, .7 mile west of the intersection of PA 120 and 872. At Grove Street, a sign denotes the trail; follow the street to the small parking lot just before the entrance to a private estate. You can reach the middle section of the trail via the unpaved but easily traversed Hunts Run Road, out of Cameron on PA 120 northwest of Driftwood. The northern terminus is near Sizerville State Park on East Cowley Run Road, .1 mile east of the last maintenance building as you pass through the park; the trailhead is at a grassy parking area next to a large sign denoting the area's flora and fauna. Also from the southern terminus at Sinnemahoning, the intrepid backpacker can connect with the Donut Hole Trail by walking about a mile east on PA 120 to the village of Jericho; and the Quehanna Trail (via the Old Sinnemahoning Road Trail) by walking over the river bridge to a side street in the village of Wyside.

Note: Do not confuse the Bucktail Path with the Bucktail Trail, a commemorative name that has been given to PA 120 from Emporium to Lock Haven as a scenic byway.

Permits may be required to camp in the state forest. For more information, contact Elk State Forest, 258 Sizerville Rd., Emporium, PA 15834, (814) 486-3353, www.dcnr.state.pa.us/forestry/stateforests/elk.aspx. Camping and other amenities are available at Sizerville State Park. For information, contact Sizerville State Park, 199 E. Cowley Run Rd., Emporium, PA 15834-9608, (814) 486-5605, www.dcnr.state.pa.us/stateparks/parks/sizerville.aspx.

The point-by-point Bucktail Path (BP) description below is based on the 1998 guide *Hiker's Guide to the Bucktail Path* by Jim and Ginny Owen (still available from Keystone Trails Association), combined with notes and updates from a 2005 through-hike and trail observation project.

BP Section 1: Sinnemahoning to Brooks Fire Tower (9.8 miles)

From the parking lot at the end of Grove Street, go down a driveway and cross Grove Run as best you can. Follow the orange blazes left and then right on an active forestry road. Begin a 2.1-mile climb up the Left Fork of Grove Run. At the top, bear left off the logging road; then quickly bear right to skirt the edge of the plateau and enter Johnson Natural Area, featuring several outstanding views over the Driftwood Fork of the Sinnemahoning. Johnson Run Natural Area contains a protected grove of old-growth forest featuring giant hemlock and several noteworthy species of hardwoods.

In this area, the BP follows a series of grassy lanes; watch the blazes carefully. At 3.8 miles, the trail briefly leaves a grassy road to climb over a knob and then returns to the lane again. Turn right onto a pipeline swath at 4.8 miles. Follow the pipeline for the next 2.3 miles, over Grove Hill and past a crossing of Ridge Road. At 7.1 miles, the trail turns left off the pipeline (it will return to the pipeline for brief spells several times over the next few miles). Next, the trail ascends an open blueberry-covered hill with good views. At the top, the trail is briefly on a dirt road before turning again into the woods. Then it heads downhill for .4 mile and makes a sharp right turn onto a trail that goes along the head of Square Timber Run to Ridge Road near the intersection with Brooks Run Road. The BP then crosses both roads. According to the forest district guide, there is an excellent spring about .5 mile east on Brooks Run Road. The BP climbs to the old Brooks Fire Tower at 9.8 miles.

Alternate to Section 1: Except for Grove Run near the southern trailhead, the southernmost 10 miles of the BP are completely dry. This section features good views over the Sinnemahoning canyon in the Driftwood area, but it also has 2.3 miles of monotonous walking along a pipeline swath. You may wish to bypass this section via a trail that ascends Lick Island Draft from PA 872, starting on that road 4 miles north of its intersection with PA 120. There is no developed trailhead on PA 872, but offering a few bills to a local homeowner for parking privileges should solve that problem. On the upper end of Lick Island Run, follow the western side of the run on the yellow-blazed trail, leading through a pretty ravine with camp-sites. Request the excellent Brooks Run Division Trail Map from the Elk State Forest district office (contact information above) to plan this alternate hike.

BP Section 2: Brooks Fire Tower to Hunts Run Road (10.4 miles)

Brooks Fire Tower cannot be climbed, though its pretty lawn makes for a good resting spot. The BP descends the hill to the Right Fork of Brooks Run, which at 10.2 miles is the first water since Sinnemahoning, other than the spring near the trail on Brooks Run Road. There are several possible campsites under hemlocks here, plus dependable water. After crossing two branches of Brooks Run, the trail continues downstream to the third branch, which it follows back up on a grassy road with good camping. Farther on, the trail recrosses the pipeline; then at 12.4 miles it crosses Ridge Road at the intersection with Stillhouse Road.

In this area, the BP is on and off the pipeline swath repeatedly until finally leaving it for good at 12.8 miles, near the head of Russell Hollow. The trail crosses the hollow and turns up the far side to follow a dividing ridge, then makes a long, sometimes steep descent along an intermittent stream. Watch the blazes carefully as the trail uses a series of intersecting old grades. The BP turns down a camp driveway to cross Whitehead Run Road at 15.5 miles. The trail follows White-head Run upstream past five wet crossings, and then turns left up Rock Run at 16.1 miles. This moderate climb has seven stream crossings, with wet areas and some really nice waterfalls. The top of the ridge is a moderately flat walk in open woods for .7 mile before beginning a steep and somewhat rocky descent of beau-tiful Moore Draft to Hunts Run Road. After proceeding down another hunting camp driveway, the BP emerges on Hunts Run Road at 20.1 miles.

BP Section 3: Hunts Run Road to Sizerville State Park (13.9 miles)

The BP jogs briefly to the right on Hunts Run Road, turns left back into the woods, then turns right (upstream) to a bridge at a now-prohibited car campsite. Cross the bridge, proceed to a hunting camp, and then turn left over the camp's small footbridge onto an old railroad grade that travels upstream along McNuff

Branch. Follow this run for 3.9 miles. The initially easy grade soon deteriorates, with many small wet areas and several sidehill excursions to avoid other wet areas. You reach a challenging wet crossing of McNuff Branch at 22 miles, then continue ahead upstream. The trail proceeds through open meadows and past old beaver dams and several possible campsites among the hemlock along the west side of the run.

McNuff Branch is a jewel of a valley, isolated and pleasant, with open views and many wildflowers in the spring. It features a plethora of beaver dams, as the enterprising critters are very busy in the area. Some of the dams are quite formidable constructions, stretching for more than 100 feet and holding back artificial ponds of considerable size. This portion of the Bucktail Path is featured in *50 Hikes in Central Pennsylvania* (2001), by Tom Thwaites.

At the head of McNuff Branch, the BP crosses a pipeline and then a woods road, and begins a pleasant climb to Steam Mill Road at 25.7 miles. The BP next follows two successive logging roads downhill for 1.1 miles before turning left onto trail at 26.8 miles; watch for this turn carefully. The trail goes down the hollow to Salt Run, where there is good camping. It next joins an old logging railroad grade and switchbacks uphill three times over the next 2 miles, skirting the ridgetop.

On the other side of the ridge, the BP descends on an old logging road with one switchback. At the bottom, you cross a footbridge over Crooked Run, then scramble up to Crooked Run Road at 31.8 miles. Turn left and follow this road for the next .8 mile. Just before a hunting camp, the BP turns sharply right up a hollow on an old woods road and follows the stream on a sometimes steep grade to the top of the ridge. On the other side, it descends Buffalo Switch Hollow, with five stream crossings. Most of the descent is steep and rocky. At 34.1 miles, you reach the northern terminus at a grassy parking lot on East Crowley Run Road, just to the east of Sizerville State Park.

12

Other Trails in Elk State Forest

The Brooks Run Division Trail Map, published by Elk State Forest, features trail descriptions for nine miscellaneous foot trails ranging in length from 1.8 to 7.4 miles. Many of these connect to the Bucktail Path and are blazed red, yellow, or blue. Some hug stream bottoms, and others climb arduously from one height to another. These trails are all north of Sinnemahoning. To obtain the map and brochure, contact Elk State Forest, 258 Sizerville Rd., Emporium, PA 15834, (814) 486-3353, www.dcnr.state.pa.us/forestry/stateforests/elk.aspx. The brochure notes that volunteer trail maintainers would be appreciated; contact the state forest office if you are interested.

Sproul Section

13

Chuck Keiper Trail

55.3 miles

The Chuck Keiper (rhymes with "viper") Trail (CKT) is a long distance backpacking trail that is lightly used and goes through some of the wildest and most visually arresting public lands in Pennsylvania, offering remarkable solitude. It was built starting in 1976 by the Pennsylvania Bureau of Forestry, aided by federally funded Title X workers and the Youth Conservation Corps. The trail is named for the late district game protector for Clinton County, a dedicated conservationist. The only access to the trail is via PA 144, through the eerily unpopulated and lonely plateau between Renovo and Snow Shoe.

The orange-blazed CKT passes through or near two natural areas and two wild areas. The trail system is divided into two loops—the West Loop of 32.9 miles and the East Loop of 22.4 miles—creating three- and two-day backpacking options. The two loops share a cross-connector trail, and the ultimate backpacking trip that does not use the cross connector would be 49.3 miles in length, though you should not avoid this scenic portion of the CKT system just because it is a connector trail. Some stream fords are still required, although recent sidehill work has reduced them substantially in the area of JU Branch, Burns Run, Boggs Run, and Yost Run. Much of this work has been done in recent years by Keystone Trails Association trail crews. Additional bridges were added in the East Branch area in 2007, and short access trails are planned to reach vistas over Dennison Fork and Fish Dam Wild Area. At the time of this writing, a new path known as the Garby Trail has been planned to connect the northern section of the Chuck Keiper Trail East Loop with the Donut Hole Trail at Hyner Run State Park, far away on the other side of the West Branch of the Susquehanna.

Two particularly lovely portions of the CKT, Yost Run, which has an outstanding waterfall, and Eddy Lick Run, with historical interest, are described in *50 Hikes in Central Pennsylvania* (2002), by Tom Thwaites. In Yost Run, the CKT has been rerouted onto sidehill above the stream to eliminate multiple wet crossings. The former route along the run is now a blue-blazed side trail open to hikers seeking an especially challenging and scenic route.

The most rugged parts of the trail are in the north and west, particularly in the Boggs Run area. The central cross connector passes through East Branch Swamp Natural Area, and the East Loop passes the southern tip of Cranberry Swamp Natural Area, which features a little-used but rewarding loop side trail. A striking and fascinating characteristic of the Chuck Keiper Trail system is the high plateau areas that lack an overhead forest canopy. The oak leaf roller destroyed much of the area's oak forest in 1968–72. The monster tornadoes of May 1985 and the disastrous Two Rock Run fire of April 1990, caused by careless burning at a hunting camp and destroying almost every tree over a 10,000-acre area, also damaged the health of the forest. The fire also necessitated a major trail relocation almost completely out of Fish Dam Wild Area. The high elevation of the plateau slows the growth of new trees, though some areas of the forest have recovered noticeably (yet very slowly) since the 1990 fire.

The usual starting point for the CKT is 24 miles north of Snow Shoe and 10 miles south of Renovo, on PA 144 at the parking area across from Swamp Branch Road. Other trailheads are found along PA 144, with limited nearby parking, and there is a parking lot at the trail crossing of DeHaas Road (southeast of PA 144) next to a historical marker. Camping is prohibited in the public watershed between Pete's Run Road and Dry Run Road (just west of Boggs Hollow) and in the two natural areas. Camp at least 200 feet from roads, streams, and leased hunting camps. For information on trail conditions and a free trail map and camping permit, contact Sproul State Forest, 15187 Renovo Rd., Renovo, PA 17764, (570) 923-6011, www.dcnr.state.pa.us/forestry/stateforests/sproul.aspx.

General descriptions of the West Loop and East Loop follow. Both are described in the counterclockwise direction, and for simplicity, both include the cross-connector trail.

CKT West Loop (32.9 miles)

0.0 mi. Near the PA 144 vista over Dennison Fork, start by walking on a new trail relocation parallel to the road. Note the vista over Swamp Branch to the south.

.7 mi. A monument near the road commemorates the first game refuge in Pennsylvania. Such refuges were too small, and by 1960 they were no longer necessary. Continue west around a tornado damage zone.

1.9 mi. Turn left down a hollow to Fish Dam Run. A mile later, turn right onto Fish Dam Trail (part of the CKT); then turn left to climb to Jews Run Road, with a possible campsite nearby.

5.7 mi. Just before Jews Run Road, jog left then turn right onto the JU Branch Trail (part of the CKT) and begin a descent into Burns Run Wild Area, with an excellent view at the top. Between here and the top of Owl Hollow, there were formerly twenty-six stream crossings, now mostly avoided thanks to recent sidehill construction. Campsites are nearby.

9.7 mi. Here you will find a piped spring.

10.2 mi. Turn right on Fisher Fire Road; then in .3 mile turn left on the Plantation Trail (part of the CKT). The trees in this area were planted in 1914. Campsites are nearby.

12.6 mi. After two stream crossings while descending the Second Fork of Yost Run, turn up the main fork and follow new sidehill trail above the stream. (The blue-blazed trail along the stream is the old route of the CKT, with fourteen wet crossings.) You reach an outstanding waterfall at the junction with Bloom Draft. There are campsites near a spring .5 mile beyond the waterfall.

16.4 mi. Cross PA 144 and then turn left on the old Snow Shoe to Renovo Road, now a barely discernible woods road that has long since been replaced by PA 144. Turn right past a hunting camp, then left along a pipeline, and then right again on trail along the headwaters of Eddy Lick Run. A spring appears to the left of the trail after five stream crossings, about 2.5 miles from PA 144.

19.4 mi. You reach the remains of Eddy Lick Run splash dam after four more stream crossings. The trail follows a later logging railroad grade that cut through a corner of the dam and rendered it useless, indicating that trains had made splash dams obsolete. Campsites are nearby.

19.9 mi. Turn left, uphill and away from the old railroad grade. In .3 mile, bear left on a jeep road, and shortly continue ahead on another old railroad grade.

21.4 mi. Turn right off the grade. There is a spring nearby to the right of the trail. Shortly, you reach a woods road that leads up to DeHaas Road. Parking is available at the road crossing (this spot is southeast of PA 144). In another .3 mile, enter a fire area at the Art Creelman Memorial Planting; then cross a pipeline. After another 1 mile, cross a logging road.

22.9 mi. Turn left off a jeep road just before the West Branch of Big Run. In another 200 yards, turn right and cross the run. Continue up Panther Branch, crossing it four times, with possible campsites.

25.3 mi. Bear right on a woods road at the top, and then cross Hicks Road, with possible campsites. After 1 mile, cross a stream (at the time of this writing, this bridge is scheduled to be replaced), and shortly turn right on Penrose Road. In .5 mile, turn left past the Camp Rockspar springhouse. In another .5 mile, turn right on a logging road, and later continue on a railroad grade. After a little less than 1 mile more, cross a stream on stones, then continue to two more wet crossings (these bridges are also scheduled to be replaced). Possible campsites in this area.

28.8 mi. Cross Coon Run Road. There is a spring 100 yards ahead on the right. After 1 mile, descend steeply and cross the East Branch of Big Run (the bridge here is also scheduled to be replaced).

29.9 mi. Turn left on the East Branch Trail (the CKT cross-connector) at a triple blaze point. Here the East Loop connects. In the next 1.5 miles of the cross-connector trail, cross three modern bridges installed by Keystone Trails Association in 2007, one having been carried to the site by helicopter.

31.1 mi. Pass a beaver dam. After 200 yards, turn right on Coon Run Road; cross the East Branch on the road bridge; then turn left on trail into East Branch Natural Area. Within the next mile, cross a stream and a pipeline. In this area, the trail meanders around old blowdown areas caused by the 1985 tornadoes.

32.3 mi. Meet PA 144 and turn left to reach the parking area.

32.9 mi. You reach the end of the CKT West Loop at the Swamp Branch parking area.

CKT East Loop (22.4 miles)

0.0 mi. From the parking area, head northeast on PA 144.

.6 mi. Turn right on the East Branch Trail (the CKT cross-connector). Cross a pipeline and stream while traveling alongside East Branch Swamp Natural Area.

1.5 mi. Turn right on Coon Run Road, cross the road bridge over the East Branch, and then turn left on trail. In the next 1.5 miles, cross three modern bridges installed by Keystone Trails Association (KTA) in 2007, one having been carried to the site by helicopter.

3 mi. Reach the end of the cross-connector trail at the junction with the West Loop, which goes to the right. Turn left onto the East Loop.

3.2 mi. Jog left across Beech Creek Road. Later, bear left at a fork in a woods road and continue across a salvage cut, the second such cut encountered since the West Loop junction.

4.1 mi. Turn left into the woods; then shortly cross a bridge over Rock Run, with campsites nearby. In .3 mile, bear left.

5 mi. Cross Shoemaker Ridge Road. In .8 mile, cross Clendenin Run on a log bridge; then later bear left uphill on an old road. The trail bisects a burned area.

7.2 mi. Cross Cranberry Run. A 2.4-mile loop trail around Cranberry Swamp Natural Area leads off to the left.

8.1 mi. Here the trail passes a vista over Benjamin Run.

8.9 mi. At a pipeline, turn right onto a jeep road. Do not cross the bridge here; continue instead for about .2 mile; then turn left on the jeep road and cross the car bridge over Benjamin Run.

9.1 mi. Turn left between a hunting camp and a piped spring. Go up Sled Road Hollow, sometimes on an old railroad grade, making six stream crossings. There are possible campsites in this area.

10.8 mi. At the junction with Mill Run Road, start down into Boggs Run Hollow. (A side trip up the road to the left leads to a good vista over Boggs Run.) Descend for 1 mile, with four stream crossings and two possible campsites; then reach the main branch of Boggs Run.

13.4 mi. The recent trail relocation you are now following has eliminated fifteen stream crossings in the past .5 mile. Now cross the stream and climb steeply to an old railroad grade. After two more stream crossings, start to the top on another grade. Cross a power line near the top.

16 mi. Jog left on Pete's Run Road, and then right on a jeep road. Bear right at a fork and come to a vista over Diamond Rock Hollow and Hall Run. Camping is not permitted in the next 4 miles because the area is a public supply watershed.

17.3 mi. After a steep descent, cross Hall Run and scramble up to PA 144. Cross the road and turn right on recent sidehill relocation, constructed by KTA in 2004 to eliminate nearly a mile of road walking.

18.2 mi. Turn left up Drakes Hollow on an old railroad grade. Soon look for a short, blue-blazed side trail to a waterfall. After 1.4 miles, continue ahead where the grade switchbacks. At the top of the ridge, continue ahead on a jeep road that enters from the left.

20.6 mi. Turn left on Dry Run Road. In .3 mile, continue ahead on Barney's Ridge Road, which comes in from the right.

21.1 mi. A short side trail to left, recently opened by the Bureau of Forestry, goes to Big Rocks Vista.

22.4 mi. You reach the parking area on PA 144 and the end of the CKT East Loop.

14
Eagleton Mine Camp Trail
23.8 miles

The red-blazed multiuse Eagleton Mine Camp Trail is open to hikers, cross-country skiers, and other nonmotorized users. It has two loops: the 8.9-mile East Loop and the 14.9-mile West Loop. At the time of this writing, the trail is being expanded, with portions to be designated for hikers only. Highlights include six bridges, an old still site, a railroad grade, a mountain meadow, two deer enclosures, a pristine mountain stream, and thick mountain laurel. The trail is named for the mining village of Eagleton on the old railroad, inhabited from 1845 to 1870. Eagleton Coal and Iron Company built several villages to house miners working in the nearby bituminous coalfields; some were funded by the royal family of Spain. The infamous Prince Farrington's stills, used for his bootlegging trade, were also in the area.

The trailheads are at the east and west ends of the loop system. Reach Eagleton Road via Beech Creek Mountain Road, between PA 144 and Beech Creek on PA 150, or more easily via PA 120 about 15 miles west of Lock Haven. From PA 120, follow Eagleton Road west for about 2.5 miles to a crossing under a high-voltage line, and park on the right side of the road. This is the Little Buckhorn (eastern) trailhead. The western trailhead is at the Shear Trap Trail. It would be wise to contact the forest district office for a trail map and directions to this remote area. Contact Sproul State Forest, 15187 Renovo Rd., Renovo, PA 17764, (570) 923-6011, www.dcnr.state.pa.us/forestry/stateforests/sproul.aspx.

15

Donut Hole Trail

89.7 miles

The Donut Hole Trail (DHT) is a long-distance backpacking trail paralleling the West Branch of the Susquehanna River through Sproul State Forest. It is one of the most remote and challenging of the state's backpacking trails and is for seasoned hikers only, with numerous steep climbs and unbridged stream crossings. Bridges were recently constructed or replaced over Cooks Run, Drury Run, Seven Mile Run, and Paddy Run. Extensive relocations have been made in the Bull Run, Seven Mile, and Merrimam Hollow areas, eliminating many stream crossings. The biggest remaining challenge of the orange-blazed DHT is a deep-water ford of the very wide Kettle Creek that should not be attempted during high water. A blue-blazed side trail provides a lengthy detour around this crossing.

After extensions were added to both ends of the trail by Keystone Trail Association crews in the mid-1990s, the DHT now extends 89.7 miles from Jericho (near the intersection of PA 120 and PA 872 in Cameron County) to Farrandsville (outside of Lock Haven). The west terminus in Jericho is at the end of the village's only street, off PA 120. To reach the east terminus at Farrandsville, leave Lock Haven on the PA 664 bridge over the Susquehanna, and turn left at the end of the bridge. Drive 5 miles along the river to Farrandsville. Continue for .6 mile after the road turns abruptly inland and passes a church; the trailhead is at the end of the road at a Game Commission parking lot. Access to the middle sections of the DHT is also available at Kettle Creek and Hyner Run State Parks.

At Jericho, the backpacker can walk about a mile west into Sinnemahoning to reach Bucktail Path, or walk over the river bridge and to a side street in the village of Wyside to access the Quehanna Trail, via the Old Sinnemahoning Road Trail. Early in the new millennium, this extensive interconnected trail network was expanded with the construction of the T-Squared Trail, which leads from the eastern section of the Donut Hole Trail to the Black Forest Trail. (All of these trails are described separately in this chapter.) At the time of this writing, another long-distance connector known as the Garby Trail has been proposed and will link the DHT at Hyner Run State Park with the Chuck Keiper Trail high on the plateau on the other side of the Susquehanna. Camping permits are required if you plan to stay more than one night at a specific spot.

For a fine map of the Donut Hole Trail and camping permits, contact Sproul State Forest, 15187 Renovo Rd., Renovo, PA 17764, (570) 923-6011, www.dcnr .state.pa.us/forestry/stateforests/sproul.aspx. Rock River & Trail, a local outfitter, offers shuttle service; call (570) 748-1818.

DHT Section 1: Jericho to Kettle Creek State Park (15.4 miles)

0.0 mi. From PA 120, turn north onto the township road that constitutes the only street in the village of Jericho. At the end of the road, cross a short stretch of private land very politely, watching for elk, and follow an old log road up to the top of the plateau. About .5 mile above Jericho, watch on the right for a natural rock bridge over Ellicott Run.

2.8 mi. Cross a pipeline. Just beyond, meet Montour Road and follow it east for nearly a mile. At the point where Montour Road turns north, continue east on a lesser track. Soon bear right (southeast) at a Y intersection. Shortly the trail leaves the track to switchback down into Bearfield Hollow, where campsites abound in a hemlock cove. At the bottom, turn right (upstream) and later left up a dry draw to the top of Savage Mountain. Pass a vista to the north over a private hunting-club pond, and then turn south down a prong of the ridge. In this area, the trail is the northern boundary of M. K. Goddard Wild Area.

7 mi. Turn left at a branch of Cook's Run and continue into its valley. Pass several campsites and go up the western side of the run on an old grade. Turn sharply right to cross Cooks Run on a footbridge, and continue upstream on an old road through large conifers and hardwoods. At 10.1 miles, turn sharply right (uphill) at a hunting-camp outhouse.

11.1 mi. Jog right briefly on Crowley Road; then turn left. (Cooks Run Vista is .2 mile north of this junction. See separate entry for Kettle Creek State Park below.) Skirt the edge of the plateau and reach the excellent Kettle Creek Vista to the left of the trail. Make a sharp right onto Kettle Creek Vista Road, follow it back to Crowley Road, and then turn left.

12.4 mi. Turn left off Crowley Road and begin a rough, steep descent toward Kettle Creek State Park. After a switchback, you reach a junction with blue-blazed Alice's Trail, the high-water detour for the DHT. Turn right and continue parallel to the creek. Upon reaching the creekside, cross the dam breast and make a knee-deep (even during periods of low water) ford to an island. Walk across the island and ford the creek again, emerging in the official state park campground. Turn left on the campground driveway and follow the blazes uphill to the main park road. During high water, a detour around the creek crossing can be made via Alice's Trail. This trail leads north to the park road, where you turn right and return to the DHT at the driveway to the park campground. This is a lengthy but safe detour, though hikers who are not afraid to get wet will experience a thrill at the creek crossing.

15.4 mi. Cross the park road and jog left briefly to the hikers' parking lot at the bottom of Summerson Hollow.

DHT Section 2: Kettle Creek State Park to PA 144 (10.7 miles)

15.4 mi. Climb steadily up Summerson Run, passing a campsite; then turn left over a ridge. A few rare American chestnut trees may be found here. Along the edge of the plateau, the trail is obscure as it winds past rock formations; watch the blazes carefully. Several potential vistas are overgrown.

19.4 mi. Pass the Spicewood Trail and continue 2 miles to a good vista overlooking Tamarack Fire Tower and Tamarack Natural Area (in different directions). Then begin a rough descent of Hickory Hollow.

22.3 mi. Turn right, pass a 4-foot waterfall, and cross Red Werts Bridge, an impressive steel I-beam apparatus. The trail then turns left, with campsites to the right. In .2 mile, turn right up Long Hollow. Over the top, drop steeply through switchbacks to the Left Fork of Hevner Run. George's Hollow contains possible campsites. With a short stint on an old road, make the increasingly steep climb to Tamarack Fire Tower.

24.3 mi. You reach Tamarack Fire Tower, offering incredible views. The tower site has a water pump. Continue southeast on a grassy woods road for .5 mile; then bear left and go down to PA 144, with a piped spring on the right.

DHT Section 3: PA 144 to Twelve Mile Road (17.9 miles)

26.1 mi. Turn left on PA 144, then right onto the Left Fork Trail (part of the DHT). Cross over multiple channels of Drury Run; then go up Browns Mill Hollow past possible campsites. Later, go through Pong Hollow to a right turn on a pipeline, with a view to the left.

29.5 mi. Turn left onto the Skyline Trail (part of the DHT). After descending steeply, bear left across another pipeline; then cross Hensel Fork and Hensel Fork Road.

30.7 mi. Turn right on Sandy Run Road. You will find a possible campsite just before this junction and others in the next mile down the road. Turn left and cross a bridge over Paddy Run, which is a municipal water supply, so there is no camping in this immediate area. There are two stream crossings on the way up McNerney Run.

33.5 mi. Turn right and follow Pfoutz Valley Road for .7 mile; then turn left at a camp driveway leading down to Merriman Hollow. Bear right and follow the stream past some waterfalls.

35.2 mi. You reach a good campsite at the junction of Merriman Hollow and Osborne Branch. Turn left onto the old North Bend and Kettle Creek Railroad grade. Make five wet crossings of Osborne Branch.

36.7 mi. Near the confluence of Osborne and Porter Branches, you reach the junction with the Susquehannock Trail. There are campsites in this area. The two long-distance trails share the same path for the next 8.7 miles. Stay on the left bank of Osborne Branch, passing open meadows, a gas well, and beaver dams.

38.2 mi. Bear left up Scoval Branch to a gas pipeline swath; then turn right and follow the swath northeast for .7 mile. Cross Osborne Branch again, with possible campsites. Halfway up the hill beyond the stream, turn right at a gate onto a gas maintenance road. Pass another gate and more gas roads; then drop steeply to Greenlick Road.

40.6 mi. Turn right briefly on Greenlick Road, then left on a gas road for 200 feet across Little Greenlick Run. Turn right briefly onto an old road, before bearing left into the woods. Proceed up Italian Hollow, then down into Greenlick Run. Follow this stream for the next .8 mile, with seven stream crossings and several possible campsites.

42.2 mi. Switchback left to ascend Bobsled Hollow, followed by a rocky descent of Long Hollow. Next you reach Twelve Mile Road.

DHT Section 4: Twelve Mile Road to Hyner Run State Park (14.1 miles)

44.0 mi. Near Twelve Mile Road, note the "official" trail location in a storm drain. As of 2007, there are plans to replace the bridge. Cross the Left Branch of Young Woman's Creek, with possible campsites beyond. Begin a strenuous climb up Morgan Hollow.

45.4 mi. Turn right on Fork Hill Road. Here the Susquehannock Trail leaves the Donut Hole Trail. After .7 mile, turn left at a hunting-camp driveway and descend to Bull Run, where a lengthy recent relocation has greatly improved the trail. There is a possible campsite at the junction with the main branch of the run.

48.9 mi. Cross the Right Branch of Young Woman's Creek and pass the monument for the first state forest land acquisition. Go up Seven Mile Road for .5 mile; then turn right into the woods. Cross the stream on a footbridge and continue up the hollow. There are two left turns at the top; both offer possible campsites. Turn left on Six Mile Road.

52.7 mi. Cross Dry Run Road and use a camp driveway to cross Cougar Run. Bear right on an old logging road through the rhododendron, with a possible campsite nearby.

54.8 mi. Reach Abe's Fork Road. Climb out of the steep valley on stone steps. Next drop into and climb out of a nasty little steep-sided 150-foot-deep gully. For the next 1.5 miles, the trail leads through open meadows; blazes are affixed to posts. Then bear right in a dirt area.

56.9 mi. Turn left off Log Road Hollow onto an easy, pretty trail with many possible campsites. Proceed to Hyner Run State Park at a parking area on the main park road.

DHT Section 5: Hyner Run State Park to Whetham (18 miles)

58.1 mi. Leave the park by walking northeast on Hyner Run Road. In .8 mile, turn right to cross Hyner Run, and later, turn right again. At 1.5 miles from the park, pass a gate and cabin, and then cross a bridge over a small stream. Soon turn left into the opening of Bear Pen Hollow. Close to the top of the hollow, there is a possible vista above the trail, looking west.

61.1 mi. Turn left onto a wide ski trail and parallel a power line for the next 1.4 miles. The orange DHT blazes share space with the ski trail's blue blazes. After crossing Pats Ridge Road, bear diagonally right.

63.1 mi. Cross Hyner Mountain Road near the intersection with Ritchie Road. Bear left across the Hiding Bear Ski Trail parking lot (this network has 14 miles of its own trails), and follow Ritchie Road east. Make a succession of turns, and later cross three small bridges over streams and bogs, followed by a sharp left turn onto a snowmobile trail blazed with red triangles. Watch the orange DHT blazes carefully in this area.

64.7 mi. Cross a bridge over Lick Run and turn right at a road fork. In .5 mile, you reach the top of an open plateau; then begin a long gentle descent with two right turns. Pass through a gate, and at about 2.5 miles after the first crossing of Lick Run, cross it again on an old bridge. Later turn right up a road out of the Lick Run valley. At the top, turn right again onto a grassy road leading to a gate and a road junction. After two left turns, head into the woods down to Rattlesnake Run.

69.3 mi. There are several stream crossings and possible campsites along Rattlesnake Run. Two miles after the first crossing, turn uphill very steeply to leave the run. At the top of the hollow, bear right onto a grassy woods road. Then .5 mile later, turn right again onto a dirt road known as Dark Hollow Trail on a signpost but Right Hand Sugar Camp Road on the map. After .3 mile on this road, turn left onto Sugar Camp Road. After nearly another mile of road walking, turn right onto McElhenny Trail (part of the DHT). Over the next 1.5 miles, turn left four times, with the fourth turn onto a rough foot trail contouring around the plateau edge, with occasional views west to the river. Turn right and go steeply downhill, then down the nose of the ridge. Switchback to the right onto an old road, and later left onto another old road, just above the railroad tracks.

76.1 mi. Turn left onto Whetham Road next to the railroad crossing. The former town of Whetham now contains little more than a large hunting camp building. There is a campsite about 200 yards upstream on the west bank of Rattlesnake Run, but in view of the road. You are now at the level of the West Branch, at the lowest point on the DHT other than the west and east trailheads.

DHT Section 6: Whetham to Farrandsville (13.6 miles)

76.1 mi. Follow Rattlesnake Road away from Whetham and cross a bridge. In .5 mile, turn right on Kingston Road and start uphill. In a little more than a mile from the turn, leave the road between a culvert and a parking area, turning left onto the Johnson-Ferney Trail (part of the DHT). There are possible campsites around this turn. Climb moderately on an old road. Later at a split, the trail stays left, becoming a grassy road.

79.8 mi. Turn left onto Oak Ridge Road. At .5 mile on this road, pass the Ferney Run Trail; then turn right on the next dirt road, climbing easily to the top of the ridge. In .3 mile after leaving Oak Ridge Road, bear right at a split of the old track; then in 150 yards, bear left at a fork. In 200 yards, turn right and descend into the Ferney drainage.

81.9 mi. Turn left, cross the stream, and climb steeply to an old woods road. A dry campsite is not far beyond. Nearly a mile after the Ferney crossing, make a sharp right turn into Dark Hollow, and cross the stream on an old bridge. In another mile, cross a branch of King Hollow. Soon there is a limited view of the West Branch of the Susquehanna River.

85.0 mi. Cross Old Carrier Road and continue down a grassy woods road through switchbacks. At .5 mile from Old Carrier Road, the DHT leaves the state forest and continues into State Game Land 89, where there is no overnight camping. In another 1.5 miles, the DHT continues straight on the Travel Trail, descending above Lick Run, a Pennsylvania scenic river, with some views. In another 2 miles, the trail joins a Game Commission maintenance road near Lick Run, continuing through rhododendron and hemlock.

89.7 mi. You reach a gate at the game land parking lot, just up the road from Farrandsville.

16
Kettle Creek State Park

The 1,793-acre Kettle Creek State Park serves as a base for the Donut Hole Trail (DHT). Note that the lower campground, through which the DHT passes, is separated from the main park area. The park offers two loop hikes using portions of the DHT.

Summerson–Owl Hollow Loop (4 miles): This is a moderately difficult loop. On the main park road, drive about 2.5 miles south from the dam, passing the parking area for the DHT and the lower campground driveway. Look for a sign for the blue-blazed Owl Hollow Trail on the left. Begin your hike on this trail with a moderate climb up the hollow, and then loop around to the left near the top. When you meet the orange-blazed Donut Hole Trail, turn left down Summerson Hollow, returning to the park road, where you turn left to walk back to your car.

Kettle Creek Vista Loop Hike (6.8 miles): This is a strenuous hike featuring a steep 1,200-foot climb to the stunning Kettle Creek Vista. Park at the area below the breast of Alvin Bush Dam, at a sign for trail parking; do not block the driveway to the dam. Across Kettle Creek Road, begin by hiking down the blue-blazed Alice's Trail, which meets the orange-blazed Donut Hole Trail after 1.1 miles. Turn right on the DHT and begin climbing steeply away from Kettle Creek. In another quarter mile, you will see Birch's Rocks, an outcropping named for a former park employee. Continue following the orange DHT blazes as the trail turns onto portions of Crowley Road and Kettle Creek Vista Road. At 3.4 miles, reach the main vista over Kettle Creek valley. After soaking in the view, continue out onto Crowley Road again. Leave the orange-blazed DHT and continue north on the road, coming to another vista looking west over Cooks Run valley. About .2 mile after this vista, you reach a junction with the blue-blazed Butler Trail. Go down this trail to a nature trail, and then emerge at the state park's upper campground. Find your way out to Kettle Creek Road and walk back to your car.

The park is in Clinton County, 7 miles north of Westport. For further information, contact Kettle Creek State Park, 97 Kettle Creek Park Lane, Renovo, PA 17764-9708, (570) 923-6004, www.dcnr.state.pa.us/stateparks/parks/kettlecreek.aspx.

17
Boone Road and Tamarack Tower
6 miles

The Boone Road and Tamarack Tower hike, from the first edition of *50 Hikes in Central Pennsylvania* (1979), by Tom Thwaites, is a moderately challenging and pleasant exploration of the forest between Renovo and Tamarack Natural Area. It also will challenge your pathfinding abilities.

Legend has it that Boone Road was built as a supply route in 1779 by Colonel Brodhead, during the pullback out of New York after the Sullivan Expedition to destroy the Iroquois Confederacy. Allegedly the name was chosen because the road was the eastern boundary of lands that were safe for Indian travel, and therefore it was a "boon" to the Indians. Nowhere in the Sullivan Expedition correspondence, however, is there any mention of such a project. Much more believable evidence shows that it was part of a state-sponsored road to carry settlers going northwest into the Allegheny watershed. The road fell out of use when Coudersport Pike, the ancestor of modern PA 44, was built in the early 1800s. The history of Clinton County states that the road was built by a contractor named Boone. Even though the old military tale is more colorful, the county history wins the test of evidence.

The trailhead is on PA 144, 7.1 miles north of PA 120 and 4.7 miles south of the turn at Kettle Creek. Park on the west side of the road at the sign for Cove Trail. This hike starts as a bit of a bushwhack to avoid private land. Begin by walking south along PA 144 to the Boone Road Trail sign, and 15 yards north of the sign, head straight into the woods up a steep bank. Cross Drury Run and continue on the same straight line through a small bog. At 50 yards beyond, you should find a faint footway along a swath. Follow this for about 300 yards and you should come to an old woods road–Boone Road. Turn right and begin climbing Boone Mountain through two switchbacks. Over the hill, you drop into Pong Hollow. At 1.3 miles from the highway, leave Boone Road Trail and turn right onto the orange-blazed Donut Hole Trail (DHT). Walk for a little more than a mile to the Left Fork Sandy Run Trail (part of the DHT system) and turn right, later crossing Drury Run on a bridge. Follow the DHT to Tamarack Fire Tower, which offers views and a well. Continue downhill on the DHT to the tower access road, where at 5.5 miles you meet another road. Turn left here and later turn right on a third road. In another .3 mile, turn right on the grassy Cove Trail and walk downhill to your car. For an alternate route from the fire tower, simply follow the access road down to PA 144, where you turn left and walk about .8 mile to your car.

Dutlinger Natural Area

The 1,521-acre Dutlinger Natural Area is named for a pioneer in Pennsylvania forestry, Forrest H. Dutlinger, who served for fifty years. This natural area is also known as the Beech Bottom Hemlocks because of its 158-acre stand of old-growth timber. A short hike to the old hemlocks is described in *50 Hikes in Central Pennsylvania* (2001), by Tom Thwaites.

You reach the area via a dirt road that leads north from PA 144, about 4.5 miles south of Cross Fork. This road actually begins at a short spur street parallel to PA 144, representing the highway's former route over a bridge. The dirt road goes north .5 mile to the state forest boundary at a bridgeless ford of Hammersley Fork. Park in this area and cross Hammersley Fork as best you can. There is an ancient hand-over-hand cable crossing that is recommended only for the adventurous, who are also advised to wear protective gloves. Getting wet by crossing the creek presents about the same level of risk, however. Continue following the dirt road upstream for roughly a mile, past a stone chimney, to the mouth of Beech Bottom Run. Turn left and follow Beech Bottom Run up a narrow, steep hollow for almost a mile and a 900-foot elevation gain. Reach the stand of old-growth timber near the top. This trail and others nearby are described in a natural area brochure available from Susquehannock State Forest, P.O. Box 673, Coudersport, PA 16915, (814) 274-8474, www.dcnr.state.pa.us/forestry/stateforests/susquehannock.aspx.

Long Fork Day Loop Hike, Hyner Run State Park

4.1 miles

Hyner Run State Park is only a mile north of PA 120, about 6 miles east of Renovo. For hikers using the Donut Hole Trail, it provides a pleasant base camp in a small stream valley. Nearby is Hyner View State Park, featuring a spectacular panoramic vista over the canyon of the West Branch of the Susquehanna.

Back at Hyner Run State Park, the Long Fork Day Loop Hike was developed by retired district forester Robert "Butch" Davey to augment the park's outdoor experience. This is a challenging and strenuous hike, and hiking boots are a necessity. The elevation change is 1,000 feet, and some parts of the climb are very steep. Park at the trailhead for Donut Hole Trail in the state park, and follow this orange-blazed trail north up Log Road Hollow. At 2.1 miles, turn right onto the blue-blazed Long Fork Trail and descend steeply. When you reach the forest road, turn right and return to the main park area. For more information and a park map, contact Hyner Run State Park, 86 Hyner Park Rd., Hyner, PA 17738, (570) 923-6000, www.dcnr.state.pa.us/stateparks/parks/hynerrun.aspx.

20

T-Squared Trail
6.5 miles

The new T-Squared Trail connects two premier long-distance backpacking trails: Donut Hole Trail and Black Forest Trail (see separate entries in this chapter). T-Squared Trail was named in honor of Tom Thwaites for his immense contributions to improving and writing about the trails in Sproul State Forest. In 1985, Thwaites recognized that important long-distance trails needed help, so he inaugurated the Keystone Trails Assocation Trail Crews to lead the effort. Extensive mountain laurel along the trail creates beautiful surroundings when blooming in mid to late June. T-Squared trail starts at Cougar Hollow on the Donut Hole Trail (DHT) and ends at the Black Forest Trail (BFT) at its junction with the Baldwin Point Trail.

For those not already backpacking the DHT or BFT, the easiest way to approach T-Squared is from PA 44. Approximately 2.5 miles north of the intersection with Hyner Road (to Hyner Run and Hyner View State Parks), turn left onto Dry Run Road/Benson Road. Follow Dry Run Road for about 6 miles as it arcs around to the south. Stop at the DHT crossing, and park near the camp gate across from Six Mile Road. Do not block the gate. There is a sign saying, "Hikers Welcome." Walk down the DHT about .8 mile to the T-Squared Trail sign, and turn left onto this blue-blazed trail.

Leading away from the DHT, the T-Squared Trail passes through a small grove of hemlocks before switching back to the top of the ridge, following a beautifully constructed CCC trail. After passing though dense laurel, the trail goes down into Mill Hollow, and then switchbacks up to the top of the ridge again. Next it heads into Rock Run, crosses Dry Run Road and then Benson Road, and finally goes steeply down into Baldwin Branch Hollow to reach the Black Forest Trail. Back at Baldwin Branch Hollow, the Baldwin Point Trail leads to a spectacular vista. For more information about trail conditions, contact Sproul State Forest, 15187 Renovo Rd., Renovo, PA 17764, (570) 923-6011, www.dcnr .state.pa.us/forestry/stateforests/sproul.aspx.

Northeast Section

21

Susquehannock
Trail System
83.7 miles

The Susquehannock Trail System (STS) is a remote long-distance loop trail in far north-central Pennsylvania that is maintained by Susquehannock Trail Club. The route largely follows old CCC fire trails, logging roads, and logging railroad grades. The trail is orange-blazed, with the "STS" emblem painted on trees at intervals. The STS is connected to Black Forest Trail via the North Link and South Link Trails (see separate entry below), and for 8.7 miles it shares a path with Donut Hole Trail. Along its lengthy route, the STS passes few signs of modern civilization and reaches into very remote state forest areas with a particular sense of quietude and seclusion.

The Northern Gateway, which provides access to the northern portion of the STS loop, is at the Bureau of Forestry headquarters building on US 6 about halfway between Sweden Valley and Walton. From the parking lot, an access trail leads a short distance to the main STS loop. Another access point for the northern portion of the loop is Lyman Run State Park, where a 1.5-mile access trail leads from the south end of the lake to the STS. The Southern Gateway is at Ole Bull State Park on PA 144, through which the trail passes. South of that park, the STS goes through Cross Fork (with food and lodging) and crosses PA 144 again. One highlight is the very large and remote Hammersley Wild Area, and the trail also passes through or near three state parks and three state forest picnic areas. Good cross-country skiing can be found along the northern portion of the Susquehannock Trail System, as well as on other nearby trails constructed especially for skiing near Denton Hill State Park.

For a map and trail guide, contact Pine Creek Outfitters, 5142 Route 6, Wellsboro, PA 16901, (570) 724-3003, www.pinecrk.com. An award and emblem are given to hikers who complete the entire trail; for further information, contact Susquehannock Trail Club, 5003 US 6 West, Ulysses, PA 16948. For information on camping and amenities at the Southern Gateway, contact Ole Bull State Park, 31 Valhalla Lane, Cross Fork, PA 17729, (814) 435-5000, www.dcnr.state.pa.us/stateparks/parks/olebull.aspx.

22

North Link Trail
and South Link Trail
8.5 miles and 5.9 miles

The blue-blazed North Link and South Link Trails were constructed, using old logging railroad grades to a considerable extent, to connect the Susquehannock and Black Forest Trails in an area where those two long-distance backpacking trails come close together. Both trails offer interesting hikes in themselves, with historical interest and a real feeling of remoteness. The enterprising backpacker can also create an intriguing circuit of about 24.7 miles by hiking these two connector trails and the adjacent portions of the Susquehannock Trail (2.3 miles) and Black Forest Trail (8 miles). Logging in this area is described in *Sunset along Susquehannock Waters* (1974), by Thomas Taber, which includes pictures of Big Trestle, Big Spring Trestle, and the railroad cut on the Hartman Trail. The remains of all these are encountered along the two Link Trails.

The North Link and the South Link are pictured on the maps for the Susquehannock Trail, and descriptions are included in that trail's guide. The North Link and South Link Trails are both very remote and difficult to reach by car. For the North Link, a series of roads climbing into the hills southeast of Ole Bull State Park can be used to reach the western end of the trail near its junction with Susquehannock Trail. The east end of the North Link is near the Black Forest Trail's northwest crossing of PA 44. The South Link can be approached via Benson Road to the west of PA 44. For both of these trails, the easiest access is to walk in on the STS or BFT from those trails' nearest road access points. For a map and trail guide, contact Pine Creek Outfitters, 5142 Route 6, Wellsboro, PA 16901, (570) 724-3003, www.pinecrk.com.

23

Black Forest Trail
42.1 miles

The orange-blazed Black Forest Trail (BFT) may be the most challenging and rewarding backpacking resource in Pennsylvania. This spectacular long-distance loop trail leads through and above the west side of Pine Creek Gorge in the northwest corner of Lycoming County. This very rugged trail charges into and out of the chasm several times, with many very steep ascents and descents, before leveling out on top of the plateau around PA 44. The trail features many outstanding vistas in all directions, with views over Morris Run, Big Dam Hollow, Young Woman's Creek, Baldwin Branch, Callahan Run, Naval Run, Little Slate Run, and Pine Creek. The Black Forest Trail system was constructed by the

Bureau of Forestry and is maintained by Bob Webber, a retired forest foreman and accomplished trail maintainer.

The book *50 Hikes in Central Pennsylvania* (2001), by Tom Thwaites, features three day hikes on particularly interesting sections of the Black Forest Trail. Two connector trails, the North Link and South Link, connect the BFT to the Susquehannock Trail, and the T-Squared Trail connects the BFT to the Donut Hole Trail. Near the BFT trailhead in Slate Run, you can use the Pine Creek Rail-Trail to connect with the West Rim Trail and the Mid State Trail upstream in the Blackwell area. All of these long-distance backpacking options are described in detail in separate entries in this chapter.

The primary trailhead is just outside Slate Run in the depths of Pine Creek Gorge, reached via PA 414 north of Waterville. Drive west, then north, on Slate Run Road for .8 mile to a pine plantation. The BFT officially begins and ends here. There are several other access points, particularly on PA 44 above the gorge. See the trail guide for details.

A map, guide set, and trail patch are available from Tiadaghton Forest Fire Fighters Association, P.O. Box 5091, South Williamsport, PA 17701. Obtain camping permits from Tiadaghton State Forest, 423 E. Central Ave., South Williamsport, PA 17702, (570) 327-3450, www.dcnr.state.pa.us/forestry/state forests/tiadaghton.aspx. The Black Forest Trail has been prone to horse damage; please contact the state forest office to report trail misuse.

24

Black Forest System Ski Trails

On top of the plateau above Pine Creek Gorge, the orange-blazed Black Forest Trail leads to an extensive network of blue-blazed cross-country ski trails. During the off-season, you can use these trails for loop hikes or backpacking trips of various lengths. Some of the trails are named after intriguing characters. George Will was a forest ranger who skied in this area as early as 1914. His wife, Ruth Will, officiated at the Pump Station Fire Tower for forty years. Sentiero di Shay means the "Path of Shay" in Italian, in tribute to Italian workers who built the railroad grades traversed by the Shay gear-driven locomotive in the logging era. Francis Kennedy was a longtime Tiadaghton district forester, avid cross-country skier, and member of the elite 10th Mountain Division during World War II.

George B. Will Trail (5.6 miles): Access and parking for this loop are off PA 44, a short distance north of Manor Fork Road.

Sentiero di Shay (13.4 miles): This lengthy and secluded loop intersects the BFT twice and shares short sections of pathway with the George B. Will Trail and the Blackberry Trail. The loop is easy and scenic, with just one steep climb, making it a good possibility for a long day hike or a beginner's backpacking trip. Use the Blackberry Trail parking lot.

Gas Line–Baldwin Trail (2.2 miles): This trail provides a shortcut between miles 21 and 34 of the Black Forest Trail, creating the possibility of day hikes in several variations.

Francis X. Kennedy Trail (4.6 miles): This trail begins from the northern section of the Sentiero di Shay loop and provides access to the area north of PA 44 as it swings toward Oleona.

Most of these trails are near PA 44. These and several other short ski trails in the area are featured in the Black Forest Trail guide and map, available from Tiadaghton Forest Fire Fighters Association, P.O. Box 5091, South Williamsport, PA 17701.

25
Big Pine Trail
and Big Trail Road
4.7 miles

The Big Pine Trail and Big Trail Road route is a challenging and rewarding hike in the Black Forest Trail (BFT) system. It leads one way from the Naval Run parking area (near Slate Run) along the west side of Pine Creek, then strenuously up Riffle Run to Big Trail Road, which then leads to the BFT. The trail along Pine Creek is scenic and narrow, following the creek from far above by tiptoeing along challenging rock ledges. At 1.5 miles, the trail reaches a ledge vista, then turns into a side canyon and ascends Riffle Run very steeply to the top of Pine Creek Gorge. At 2.5 miles, turn right on the rarely used Big Trail Road, and proceed for 2.1 more miles past two outstanding vistas over the gorge. The BFT meets and briefly follows Big Trail Road about a mile from that road's end at Trout Run Road. The book *50 Hikes in Central Pennsylvania* (2001), by Tom Thwaites, describes an intensely challenging and amazingly scenic 9.6-mile loop hike using the Big Pine Trail, Big Trail Road, and a section of the BFT. This particular hike may offer the ultimate Pine Creek Gorge experience. The Big Pine Trail is featured in the Black Forest Trail guide and map, available from Tiadaghton Forest Fire Fighters Association, P.O. Box 5091, South Williamsport, PA 17701.

26
Golden Eagle Trail
9.1 miles

A rugged and very beautiful loop trail, with a short entrance trail, the Golden Eagle Trail starts in the east side of Pine Creek Gorge and features a strenuous climb to pristine mountaintop streams and several outstanding vistas. The trailhead and parking lot are on PA 414, about 3.5 miles north of Cammal and 1.5 miles north of a crossing of the Pine Creek Rail-Trail. Because of heavy usage by hikers and the area's fragile ecosystem, overnight camping is prohibited along this trail. The Golden Eagle Trail is featured in *50 Hikes in Central Pennsylvania* (2001), by Tom Thwaites, and this accomplished hiking authority states that it "may be the best day hike in Penn's Woods."

Bob Webber Trail
3.7 miles round-trip

The Bob Webber Trail is a one-way scenic trail constructed in the late 1990s as a counterpart to the nearby Golden Eagle Trail. Named for the veteran forester and hiker who maintains the Black Forest Trail on the other side of Pine Creek Gorge, it leads to a stupendous view over the gorge at Wolf Run Bald Vista. There is no outlet from the vista, so after climbing up the trail, you must turn around and go back, for an in-and-out distance of 3.7 miles. The Bob Webber and Golden Eagle Trails are visible from each other's vistas. The trailhead for the Bob Webber Trail is on PA 414 along the Pine Creek Rail-Trail, at the road crossing of Ross Run. This crossing is .5 mile south of the rail-trail's crossing of PA 414.

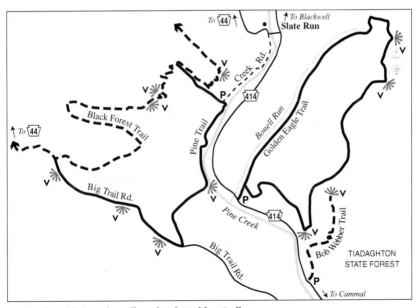

Pine Trail, Golden Eagle Trail, and Bob Webber Trail

28
Little Pine State Park

Little Pine State Park is a hikers' park, serving as a base for backpackers and featuring several noteworthy trails of its own. The Mid State Trail (see the Long-Distance Trails chapter) passes through the park, and most of the hiking and backpacking trails described in this section are nearby. In addition, 23 miles of trails within the park boundaries encircle the lake and climb the surrounding mountains. To reach Little Pine State Park, take PA 414 to Waterville; then turn onto Little Pine Creek Road and proceed to the park. For a brochure and map describing the park's trails, contact Little Pine State Park, 4205 Little Pine Creek Rd., Waterville, PA 17776, (570) 753-6000, www.dcnr.state.pa.us/stateparks/parks/littlepine.aspx.

29
Gillespie Point Trail
1 mile

The one-way Gillespie Point Trail is not an ordinary short trail. The unique cone-shaped mountain above Blackwell, a rarity among the long ridges of the Allegheny Mountains, is an area landmark that can easily be seen from far up and down Pine Creek Gorge and from several points on the Black Forest and West Rim Trails. The Mid State Trail (see the Long-Distance Trails chapter) leads up to a view from a short ridge on top of the cone; this hike is from Blackwell to the vista. The trailhead is just to the east of Blackwell off PA 414. Park at the corner of Big Run Road if there is space; otherwise, park at the canoe parking lot next to Pine Creek in downtown Blackwell and walk back through the village, following the current route of the Mid State Trail (MST).

The orange-blazed Gillespie Point Trail (as well as the MST) turns onto Big Run Road, then after about 100 yards heads steeply uphill at the bend in the road. The trail follows a rugged and precarious old wagon road up the side of Pine Creek Gorge to a bench at .6 mile, and then turns left to follow the ridgeline up to the top in another .4 mile. The view from the top is spectacular, looking up and down the Pine Creek Gorge and Babb Creek Canyon to the right. This vista was constructed by Bob Webber.

You can either return the same way or continue ahead on the MST to form a 3.8-mile loop hike, following the MST downhill to Big Run Road, then turning right and taking that road back to Blackwell. Use the MST map and trail guide. Contact Mid State Trail Association, P.O. Box 167, Boalsburg, PA 16827, www.hike-mst.org.

30

Bohen Run Falls Loop

8.2 miles

The Bohen Run Falls Loop is a rewarding hike in and above the west side of Pine Creek Gorge that leads to two outstanding waterfalls and an excellent vista. It is not advisable to make this hike during slippery conditions. The loop uses portions of the Mid State Trail (MST), West Rim Trail (WRT), and Pine Creek Rail-

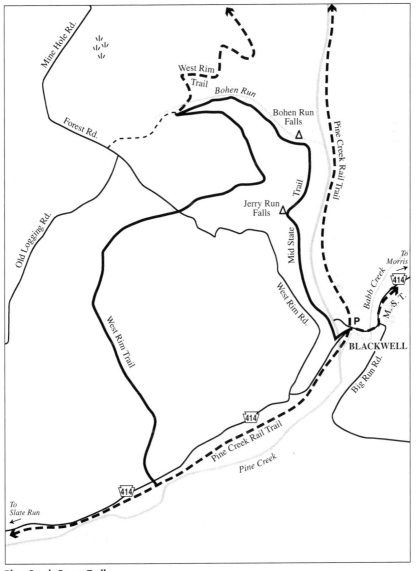

Pine Creek Gorge Trails

Trail. The first section of this hike follows the former northern end of the MST to its terminus at the WRT. At the time of this writing, the MST is being extended north to the New York border, and a new section from Blackwell up the east side of the gorge is partially complete (see the Long-Distance Trails chapter for details). The section of the MST this hike employs is scheduled to become a blue-blazed spur trail once the new northern extension is complete.

Park in the canoe parking lot in downtown Blackwell, walk over the road bridge, and then turn right and hop over the guardrail to access the current route of the MST (orange-blazed at the time of this writing, blue-blazed in the future). Initially the trail is narrow and steep-sided as it climbs above Pine Creek, but it eventually becomes easier, while still climbing. About a mile from Blackwell, walk carefully along a ledge above the beautiful Jerry Run Falls. This is an uncommon "buttermilk" falls, in which the water spreads out evenly across a wide rock face. About .3 mile later, you come to a blue-blazed side trail that leads to nice campsites along Pine Creek and then climbs back up to the main trail. Next, you reach the spectacular Bohen Run Falls, viewed from a nearly vertical 50-foot cliff. Continue climbing up Bohen Run on an old slate quarrying road to the junction with the orange-blazed WRT and a blue-blazed side trail. This spot is the original northern terminus of the MST, 261 miles from Maryland.

Turn sharply left on the WRT and proceed to the vista over Blackwell. This is one of the great natural overlooks in Pennsylvania; on a clear day, you can see over the long ridges of the Appalachian Mountains beyond Williamsport, more than 30 miles away. Next, cross West Rim Road and proceed through a high plateau forest, where some logging has taken place in recent years. The trail soon begins a descent back into Pine Creek Gorge via the beautiful Lloyd Run Hollow. You reach PA 414 across from the Rattlesnake Rock parking area. Walk through the lot and find your way to the Pine Creek Rail-Trail, where you turn left and walk about 1.8 scenic and easy miles back to the Blackwell parking lot.

31
West Rim Trail
30.5 miles

The West Rim Trail (WRT) is a very scenic long-distance trail that mostly follows the western edge of Pine Creek Gorge, from Ansonia to near Blackwell. Parts of the WRT pass through mixed Allegheny hardwoods, featuring white ash, cherry, and hemlock. In other areas, the trail winds along ridges of oak forest with abundant mountain laurel, and it also passes through boggy meadows near beaver dams. You will encounter some challenging topography when the trail departs from the edge of the main gorge to traverse side canyons. Best of all, the sections of the WRT along the main gorge lead to many outstanding vistas, some well over 1,000 feet above Pine Creek.

The WRT is currently connected to the northern end of the Mid State Trail; in the future, that section will become a blue-blazed connector between the WRT and the new northern extension of the MST on the other side of the gorge. Meanwhile, intrepid backpackers can reach the Black Forest Trail from the southern end of the WRT by following a section of the Pine Creek Rail-Trail downstream to Slate Run. A backpacking trip on a portion of the WRT is also featured in *50 Hikes in Central Pennsylvania* (2001), by Tom Thwaites.

The WRT's northern terminus is at a forestry maintenance building approximately 1 mile south of US 6 on Colton Road, outside of Ansonia. The southern terminus is along PA 414 at Rattlesnake Rock parking area, 2 miles south of Blackwell. The trail was initially laid out by a forestry student, and the Bureau of Forestry continues to maintain it. The main trail is orange-blazed, and several access trails that lead in from nearby roads are blue-blazed. For a map and trail guide, contact Pine Creek Outfitters, 5142 Route 6, Wellsboro, PA 16901, (570) 724-3003, www.pinecrk.com. For a map and guide to short trails in the Ansonia area near the WRT's northern terminus, contact Tioga State Forest, One Nessmuk Lane, Wellsboro, PA 16901, (570) 724-2868, www.dcnr.state.pa.us/forestry/stateforests/tioga.aspx.

32

Pine Creek Rail-Trail
62 miles

During the industrial era, railroads provided the only access to the remote depths of Pine Creek Gorge, and to this day some areas are still unreachable by road. The railroad line from Jersey Shore to Corning, New York, offered wonderful views and natural solitude that once were available only to railroad engineers. But since the abandonment of the rail line in the 1980s, outdoor lovers can traverse the remote bottom of the gorge by hiking, biking, or skiing. The old railroad bed has been transformed piece by piece into a long-distance recreational trail known as Pine Creek Rail-Trail.

The first segment of the rail-trail formally opened in 1996, and extensions have been opened in the years since. At the time of this writing, the trail reaches 62 miles from Ansonia in the north to Jersey Shore in the south, with a planned northern extension toward the New York border. The rail-trail is also a key link in the growing Pennsylvania Wilds backpacking network, connecting the West Rim and Mid State Trails at Blackwell with the Black Forest Trail at Slate Run. The rail-trail is intended for hikers and mountain bikers; horseback riding is allowed on a parallel path for about 9 miles between Ansonia and Tiadaghton. Leashed dogs are permitted. The trail can be used from half an hour before sunrise to half an hour after sunset. Camping is allowed along many sections of the trail with a permit, though in some sensitive areas, camping is prohibited. The official trail map denotes camping and noncamping areas precisely.

You can access the northern end from the Big Meadow parking area along US 6 in Ansonia or the Darling Run parking area on PA 362 a short distance south of US 6. There is no road access for about the next 19 miles south to Blackwell, offering a long and secluded trip for hikers, bikers, and skiers. From Blackwell south to Jersey Shore, the trail follows PA 414 closely, with access at several different parking lots along this road. For a trail map and camping permits, contact Tioga State Forest, One Nessmuk Lane, Wellsboro, PA 16901, (570) 724-2868, www.dcnr.state.pa.us/forestry/stateforests/tioga.aspx.

33

Colton Point and
Leonard Harrison State Parks

Colton Point and Leonard Harrison State Parks are located on opposite sides of Pine Creek Gorge west of Wellsboro. Both offer spectacular vistas into the gorge and over the plateau areas above. The creek is plainly visible, with a parallel gray stripe that is the Pine Creek Rail-Trail. When Pine Creek can be waded at times of low water, Turkey Path Trail connects the two parks. This rugged but developed trail starts at Leonard Harrison and descends 1 mile along a run with a major waterfall, down to Pine Creek Rail-Trail along the creek. After wading across the creek, you can climb to the lookout at Colton Point via unmarked trails. Colton Point is also a good base for hiking the West Rim Trail, which passes through the park and past some of its vistas.

For further information on all these hiking opportunities, contact Leonard Harrison State Park, 4797 Route 660, Wellsboro, PA 16901, (570) 724-3061, www.dcnr.state.pa.us/stateparks/parks/leonardharrison.aspx. For specific information on Colton Point State Park, write to Colton Point State Park, c/o Leonard Harrison, at the same mailing address or call the same phone number. The website for Colton Point is www.dcnr.state.pa.us/stateparks/parks/colton point.aspx.

Bee Tree Ski Trail

6.6 miles

The Bee Tree Ski Trail begins at the Ansonia parking lot serving the northern terminus of the West Rim Trail (WRT) and follows that orange-blazed trail for .4 mile to Strapmill Hollow. Here the blue-blazed Bee Tree Trail leaves the WRT and crosses Colton Road, then continues through the forest parallel to upper Pine Creek and US 6. After crossing Bee Tree Hollow, the trail reaches Steele Hollow and climbs its east side to the height-of-land. The trail then descends the west side of the hollow to a parking lot near Rexford. This is not an easy ski trail, and during the off-season the hike is fairly challenging as well. The Bee Tree Ski Trail is visible on the map for the West Rim Trail (see separate entry above). For more information and a map dedicated to the trail, contact Tioga State Forest, One Nessmuk Lane, Wellsboro, PA 16901; (570) 724-2868, www.dcnr.state.pa .us/forestry/stateforests/tioga.aspx.

Sand Run Falls Trail

7 miles

Sand Run Falls Trail is an easy and scenic hike to an impressive waterfall. The orange-blazed trail generally parallels Sand Run Creek and turns around at the 30-foot waterfall, which you reach via a short but challenging side trail down a minor cliff. The trail was built in 1993 and is maintained by Boy Scout Troop 24 of Wellsboro. Drive 12.5 miles southeast from Wellsboro on SR 2018 and SR 2016, or 3.5 miles west on SR 2016 from US 15 near Blossburg.

REGION 8

Endless Mountains

Region Editors: Joe and Lorraine Healey

The Endless Mountains Region consists of the highlands in the northeastern corner of Pennsylvania. This region is bordered on the north by the New York state line; on the east by the Delaware River to Atco; on the south by PA 652 to Indian Orchard, US 6 to Scranton, and US 11 to Northumberland; and on the west by US 15 to the New York border.

Community names in this region provide an index to history. Evidence of Indian habitation remains in the poetic Sheshequin, Wyalusing, Mehoopany, and Tunkhannock. Settlers from Connecticut brought names such as New Milford and Windham Center, as well as classical names like Troy, Athens, and Rome. In the late eighteenth century, refugees from the French Revolution settled at Azilum on the Susquehanna River. The execution of their beloved Queen Marie Antoinette back in France resulted in the dispersal of the refugees, who founded LeRaysville, Dushore, and Laporte. Azilum is now a state historic site, with reconstructed log cabins and a nineteenth-century farmhouse museum. Songwriter Stephen Foster lived in Athens and Towanda; the song "Camptown Races" was based on his experiences at local horse races. Joseph Smith, the founder of Mormonism, interpreted the Golden Tablets at Oakland in Susquehanna County and drew his first followers from that area.

This region features rolling hills formed by the erosion of an ancient seabed that has since risen and become the Allegheny Plateau. In the southwestern part of the region, the plateau was warped by the geologic building of the Appalachian Mountains, forming rugged highlands that are heavily forested and sparsely populated. In a much more recent era by geologic standards, northeastern Pennsylva-

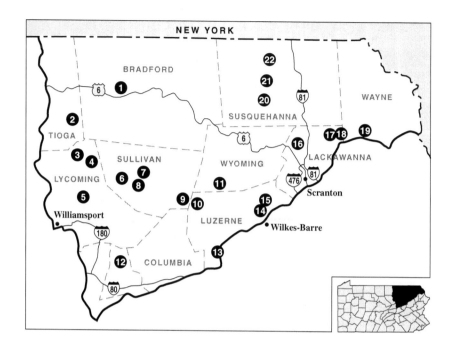

nia was scoured by glaciers, resulting in hundreds of lakes and ponds. Many of these bodies of water are now the inspiration for parks that make good hiking destinations.

Many local regional hiking guides and books of historical interest are available for the Endless Mountains region. For further reference, *Hiking the Endless Mountains: Exploring the Wilderness of Northeast Pennsylvania* (2003), by local hiker Jeff Mitchell, describes a variety of family-friendly day hikes and a few extended backpacking trips in the region.

Two recent natural events have had an impact on the hiking trails in this region. Defoliations by the elm spanworm in 1993–94 were followed by the anthracnose fungus, resulting in the death of vast numbers of trees. This has increased the amount of sunlight reaching the forest floor, causing briars and stinging nettles to thrive and compounding the challenges of trail maintenance. The Old Loggers Path and the Loyalsock Trail are experiencing difficulties with dense undergrowth, and other trails will probably be affected by this ongoing problem.

1

Mount Pisgah State Park
and County Park

The 1,302-acre Mount Pisgah State Park is midway between Troy and Towanda in Bradford County, situated along Mill Creek at the base of 2,260-foot Mount Pisgah 2 miles north of US 6. Three principal trails of the park's 10-mile hiking system are accessible from the parking lot at the beautiful 75-acre Stephen Foster Lake, named after the famed composer, in the heart of the state park. The summit of Mount Pisgah, featuring marvelous scenic vistas of Bradford County in almost all directions, is protected as a county park and has limited day-use facilities. To the east of the state park, State Game Land 289 can be reached from Mount Pisgah via a number of spur trails diverging from the Oh! Susanna Trail.

Mill Stream Trail (1 mile): This pleasant stroll starts from the parking lot. Cross the paved road to the lake; then follow the shoreline through large hemlock, sugar maple, basswood, and white ash on the original farm woodlot. More than ten varieties of ferns grow among the large boulders on the steep slope above the trail, and woodland wildflowers are numerous in the spring. At the upper end of the lake, the trail turns uphill and circles back to the parking lot. The upper section of the trail consists of old pastures now progressing to early successional woodland.

Oh! Susanna Trail (2 miles): Who else but Oh! Susanna could ramble up and over the rolling hills encircling Stephen Foster Lake? Begin by crossing the pedestrian bridge spanning the narrow upper end of the lake, and stroll across the mowed meadow toward the swimming pool. Then travel in a northeasterly direction across the level day-use area to a narrow notch and footpath through the woodlot above the lake. The path eventually joins a paved road that meanders through open meadows ablaze with summer and early-fall flowers. Follow the road to its end at the dam, where a wide footpath continues through mixed hemlock and hardwood forest before eventually returning to the parking lot.

Ridge Trail (6 miles): From the parking lot, this trail climbs to the summit of Mount Pisgah. Travel the maintained path away from the lake to the sign denoting the beginning of the Ridge Trail. This trail has some steep sections, so prepare for a strenuous yet exhilarating climb. The trail at first traverses open fields, which are long-abandoned pastures, but soon begins to climb the wooded, boulder-strewn slopes. You reach an open plateau near the trail's end, after an ascent of more than 1,000 feet. The trail follows the edge of old fields on the plateau, then crosses into the county park. Continue on the moderately challenging county park trail to the summit of Mount Pisgah and its spectacular vistas. From here, retrace your steps to the parking lot way back down the mountain.

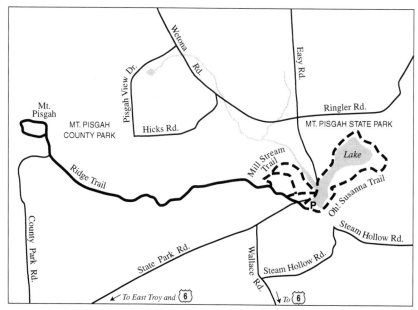

Mount Pisgah Parks

No maps are available for the county park, but you can obtain maps of the state park along with other information by contacting Mount Pisgah State Park, RD 3, Box 362A, Troy, PA 16947, (570) 297-2734, www.dcnr.state.pa.us/state parks/parks/mtpisgah.aspx.

2
Tioga State Forest

The western portion of Tioga State Forest is more famous for the West Rim Trail and Pine Creek Gorge (see the Pennsylvania Wilds Region chapter). But there are also many hiking possibilities in the rest of the forest district east of US 15. Short hikes in the forest's Armenia Division (Upper Tioga River) start at the Armenia Ranger Station, on SR 2021 in southeast Tioga County, 1.2 miles north of Gleason on PA 414. The trails are unmarked, so the USGS map for the Gleason quadrangle is recommended for hikers. Please do not block gated lanes. During hunting seasons, October through January, wear safety orange clothing.

Wynne Wildlife Area (.8 mile): The Armenia Ranger Station and adjacent wildlife management area are on land originally settled in 1842 by the Wynne family. Through the generations, these immigrants from Ireland cleared land for fields of potatoes, oat, and buckwheat, plus pastures and apple orchards. In 1940, the Federal Resettlement Administration purchased the farm, adding to its 14,000-acre Armenia Mountain Project acquisitions. In the mid-1950s, the government deeded the entire project to the Pennsylvania Bureau of Forestry, which now primarily manages the 180-acre Wynne Wildlife Area. Management tactics enhance and retain a diversity of vegetation favorable to wildlife and prevent the area from reverting to a dense stand of northern hardwoods. Travel north on SR 2021 from Gleason, and immediately after passing the ranger station, turn left onto a dirt road. Continue .1 mile and park near the gate on the left.

Walk around the gate and follow the logging lane for a quarter mile. The area on the left was cleared of virgin hemlock in the mid-1800s and tilled for crops until 1940; then it was planted in strips of red pine, red oak, and jack pine. The lane turns 90 degrees right and continues 200 yards to the edge of a salvage clear-cut. A stand of dying trees was cut in 1995, and the area was fenced to keep deer at bay until a new forest becomes established. According to Wynne family records, the virgin hemlock in this area were cut in 1880 for bark, which brought far more income than wood. The site was not farmed and thus regenerated to northern hardwoods. Back at the bend, leave the lane and enter a small field. Here, goldenrod and trees had been encroaching until 1990. Now annual mowing maintains more favorable wildlife forage. The earthen mounds were seeded with staghorn sumac, a winter bird food, in 1997.

The service lane leads from the eastern edge of the field into a "wild" apple orchard, once a pasture fertilized with apple seeds by cattle. Daylighting, cutting the encroaching native trees to create open areas, enhances the growth of apple trees, honeysuckle, brambles, and blueberries throughout the orchard. Continue on the service lane; the brushy area on the right was established by felling trees and erecting a deer fence. The lane to the right leads to small aspen regeneration cuttings, mowed areas, and views of the farmland near Gleason. Back at the main service lane, continue east and north toward the ranger station. The dense hardwood stand on the hillside is a good example of the power of plant succession—the entire hillside was an active apple orchard in the late 1800s. Follow the ranger station's fence back toward SR 2021. En route to the parking spot, turn right and enter a red pine plantation. The flat slab rock about 50 yards from the road served as the foundation for the Wynnes' log cabin in 1842.

Fallbrook Falls (.5 mile): In the late 1800s, the coal-mining town of Fallbrook was Tioga County's largest community, with 2,300 residents. The Fallbrook Railroad switchbacked down Fallbrook Hollow, then followed the Tioga River north, carrying 5 million tons of its bounty to Corning between 1859 and 1904. During an economic lull in 1864, mine strikes and general chaos became so rampant that the Bucktail Regiment was called in to restore order. In 1871, the community was ravaged by smallpox, and the next year, it was threatened by a forest fire. By 1908, Fallbrook was no longer a town, and the school closed in 1945. Today there are several hunting camps but no residents.

Travel north on SR 2021 about 3 miles from Armenia Ranger Station, to the stop sign at County Bridge State Forest Picnic Area. Turn left on T930 (toward Blossburg) and continue 2.5 miles to the old Fallbrook town intersection. Cross the concrete bridge and park on the left near the forestry gate. Walk down on the gated lane, and shortly turn left and cross the stone arch footbridge to Fallbrook Falls. Another footbridge once led to the railroad tracks on the opposite side of the glen. Travel uphill from the overlook rail to find the abandoned park. The service lane leads to the gate.

Armenia Mountain Snowmobile Trail: From the Armenia Ranger Station, travel north on SR 2021 approximately 3 miles to County Bridge State Forest Picnic Area. Turn left on T930 (toward Blossburg). Travel 1 mile and park near the intersection with Ridge Road. Loop hikes of 3 miles or longer are possible from this point, on gentle grades through northern hardwood forests and pine and larch plantings in reclaimed coal strippings.

For a free public-use map, contact Tioga State Forest, One Nessmuk Lane, Wellsboro, PA 16901, (570) 724-2868, www.dcnr.state.pa.us/forestry/stateforests/tioga.aspx.

Tiadaghton State Forest

The section of Tiadaghton State Forest east of US 15 offers many hiking opportunities for those who like to go off the beaten path. The Grays Run area, between US 15 and PA 14, offers great natural solitude and enjoyable hiking, with former CCC and logging trails to Sugar Camp Mountain, Elk Knob, Round Top, and Bodine Mountain. McIntyre Wild Area, east of PA 14 near Ralston, is laced with numerous trails. In the coal-mining ghost town of McIntyre, you can find old house foundations, former streets, orchards, and mining holes. You can use former roads and railroad grades to reach overlooks of Rock Run and Lycoming Creek. There are picturesque waterfalls on all the streams in McIntyre Wild Area. For a free map, contact Tiadaghton State Forest, 423 E. Central Ave., S. Williamsport, PA 17702, (570) 327-3450, www.dcnr.state.pa.us/forestry/stateforests/tiadaghton.aspx.

Old Loggers Path
27.8 miles

Old Loggers Path is an orange-blazed long-distance backpacking trail that follows former railroad grades, logging roads, bark trails, and other remnants of old industrial transportation, hence the name. The trail is a circuit through remote areas in northeastern Lycoming County. Highlights of the trail are the many revealing cuts on the railroad grades; Rock Run, one of the prettiest streams in Pennsylvania; and vistas over McIntyre Wild Area, Pleasant Stream, and the Loyalsock Trail region.

This area and many others like it have been described in a series of historical books on logging railroads. This region, including Masten, is included in *Ghost Lumber Towns of Central Pennsylvania* (1970), by Thomas Taber. Old Loggers Path is located entirely on state forest land that formerly belonged to the Central Pennsylvania Lumber Company. The trail takes advantage of the engineering expertise of the early logging railroaders by following the moderate grades up and down the rugged landscape. For a detailed description of a backpacking trip on the entire Old Loggers Path, see *50 Hikes in Central Pennsylvania* (2001), by Tom Thwaites.

To reach the starting point, go 2.7 miles southwest of Ellenton on LR 41110 or 9.4 miles up Pleasant Stream Road from PA 14 at Marsh Hill. Look for parking near the stop sign in Masten, a ghost lumber town. The starting point is a short distance down Pleasant Stream Road. The route from Ellenton is the only access in the winter, as all other roads are usually blocked by snow. Keystone Trails Association sponsors a patch for this trail. A trail map is available from Loyalsock State Forest, 274 Arbutus Park Rd., Bloomsburg, PA 17815, (570) 387-4255, www.dcnr.state.pa.us/forestry/stateforests/loyalsock.aspx.

5

Loyalsock Trail
59.3 miles

The name Loyalsock is derived from the Native American name *Lawi-Saquick,* meaning "Middle Creek," because the creek now known by that name is situated between Muncy Creek and Lycoming Creek. Loyalsock Creek rises in Wyoming County and empties into the Susquehanna River at Montoursville. The scenic and challenging Loyalsock Trail (LT) runs roughly parallel to its namesake creek. The LT frequently climbs up and down ridges and mountaintops, passing many waterfalls, lakes, ponds, and historic places. The trail is known for its many fine vistas. Beware of stinging nettles and briars, which are becoming a serious challenge along this trail.

The Loyalsock Trail is maintained by the Alpine Club of Williamsport. The group marks the main trail with high-quality 2-by-6-inch yellow rectangles with 1-inch horizontal red stripes. Originally the trail was marked by tin can lids painted red with a yellow "LT," and many of these are still present. Side trails are marked with yellow can lids bearing a red X. Lead-in trails are marked with blue metal disks. Side trails marked with white blazes are not actively maintained.

The western terminus of the LT is on PA 87, 8.6 miles north of I-180/US 220 at Montoursville. The eastern terminus is on Mead Road just off US 220 near Ringdale. The trail is shown on the public-use map for Loyalsock State Forest. The Alpine Club publishes a detailed guidebook with maps that divide the trail into eight sections, all with road access at each end. The club also offers an embroidered LT patch, which anyone who has hiked at least 10 miles of the trail can purchase. Contact Alpine Club of Williamsport, P.O. Box 501, Williamsport, PA 17703, www.lycoming.org/alpine.

6
Loyalsock State Forest

Loyalsock State Forest has 80 miles of trails, all marked with red circles with signs at trailheads, and are shown on the state forest public-use map. By themselves, they provide various hiking opportunities and loops. But there are also possibilities for more challenging loop hikes in conjunction with the Loyalsock Trail, the Worlds End State Park trails (see separate entry below), and Old Loggers Path. Worlds End State Park makes a good base for hiking the state forest trails. For a public-use map, contact Loyalsock State Forest, 274 Arbutus Park Rd., Bloomsburg, PA 17815, (570) 387-4255, www.dcnr.state.pa.us/forestry/stateforests/loyalsock.aspx.

7
Worlds End State Park

Worlds End State Park is a stunning hikers' park featuring a number of short trails intersecting the long-distance Loyalsock Trail (see separate entry above). Worlds End was founded in 1932 and retains a rustic atmosphere. Most of the facilities are located in a deep scenic gorge along Loyalsock Creek, 650 feet lower than the surrounding plateau. The trails mostly start in the valley and climb steeply; some are very challenging, and many have scenic vistas.

High Rock Trail (1 mile): This yellow-blazed trail starts at the park office and ends on PA 154 below the swimming area. The trail leads along Loyalsock Creek through a mixed northern hardwood forest, taking in High Rock Cliff, High Rock Falls, High Rock Vista, and many rock outcroppings. The trail shares the same route as the Loyalsock Trail (LT) from the cabin bridge to the vista. The terrain is rugged and rocky and includes a steep section called the Rock Stairs.

Canyon Vista Trail (3.5 miles): Starting along Mineral Springs Road by the campground, this blue-blazed trail climbs to the spectacular Loyalsock Canyon Vista. The trail intersects the LT partway up, and after a fairly level stretch, it joins the Link Trail for the final .3-mile climb.

Double Run Nature Trail (1.2 miles): Blazed with white circles containing the letters "DR," this trail starts across from the chapel on PA 154 and splits at the branches of Double Run, loops up the west branch of the creek, and returns down the east branch. This is a gradually sloping, leisurely walk along a small, cascading mountain stream with many pools and waterfalls.

Worlds End Trail (3.3 miles): This trail heads south from the park office and climbs steeply to the plateau. Then, passing over fairly flat terrain, it crosses Coal Mine Road and ends at the LT. You can extend the 3.3-mile one-way trail into a 10.5-mile loop by returning to the park via the LT. Orange disks with the letters "WE" mark the trail. The pathway from the office to Pioneer Road carries both this trail and the Loyalsock Trail. A vista overlooking the steep-sided gorge around the park gives you an idea of how the park received its name.

Link Trail (8.5 miles): This scenic path is a spur trail of the LT system, marked with yellow tin can lids with a red X. The Link Trail starts at the cabin bridge and ends upstream at the steel Rock Run Road bridge over Loyalsock Creek. At the junction of the two branches of Double Run, the Loyalsock Trail and the Link Trail share a stream crossing. In high-water periods, this stream crossing may be difficult.

Worlds End State Park is on PA 154 between Forksville and Laporte. All overnight trail users must park at the office, and vehicles must be registered with the staff. Hikers arriving after hours should drop a copy of their itinerary through the door slot. For a recreation guide showing the park's trail network, contact Worlds End State Park, P.O. Box 62, Forksville, PA 18616, (570) 924-3287, www .dcnr.state.pa.us/stateparks/parks/worldsend.aspx.

8

Eagles Mere

Native Americans believed that Eagles Mere Lake was once a great abyss where the soul passed into the afterlife. A belligerent and discontented chief known as Stormy Torrent decided to do the forbidden: enter this chasm, converse with the souls of his illustrious ancestors, and return with divine wisdom. As thousands watched on the appointed day, Stormy Torrent, accompanied by a beautiful princess from the shores of Lake Erie, descended a long flight of steps into the abyss. When they disappeared from view, the heavens darkened, and lightning and thunder rolled across the mountain. An awful downpour followed, filling the abyss to form a lake.

At the turn of the century, Eagles Mere was a thriving resort with many stately homes and three massive hotels. Still popular as an upscale summer residence for those seeking both natural beauty and recreation, the town is surrounded by many hiking trails through unspoiled forests and across mountain slopes. Many paths remain pristine and untouched after more than a century. For example, Laurel Path first opened in 1895.

Laurel Path (2 miles): This unmarked trail encircles Eagles Mere Lake, passing all the boat landings and sometimes following immediately along the shore. Halfway along the east side of the lake is Lovers Rock, where it is said that the spirit of the lake may be seen.

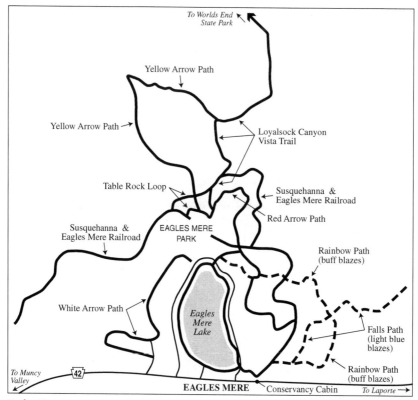

Eagles Mere

Red Arrow Path (1.3 miles): This path runs from the end of Mineral Springs Avenue in Eagles Mere Park to the bathing beach, with three route choices. The start at Mineral Springs Avenue can be confusing, because this trail and the Loyalsock Canyon Vista Trail are both blazed red. Facing north, the Red Arrow Path passes to the right. This path features several interesting rock formations, including a rock labyrinth.

Green Arrow Path (.9 mile): Passing from Eagle Rocks on Red Arrow Path to the Crestmont Inn, this green-blazed trail features Sullivan View, looking toward a pleasing range of forest-covered mountains to the east.

White Arrow Path (1.5 miles): Marked with white blazes, this trail connects the athletic field near the bathing beach to the end of Prospect Avenue, passing Prospect Rocks and the golf course en route.

Yellow Arrow Path (2 miles): This trail goes from Johnson Lane in Eagles Mere to Shanerburg Road, and then back to a junction with the Loyalsock Canyon Vista Trail.

Loyalsock Canyon Vista Trail (3.8 miles): This red-blazed trail extends from the end of Mineral Springs Avenue in Eagles Mere Park to a junction with the Loyalsock Trail (see separate entry above) just north of Shanerburg Road. From the junction, follow the Loyalsock Trail to a vista that overlooks the canyon of Loyalsock Creek and Worlds End State Park.

Buff Trails: These are Eagles Mere Conservancy trails, mostly originating from the railroad bed and marked with buff-colored blazes. Buff A (the Margaret Estey Trail) goes from the conservancy cabin on Outlet Pond across Lakewood Avenue, and connects to Laurel Path. Buff B runs east from the railroad bed in a long loop, returns to cross the railroad bed, and continues to Red Arrow Path. Buff C (.4 mile) is a crossover trail with Buff B. Buff D (1.3 miles) follows the railroad grade to Sullivan View and connects there with Green Arrow Path.

Eagles Mere is on PA 42 in Sullivan County. The Eagles Mere Conservancy has published an updated map for old trails plus new ones recently added by the organization. Most of these trails are not on public land, so no assumption can be made concerning the legality or safety of using them. Copies of the guide are available at the conservancy's log cabin by Outlet Pond (summer only). For more information, contact Eagles Mere Conservancy, P.O. Box 64, Eagles Mere, PA 17731, (570) 525-3385, www.eaglesmere.org/emconservancy.html.

9

State Game Land 13, North Mountain

The story is told that on the third night of a February blizzard during the Civil War, a lone man in a sleigh climbed North Mountain up Fishing Creek gorge. The folks in Jamison City saw him pass through, as he had done regularly many times before; gossip said that he was a wealthy bachelor visiting a lady whose husband was away at war. As he neared the summit that night, a cold gust of wind chilled him despite layers of blankets. Suddenly along the road there appeared what at first seemed like a huge shimmering icicle, but then became a glistening man with long white hair and beard. The creature sprang into the passing cutter, clenching the terrified driver's throat. As the screaming horse raced up the mountain, the sleigh spilled, throwing its contents into a snowdrift. When the bachelor finally pulled himself from the snow, he found both the horse and the apparition gone. Weak and badly injured, he struggled through the bitter cold to his lover's home, where he died several days later.

The mysterious aura of North Mountain has inspired many tales like this, some of which are found in *North American Mementos* (1920), by Henry Wharton Shoemaker. The imagination of the local people also put North Mountain in the history books. During the Civil War, rumors spread that the Confederates, aided by Southern sympathizers on the upper reaches of North Mountain, had broken Union lines and built a fort on the mountain's rocky ramparts. A detachment of 1,000 Union soldiers went to the location, entering the valley with bands playing and banners waving. The troops searched the mountain thoroughly for the alleged fort and its 500 defenders but found only a group of startled berry pickers.

Hikers will find the scenery of North Mountain as enjoyable as its history and folklore. State Game Land 13, at a big 49,527 acres, is in Sullivan and Columbia Counties. The terrain is mountainous and wooded, with numerous waterfalls, similar to nearby Ricketts Glen State Park (see separate entry below). For a special sportsmen's recreation map or further information, contact the PGC Northeast Region Office, P.O. Box 220, Dallas, PA 18612-0220, (570) 675-1143.

10
Ricketts Glen State Park

Ricketts Glen State Park, located at the junction of Luzerne, Sullivan, and Columbia Counties 30 miles north of Bloomsburg, is a 13,050-acre scenic paradise. Two state routes, PA 487 and PA 118, provide access to the park, which was named for Col. Robert Bruce Ricketts, a land baron of the nineteenth century. Although the area was approved as a national park site in the 1930s, World War II brought an end to this plan, and the commonwealth acquired the land for a state park. The major feature of the park is Kitchen Creek and its tributaries, which tumble down the Allegheny Front about 1,000 feet over a distance of 3 miles, forming nearly two dozen named waterfalls and many more small ones. The tallest is an awe-inspiring 94 feet. The park features the greatest concentration of named waterfalls in any small area in the eastern United States. Glen Ganoga and Glen Leigh join at Waters Meet, and the creek continues downward to PA 118. The prime attraction for hikers is 20 miles of trails, varying from fairly level to very steep and strenuous.

Falls Trail (6.7 miles): This incredibly scenic trail is the jewel of the state park, and forms a loop (with the entrance trail from PA 118) that takes you to twenty-one of the park's most spectacular waterfalls. This trail has some very steep and difficult sections. If you plan to hike the Falls Trail, you should be prepared and in good physical condition, and wear sturdy hiking boots. Many people have been severely injured on this trail, often by unwisely trying to tackle the cliffs surrounding the waterfalls. The trailhead is at a parking lot on PA 118.

Highland Trail (1.2 miles): This trail connects with both sides of the Falls Trail at the top of the mountain, forming a portion of the Falls Trail loop hike described above. The Highland Trail also extends from both sides of that loop and can be reached from the parking lot behind the park office.

Cherry Run Trail (4.6 miles): This trail starts behind the cabins at dry Lake Leigh and travels up to Mountain Springs Road.

Old Bulldozer Road Trail (2.9 miles): This trail starts at the parking lot on PA 118 and ascends very steeply to the top of the mountain, ending at dry Lake Leigh.

Mountain Springs Trail (.6 mile): This trail runs from the Bulldozer Trail to Mountain Spring Dam, where ice was harvested in the early twentieth century.

Old Beaver Dam Trail (1.3 miles): This trail starts at the Highland Trail and goes out to PA 487. For a longer 2.8-mile loop hike, cross PA 487 to Grand View Fire Tower Road, and hike up and around the Grand View Trail.

Ganoga View Trail (1.9 miles): This trail begins on PA 487 and ends at Old Beaver Dam Trail. Use Old Beaver Dam Trail, Grand View Trail, and Ganoga View Trail for a pleasant 6-mile hike.

For a longer hike of 10.6 miles, hike the Cherry Run Trail to Mountain Springs Road. Go right on the road and follow it to the dam. Cross in front of the dam and continue to the Mountain Springs Trail. For further information and a park brochure with a map, contact Ricketts Glen State Park, 685 State Route 487, Benton, PA 17814, (570) 477-5675, www.dcnr.state.pa.us/stateparks/parks/rickettsglen.aspx.

11

State Game Land 57

The 38,000-acre State Game Land 57 is in Luzerne and Wyoming Counties, north and east of Ricketts Glen State Park (see separate entry above), and features several marked and unmarked trails. No camping is permitted on state game lands.

Meat Trail (2 miles): The yellow-blazed Meat Trail, so named because hunters frequently use it to remove their deer, traverses an incline and crosses Mehoopany Creek on a suspension bridge. At the southern end of the trail, you can extend your hike by continuing on adjacent service roads. The trail is accessible from LR 65046. Park at the game land lot.

High Knob Trail (6 miles): This fairly level trail, marked with yellow blazes, includes landscapes varying from forests to wetlands. The trail is accessible during hunting season via service roads out of Noxen.

Joe Gmiter Trails: These four loop trails, ranging from 3.3 to 10.5 miles, were built by the Susquehanna Trailers Hiking Club under the supervision of the Game Commission and named for the longtime president of the club. Elevations range from 1,200 to 1,700 feet. Some parts of the trails border a horse farm, beaver pond, and old logging roads, and you can see a great variety of wildlife and trees. Each trail is blazed in a different color, and all hikes are counterclockwise because of restrictions against painting blazes on both sides of trees. These trails start and finish in a parking area 3 miles from Noxen. Maps are available from Harry West, Box 33-C, Noxen, PA 18636. See also susquehanna_trailers.tripod.com.

For an unmarked 13-mile hike, start at the entrance to Mountain Springs off PA 487. The hike leads down to the iron bridge in Stull, mostly on an old railroad grade. Timber and ice were harvested here on Colonel Ricketts's property.

12
Montour Preserve

The 966-acre Montour Preserve, owned by Pennsylvania Power and Light, is free for use by the public. Located near Washingtonville in Montour County, the preserve is open year-round for nature study, environmental education, and outdoor recreation. Many of the activities center around 165-acre Lake Chill-isquaque and the preserve's hiking trails. A visitors center features exhibits of birds of prey, fossils, fish, and waterfowl. Trails range in length from .3 to 4.5 miles. For maps and guides, contact Montour Preserve, 700 Preserve Rd., Danville, PA 17821, (570) 437-3131, www.pplweb.com/montour+preserve/things+to+do/hiking.

13
Mocanaqua Loop Trail

Mocanaqua Loop Trail is an Earth Conservancy trail network opened on National Trails Day, June 7, 2003. The network contains four individual loop trails that together comprise about 9 miles of varying terrain along the northern reach of Penobscot Mountain. The four loops all traverse the mountainside and the ridgetop area, where there are several scenic overlooks, and three of the four contain physically challenging terrain. All these trails are intended for nonmotor-ized uses only, but be aware that ATVs are seen and heard frequently, though they may be using their own trails.

The trailhead in Mocanaqua includes restrooms, picnic tables, benches, bicy-cle racks, a water fountain, and a grill. From US 11, turn onto the Shickshinny Bridge (PA 239) toward Mocanaqua, and take the first left after crossing the bridge. The trailhead and parking are at the end of this short dead-end street. For further information, contact Earth Conservancy, 101 S. Main St., Ashley, PA 18706, (570) 823-3445, www.earthconservancy.org/projects/recamenities.

14
Back Mountain Trail

The Back Mountain Trail was originally built in the 1880s by Albert Lewis, a local entrepreneur who delivered ice from Mountain Springs Lake in the Endless Mountains to urban markets. He sold his successful rail line to the Lehigh Valley Railroad Company, which expanded the service to include lumber, leather goods, and anthracite coal. The railroad was abandoned in 1963, and in 1996 the Anthracite Scenic Trails Association acquired the corridor and arranged for public use with Luzerne County.

Since then, 2.2 miles of the corridor have been converted to trail, enabling bicyclists and hikers safe access through a cut in the mountains between the Wyoming Valley floor and the many Endless Mountains communities. Variety is the spice of the trail, with a waterfall, lengthy shady stretches, far-reaching views, and flower-filled meadows. The trail currently runs from Luzerne to Trucksville. In its final form, it will run 14 miles from Luzerne to Harveys Lake, and plans have been made for connections with many of the other trails in the area. The Luzerne trailhead is on Parry Street at the "Gateway to the Back Mountain" kiosk. For further information, contact Anthracite Scenic Trails Association, P.O. Box 212, Dallas, PA 18612, (570) 675-9016, bmt.editthispage.com.

15
Frances Slocum State Park

The 1,035-acre Frances Slocum State Park is in Luzerne County, 5 miles from Dallas and 10 miles from Wilkes-Barre. The park is named for a young Quaker girl who was kidnapped by Indians. For those wishing for a peaceful walk, a network of hiking trails will take you to many points of interest.

Frances Slocum Trail (.7 mile): This blue-blazed trail starts at the boat rental parking lot and loops around to the rock shelter where the Indians held their young captive overnight. The trail circles back to the parking lot.

Lake Trail (1.4 miles): This red-blazed trail starts at the bridge on the campground road and follows the lakeshore through the boat launch area. The other end loops back onto itself after meeting the Frances Slocum Trail.

Deer Trail (3.8 miles): This yellow-blazed trail starts at the visitors center. If you like stone walls, you will love this trail. Spur trails are blazed yellow with black slashes, allowing for shorter loops of 1.3 and 2.5 miles. The Deer Trail is maintained by the Susquehanna Trailers Hiking Club.

Larch Tree Trail (2 miles): This orange-blazed trail starts at the second gate down the campground road and forms a large loop.

Campground Trail (1 mile): This white-blazed trail begins behind the group camping area at a stone wall and continues through woods along a gas pipeline. The other end of the trail is at the Stony Point Campground parking lot.

A loop hike incorporating many of the park's more interesting features is also included in *50 Hikes in Eastern Pennsylvania* (2003), by Tom Thwaites. For further information or a park brochure with map, contact Frances Slocum State Park, 565 Mt. Olivet Rd., Wyoming, PA 18644, (570) 696-3525, www.dcnr.state.pa.us/ stateparks/parks/francesslocum.aspx.

Lackawanna State Park

The 1,411-acre Lackawanna State Park is 10 miles north of Scranton in Lackawanna County. It is easily accessible from I-81 at Exit 60 or 61. More than 6 miles of hiking trails, restricted to foot travel only, are sprinkled throughout the park. For further information or a park brochure with map, contact Lackawanna State Park, RR 1, Box 230, Dalton, PA 18414, (570) 945-3239, www.dcnr.state.pa .us/stateparks/parks/lackawanna.aspx.

D&H Rail-Trail

38 miles

The D&H (Delaware and Hudson) Rail-Trail runs through historic areas of Lackawanna and Susquehanna Counties, from Simpson to the New York border just north of Lanesboro. The trail begins under the viaduct and proceeds north, with the scenic Lackawanna River on your right, passing through Forest City, Union Dale, Herrick Center, Ararat, Orson, Thompson, Starucca, and Stevens Point on the way to Lanesboro. The Delaware and Hudson Gravity Railroad was the trial site of the first operational steam locomotive in the United States. The engine traveled 3 miles. From this humble beginning, the line became a workhorse, shipping coal to the entire Northeast. For a map or further information, contact Rail-Trail Council of Northeastern Pennsylvania, P.O. Box 123, Forest City, PA 18421, (570) 785-7245, www.nepa-rail-trails.org.

O&W Rail-Trail

30 miles

Like other railroads and canals in the region, the Scranton line of the O&W (Ontario and Western) was constructed to haul coal. When coal was no longer king, the need for the railroad ceased, and the track was abandoned in 1957. This trail begins in Simpson, along with the D&H Rail-Trail (see separate entry above). The O&W Trail runs along the east side of the Lackawanna River, paralleling the D&H Rail-Trail for about 10 miles to Stillwater Dam, just north of Forest City. The trail then diverges to the northeast and east through Herrick Township, Pleasant Mount, Orson, and Poyntelle.

The southern section of the trail has not been improved. The northern 6 miles, owned by Preston and Buckingham Townships in Wayne County, have been improved. Access this area via PA 370 in Lakewood, at the train station in the center of town. The remainder of the O&W Railroad north to Hancock, New York, is owned by the various townships. For a map or further information, contact Rail-Trail Council of Northeastern Pennsylvania, P.O. Box 123, Forest City, PA 18421, (570) 785-7245, www.nepa-rail-trails.org.

19

Prompton State Park

Prompton Dam is near Route 6 at Waymart. The state park is currently operated in cooperation with the U.S. Army Corps of Engineers, and Prompton Lake is the focal point of the park. There are 9 miles of hiking trails of moderate difficulty. One encircles the lake, with various offshoot trails on the eastern side. Many bald eagles have been sighted at Eagle Pass on the far side of the lake, 2 miles off the main trail. You can also get a bird's-eye view of the area's windmills from the parking area. A large trail map is posted at the pavilion at the lake entrance off PA 170. For more information, contact Prompton State Park, c/o Lackawanna, Dalton, PA 18414, (570) 945-3239, www.dcnr.state.pa.us/state parks/parks/prompton.aspx.

20

Woodbourne Forest Preserve

In 1956, this preserve became the first property protected by The Nature Conservancy in Pennsylvania. Pioneer conservationists Francis R. Cope Jr. and his family donated almost 500 acres to the organization. Nestled in the heart of Susquehanna County, Woodbourne protects one of the few remaining examples of old-growth forest in eastern Pennsylvania. Thanks to the continued generosity of the Cope family and further land purchases by The Nature Conservancy, the preserve's size has increased to its current 654 acres. A stewardship committee of dedicated volunteers manages the preserve. A 1-mile nature trail leads to many marked points of interest. With new trails built by Keystone Trails Association in 2006, Woodbourne boasts more miles of wilderness paths open to the public than at any other site in Susquehanna County. Campfires and overnight camping are not permitted in the preserve.

A 4.9-mile hike follows Woodbourne Forest's longest trail, the blue-blazed Cope's Ramble, beginning at the picnic pavilion adjacent to the parking area 1 mile north of Dimock on PA 29 (which is 16 miles north of Tunkhannock and 5 miles south of Montrose). A sign beside the highway marks the preserve's parking area. Follow the blazes downhill from the pavilion, across the meadow and to the edge of the swamp. At the wetlands, the blue-blazed trail departs from the yellow-blazed and orange-blazed paths. Cope's Ramble crosses gravel Baker Road twice and takes you to enormous red oak, eastern hemlock, white ash, sugar maple, basswood, and black cherry trees, as well as several interesting old fieldstone walls that are the surviving sentinels of long vanished farms and homesteads. Wear sturdy hiking shoes for this hike. For further information, contact Woodbourne Forest and Wildlife Preserve, RR 6, Box 6294, Montrose, PA 18801, (570) 278-3384, www.nature.org/wherewework/northamerica/states/pennsylvania/preserves/art826.html.

21
Endless Mountain Riding Trail
14 miles

When the Montrose Branch of the Delaware, Lackawanna, and Western Railroad was abandoned in 1944, a retired judge bought the right-of-way for $1. Since the judge was a horse enthusiast, the railbed was used by a local equestrian club. The Endless Mountain Riding Trail begins in Montrose behind the Humane Society building on PA 706 (Grow Avenue), and the corridor is heavily forested for much of its 14-mile length. Highlights include a 60-foot waterfall, an old depot, and bird watching opportunities. The trail proceeds east from Montrose to Heart Lake, then south along Martins Creek to Allford. For further information, contact Endless Mountain Bike Club, c/o New Milford Bike, 195 Main St., New Milford, PA 18834, (570) 465-2169.

22
Salt Springs State Park

Salt Springs State Park in Susquehanna County is 7 miles north of Montrose, on Salt Spring Road west of Franklin Forks on PA 29. A stand of virgin hemlocks, estimated at 600 to 700 years old, is a focal point of the 400-acre park. Three hiking trails traverse the park, totaling about 5 miles. For further information or a park brochure with map, contact Salt Springs State Park, c/o Lackawanna, Dalton, PA 18414, (570) 945-3239, www.dcnr.state.pa.us/stateparks/parks/saltsprings.aspx.

REGION 9

Pocono Highlands

Region Editor: Wayne Gross

Contributors: Stephanie Croteau, Shirley Gross, Roy Kleinle,
Rosemary Miller, Tom Miller, John Motz, Joel Wilkinson

The Pocono Highlands Region encompasses the well-known hills of that name in northeastern Pennsylvania. The region is bordered on the east by the Delaware River; on the south by I-80 and US 209 to Jim Thorpe; on the southwest by PA 93 to Nescopeck; and on the north by US 11, US 6, and PA 652 to the Delaware River.

The Pocono "Mountains" are not really mountains, but a rugged plateau with deep, river-carved canyons. The Poconos are bounded on the north by the highlands of the Endless Mountains region, on the east by the escarpment leading down to Delaware Water Gap, on the west by the Moosic Mountains, and on the south by the Ridge and Valley Province formed by the Appalachian Mountains. There is little extreme elevation change in the Poconos other than at the escarpment. On the east side of the escarpment in particular, waterfalls cascade off the plateau through scenic gorges down to the Delaware River between Milford and Stroudsburg.

The Poconos are an area unique to the commonwealth. Because they are home to Pennsylvania's largest concentration of globally rare plants, animals, and ecosystems, The Nature Conservancy has placed the Poconos on its list of the world's "Last Great Places." The area is home to oak-pine-heath ecosystems that are not found anywhere else in the world. The Poconos also bear the stamp of the most recent glaciation, with many noteworthy kettle lakes such as Bruce Lake in Pike County, Deep Lake in State Game Land 38, and Lake Lacawac near

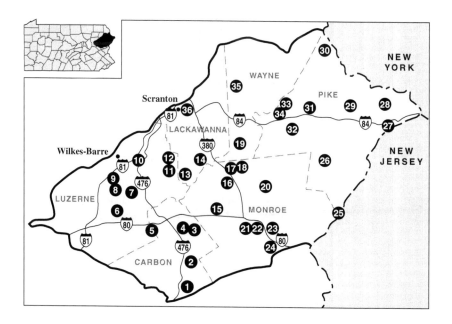

the artificial Lake Wallenpaupack. A giant glacial pothole is found at Archibald State Park north of Scranton. Hickory Run State Park in Carbon County features a boulder field left behind by glaciers. Erratics, moraines, striations, and other glacial features can be found throughout the region by the careful observer.

The high altitudes of the Poconos also harbor many bog ecosystems of a type more common far to the north, and the cool microclimates of the bogs have aided in the retention of many regionally rare plants and animals. The northern hardwood forests of the Poconos also resemble forests much farther to the north. The unique tamarack, a conifer that drops its needles in winter, and the stately black spruce, a mostly Canadian species, surround the region's many bogs. The bogs of Pike and Monroe Counties also feature sphagnum moss and pitcher plants, which have evolved to capture insects in order to gain the mineral nourishment that the bogs lack. Leatherleaf, sedge, sundew, bog rosemary, and cottongrass also abound in the bogs.

Early settlers tried farming in this region but were ultimately discouraged by the rocks and thin soil. Old decayed stone walls bespeak earlier attempts to tame the land and bear mute evidence of failure and broken dreams. This saved the Poconos from the fate common to most areas within 100 miles of New York and Philadelphia. Development came later and was based on recreational facilities and vacation homes in a scenic landscape that had not been covered with agriculture and industry.

Though the area abounds in state forests and game lands, most of these public lands are scattered and noncontiguous. For the enterprising hiker, the game lands are laced with access roads and trails. The 45-mile Thunder Swamp Trail

System in southern Pike County was laid out by state forest personnel with help from the Young Adult Conservation Corps (YACC). The Pinchot Trail System was laid out in Lackawanna County under the sponsorship of the YACC and the Youth Conservation Corps. These trail systems have been the destination of many Keystone Trails Association Trail Care weekends to install bridges and perform trail maintenance.

The Poconos are an excellent place to hike during all four seasons. In spring, you are surrounded by beautiful waterfalls enhanced by snowmelt, the sounds of birdsong, and an abundance of wildflowers. Summer provides you with cool green refuges from the summer heat. Fall offers pleasant weather and beautiful colors. Winter features the unique beauty of the snow-covered landscape. Though the elevation changes of the Poconos put no great strain on the hiker, the rocks will, and you are well advised to wear sturdy shoes and carry a walking stick, which will provide great assistance in the rock fields.

1

Beltzville State Park

The focal point of the 2,972-acre Beltzville State Park is the 949-acre Beltzville Lake. Around the lake are 15 miles of hiking trails along wooded pathways and old roads. Points of interest along the trails include the remains of a gristmill raceway, a slate quarry from the 1700s, and a waterfall in Wild Creek Cove. Portions of the trail system can be used for cross-country skiing. Beltzville State Park is located off US 209, east of the Northeast Extension of the Pennsylvania Turnpike (I-476) at Exit 74. Follow signs to the park. For more information, contact Beltzville State Park, 2950 Pohopoco Dr., Lehighton, PA 18235, (610) 377-0045, www.dcnr.state.pa.us/stateparks/parks/beltzville.aspx.

2

Weiser State Forest, Penn Forest Area
4.5 miles

To reach the parking area for the Penn Forest Area, a Carbon County state forest district, follow PA 903 north from Jim Thorpe for 6.5 miles. Turn right and follow Reservoir Road (LR 13012) for 1.7 miles, crossing I-476. Turn left and follow a dirt road for .5 mile through Bethlehem Water Authority land. Park along the road near the gate and sign for Weiser State Forest. Follow the gravel road north through the forest. The terrain is flat amid a mixed oak forest. In 1.6 miles, reach an intersection with another gravel road. To the left, the gravel road leads .4 mile to a gate. Return to the parking area via the first gravel road. This route is excellent for cross-country skiing in the winter. For more information, contact Weiser State Forest, P.O. Box 99, Cressona, PA 17929, (570) 385-7800, www.dcnr.state.pa .us/forestry/stateforests/weiser.aspx.

Delaware State Forest
and State Game Land 129

On the edge of the Pocono Plateau, the 3,500-acre State Game Land 129 and a small adjacent portion of Delaware State Forest offer hiking experiences similar to those at Big Pocono State Park and State Game Land 38 nearby. The western edge of State Game Land 129 borders Hickory Run State Park. Within the state forest tract is the Pohopoco Fire Tower, on Pimple Hill on the west side of PA 115. This point provides a view south to Blue Mountain (which carries the Appalachian Trail on its crest), Delaware Water Gap, Wind Gap, and Lehigh Gap. To the east is a view of Long Pond and the edge of the Pocono Plateau, toward the fire tower at Big Pocono State Park. To the west is a view of Lake Mountain and the Pocono Plateau. For more information on the state forest, contact Delaware State Forest, HC 1, Box 95A, Swiftwater, PA 18370, (570) 895-4000, www.dcnr.state.pa.us/forestry/stateforests/delaware.aspx.

Hickory Run State Park

The 15,483-acre Hickory Run State Park, on the Pocono Plateau, features a unique boulder field that has been named a national natural landmark. The 16-acre field was left behind by glaciers, with boulders up to 16 feet long. The plain of rocks is uninterrupted by vegetation. Hickory Run State Park has numerous hiking opportunities, including the Boulder Field Trail, Hawk Falls Trail, Sand Spring Trail, Fireline Trail, Deer Trail, Lake Trail, Leonardsville Trail, and many others. A guide to these trails is available from the park office. From I-80, take Exit 274 and drive east on PA 534 for 6 miles. From the Northeast Extension of the Pennsylvania Turnpike (I-476), take Exit 95 and drive west on PA 940 for 3 miles; then turn east on PA 534 and proceed for 6 miles. For a recreational guide with map, contact Hickory Run State Park, RR 1, Box 81, White Haven, PA 18661, (570) 443-0400, www.dcnr.state.pa.us/stateparks/parks/hickoryrun.aspx.

5

Lehigh Gorge State Park
26 miles

The focus of the long, narrow 4,548-acre Lehigh Gorge State Park is the Lehigh River Gorge. Excellent hiking opportunities are available on 26 miles of the abandoned railroad grade paralleling the Lehigh River. The access points at Port Jenkins, White Haven, Rockport, and Jim Thorpe allow for different hike lengths. You can see the beauty of the gorge in all four seasons, and Glen Onoko Falls is of special interest. Lehigh Gorge is part of the Delaware and Lehigh Canal National Heritage Corridor, and the abandoned railroad grade is one component of the proposed 150-mile Delaware and Lehigh Trail from Bristol to Wilkes-Barre (see the Long-Distance Trails chapter). The railroad grade is also excellent for cross-country skiing and biking.

To reach the northern access area at White Haven, take Exit 273 off I-80. Follow PA 940 east to the Thriftway store, go through the Thriftway parking lot, and bear left to the state park access area. To reach the central access area at Rockport from the south, follow US 209 southbound from Jim Thorpe, then PA 93 northbound. Turn onto SR 2055 (Lehigh Gorge Drive), and continue through Weatherly to Rockport at SR 4014. Rockport is also accessible from the north by following PA 940 west from Exit 273 off I-80, then turning left onto SR 2055 (Lehigh Gorge Drive) and continuing to Rockport. For more information on the state park segment, contact Lehigh Gorge State Park, RR 1, Box 81, White Haven, PA 18661, (570) 443-0400, www.dcnr.state.pa.us/stateparks/parks/lehighgorge.aspx.

6

Nescopeck State Park
and State Game Land 187

The 2,981-acre Nescopeck State Park is adjacent to 7,880-acre State Game Land 187, creating a large protected area with 19 miles of hiking trails. The state park, located between Nescopeck Mountain and Mount Yeager, has thirteen interconnecting trails that access the 9-acre Lake Frances and 6 miles of Nescopeck Creek. The trails are also suitable for cross-country skiing in the winter. From I-80, take Exit 262 to PA 309 south. After about .8 mile, turn left onto Honey Hole Road. The park begins a short distance east of the I-80 underpass. Travel about 6 miles farther on Honey Hole Road to the Lake Frances Day Use Area on the right opposite Lake Frances Road. For more information, contact Nescopeck State Park, 1137 Honey Hole Rd., Drums, PA 18222, (570) 403-2006, www.dcnr.state.pa.us/stateparks/parks/nescopeck.aspx.

State Game Land 119
7 miles (round-trip)

The 7,945-acre State Game Land 119 in Luzerne County features a 3.5-mile portion of the Lehigh and Susquehanna Railroad corridor. From PA 437 near Glen Summit, follow Church Road into the game land. A side trail at the parking area leads uphill 100 feet to the railroad corridor. The trail proceeds east through the game land, crossing Little Nescopeck Creek and providing views south to Mount Yeager. At the edge of the game land, the trail passes by Moosehead Lake. At the boundary, you can retrace your route for a 7-mile in-and-out hike. This section of the railroad is part of the Delaware and Lehigh Canal National Heritage Corridor (see the Long-Distance Trails chapter).

State Game Land 207
6 miles

The 1,400-acre State Game Land 207 is on Penobscot Mountain in Luzerne County. To reach the parking area, follow PA 309 north for .3 mile from its intersection with PA 437 in Mountain Top. Turn left onto Brown Street and go .1 mile to a parking area at the bend of the road. Walk around the gate and follow the railroad grade into the game land, passing through a mixed oak forest. On the right, the mountainside descends steeply to PA 309 as the grade passes through Solomon Gap. There are limited views of Penobscot Mountain to the right. After the second power line, a rock cut on the right provides a view of Wilkes-Barre, Wyoming Valley, and the distant mountains. There is also a view down Solomon Creek Valley and the site of the Ashley Planes (see separate entry below). Follow the grade to the edge of the game land and return to your car. This route is excellent for cross-country skiing in the winter.

Ashley Planes
5 miles

Constructed by the Lehigh and Susquehanna Railroad, the Ashley Planes are listed on the National Register of Historic Places and were considered an engineering marvel in the mid-1800s. The three steep inclined planes were built to raise coal-laden railcars 1,000 feet above the Wyoming Valley floor, through

Solomon's Gap to the crest of Penobscot Mountain at Mountain Top. The railroad transported the coal to the Lehigh Canal, which led to the Delaware Canal and ultimately to market in Philadelphia and New York. The steam-powered planes remained in service until 1954.

Today the inclined railroad is gone, but the wide and steep abandoned corridor, with a footpath of crushed stone and grass, is a challenging hiking route. From the bottom of the mountain, Plane 3 ascends to a tunnel under I-81. Plane 2 ascends to the bottom of Plane 1. Halfway up, Plane 1 crosses to the east side of PA 309 and ascends to Mountain Top. A hike to the summit and back down is approximately 5 miles.

Access is at the base of the mountain in Ashley and at the top in Mountain Top. Ashley Planes is part of the Delaware and Lehigh Canal National Heritage Corridor (see the Long-Distance Trails chapter). A detailed guide and maps are included in *Guide to the Lehigh Canal, Lower and Upper Divisions, with the Ashley Planes, and the Penn Haven Planes, and the Switchback Railroad,* by David G. Barber, available from the National Canal Museum, 30 Centre Square, Easton, PA 18042, (610) 559-6613, www.canals.org.

Seven Tubs Natural Area
2.5 miles

The 550-acre Seven Tubs Natural Area is in Luzerne County. Wheelbarrow Run, flowing through rock formations smoothed by water and the passing of time, creates beautiful cascades. The trail along the Tubs is about .5 mile in length. The 2-mile blue-blazed Audubon Trail forms a loop hike. To reach the parking area, follow PA 115 south for 1.4 miles from Exit 47 off I-81 near Wilkes-Barre. The entrance to the natural area is on the right. Follow the road to the parking area; handicapped parking is found farther down the road. The area is open from Memorial Day to Labor Day. For more information, contact the Luzerne County Parks Department at (570) 331-7046, www.luzernecounty.org.

State Game Land 91
4.8 miles

The 16,590-acre State Game Land 91 encompasses a northern hardwood forest and the 4.8-mile Meadow Run Railroad grade. The game land is adjacent to Lackawanna State Forest and the Pinchot Trail System. To reach the trail, follow PA 115 north of Blakeslee for 9.5 miles. Turn right onto Meadow Run Road at the blinking light and go 3.3 miles. A gravel game land parking area is on the right. Walk across the road and follow a grassy woods road a short distance to a footbridge across Meadow Run. Follow the abandoned railroad grade downstream, amid hemlock, maple, and cherry trees. The grade takes you through an area with many dead standing trees, the result of beaver activity. Farther on, it passes a meadow on the left and a pond created by past beaver activity on the right. After crossing two pipelines, the grade goes through a number of swamps. Meadow Run meanders through the forest, at times directly adjacent to the railroad grade. At 1.6 miles, the grade becomes overgrown.

For a challenging hike, continue following the grade as it becomes indiscernible, eventually leading to wild and scenic cascades on Meadow Run. The trail all but disappears, so keep an eye out for the telltale ruts of an old railroad grade and pieces of scattered coal. The trail eventually leads another .8 mile to the edge of the game land adjacent to private property along Meadow Run. Do not trespass. Return to the parking area via the railroad grade.

12
Pinchot Trail System
25 miles

The Pinchot Trail System was built by the Sierra Club's Northeast Pennsylvania Group through Lackawanna State Forest in the southernmost corner of Lackawanna County. This loop trail is excellent for a beginner's backpacking trip or for day hikes. There are a few steep grades and numerous creeks and swamps on terrain typical of the Pocono Plateau. A side trail leads to Pine Hill Lookout, with beautiful 360-degree views of the surrounding landscape. The areas of Painter Creek and Choke Creek (see separate entry below) are particularly beautiful, and there is also good cross-country skiing on the trail. Overnight camping is permitted throughout the trail, per area guidelines. A no-fee camping permit is required and can be obtained from the state forest office.

To reach the Pinchot Trail, take Exit 178 off I-81, and follow PA 315 through Dupont (away from the airport). After 1.1 miles, turn left at the traffic light onto Suscon Road and continue for 12.2 miles. The trailhead is on the left side of the highway, about 1 mile east of the county line. For information and maps of the Pinchot Trail System, contact Lackawanna State Forest, 401 Samters Building, 101 Penn Ave., Scranton, PA 18503, (570) 963-4561, www.dcnr.state.pa.us/forestry/stateforests/lackawanna.aspx.

13
Choke Creek Trail
5.5 miles

The Choke Creek Trail uses part of the Pinchot Trail System (see separate entry above) and provides a lovely walk through several different types of Pocono terrain The trail starts at a small parking area on the south side of Tannery Road, about 2 miles west of its intersection with LR 665 near Thornhurst. The first portion of the trail meanders through rocky, poorly drained upland with blueberries, rhododendron, mountain laurel, and sheep laurel. A short segment leads along a steep sidehill through a grove of balsam fir, then down along Choke Creek. This bubbling stream is stained coffee brown from the tannic acid of rotting organic matter in the swamps at its source. After paralleling the stream for about a mile, the trail heads northeast along the state forest boundary line, goes uphill past large red oaks, and levels off to cross the headwaters of Butler Run. The trail then follows an old woods road, turns northwest onto Tannery Road, and returns to the parking lot. For information and maps, contact Lackawanna State Forest, 401 Samters Building, 101 Penn Ave., Scranton, PA 18503, (570) 963-4561, www. dcnr.state.pa.us/forestry/stateforests/lackawanna.aspx.

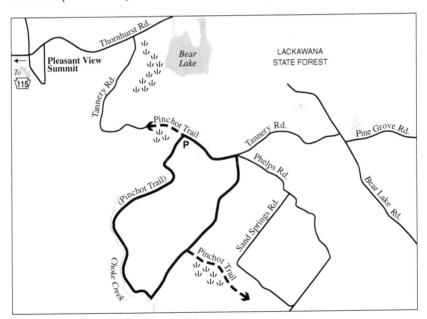

Choke Creek Trail

14
State Game Land 135

The 3,000-acre State Game Land 135 encompasses northern hardwood forests adjacent to Lackawanna State Forest and the Pinchot Trail System. An abandoned railroad grade passes through the game land, offering access to several areas of scenic and historical interest.

Wilkes-Barre and Eastern Railroad Grade to Ash Creek (1.7 miles): To reach the parking area for this hike, follow River Road (SR 2013) 4.7 miles north from its intersection with Bear Lake Road in Thornhurst. Then turn left and follow SR 2017 for 1.3 miles, passing a pond on the right. Turn left onto a dirt road and follow it a short distance to a game land gate. Hike down the grassy woods road a short distance to a T intersection with the abandoned Wilkes-Barre and Eastern Railroad grade. This is the same grade that passes through State Game Lands 127 and 38 and Big Pocono State Park (see separate entries below). Turn right and follow the grade north through the hemlock and northern hardwood forest, passing two cabins along the way. Before the game land boundary, veer left onto a woods road, which narrows to a trail. Follow the trail for several hundred yards to an open swamp and meadow containing Ash Creek. An old beaver dam at the south end created the swamp. This trail is great for cross-country skiing in the winter.

Buckley Run and Fenner Mill Run (6 miles): Reach the parking area for this hike by following Bear Lake Road (LR 665) west for 3.8 miles from Thornhurst. Then turn right on gravel Pittston Road in Lackawanna State Forest and go 1 mile. Turn right and follow gravel Sassafras Road for 1 mile to the state forest boundary. Continue .8 mile on the dirt road in the game land to the parking area. Walk down the grassy woods road eastbound through maple, beech, birch, sassafras, and cherry trees. Cross Buckley Run, and ascend then descend to Fenner Mill Run. A small beaver dam has created a swamp upstream of the crossing. At the intersection with another woods road from the left, continue to the right and cross Ash Creek on a bridge. At the intersection with the abandoned Wilkes-Barre and Eastern Railroad grade, turn left and follow the grade north, paralleling Ash Creek as it flows through another swamp created by beavers. The grade continues north for .5 mile through a hemlock forest to a gate at the game land boundary. Here the grade continues south for a quarter mile to private property. Backtrack to the T intersection, and follow the woods road back to the parking area. This trail is great for cross-country skiing in the winter.

15
State Game Land 318
(Lost Lakes)

The 852-acre State Game Land 318 was purchased by The Nature Conservancy and donated to the Pennsylvania Game Commission. Reach the parking area for this hike via PA 940, 5 miles west of I-380. Turn left and follow Stony Hollow Road for .5 mile to a gravel parking area on the left side. This loop hike includes the 1-mile Commander John Butler Trail, starting at the sign in the parking area. The trail leads to a grassy woods road. Follow the woods road and ascend for about .8 mile. At a fork in the road, bear right where you find a red "CJB" painted on a tree. Follow this trail a short distance to another woods road and turn left. This woods road leads several hundred yards to a beaver pond and ends at the dam. A man-made dam from bygone years is still visible as the foundation for the beaver dam. This is a nice spot, with the pond nestled amid hemlocks, black spruce, beech, maple, yellow birch, cherry trees, and blueberry. Rhododendron blooms in July. Return on the woods road. At the junction with the CJB Trail, you can either turn right and follow that trail back to the parking area, for a total hike of 2 miles, or continue straight on the woods road, which descends through the hemlock forest to Stony Hollow Road, where you turn right and go .3 mile to the parking area.

16
State Game Land 127

The 25,527-acre State Game Land 127 features many hiking opportunities among its northern hardwood forests, wetlands, creeks, and ponds. The game land is in Monroe County, west of I-380 and north of PA 940, and to the south and west of Gouldsboro and Tobyhanna State Parks. Access is via PA 940, PA 423, and PA 507. You may see black bears, deer, wild turkeys, grouse, snowshoe hares, ospreys, and other wildlife. The area has mostly level and gently rolling trails. You can combine numerous unmarked trails on grassy woods roads in many different ways.

Artillery Ridge Trail (8 miles): This trail follows Artillery Ridge Road along the ridge of the same name, through northern hardwood forests to Artillery Ridge Tower. As is common on the Pocono Plateau, this "ridge" is just slightly higher than the surrounding land. Start from the first game land parking area on the right along PA 423, 2.5 miles north of PA 940. Follow Artillery Ridge Road about a mile to a side trail that leads through dense vegetation to Jimmy Pond. At approximately 4 miles, you reach an old tower that was used as a lookout during military exercises in the early twentieth century. Unfortunately, there are no views from the tower. A little farther is a game land food plot along I-380. You will see wild turkeys if you are lucky. Backtrack 4 miles to the parking area. This is a good cross-country ski route as well.

Warnertown Dam and Falls (4.5 miles): Park at a game land parking area along PA 423, approximately 3 miles north of PA 940, on the right after a power-line crossing. The hike starts on the other side of the highway. Follow the grassy Hay Road parallel to Tobyhanna Creek. At 1.5 miles, Hay Road intersects Warnertown Dam Road, which leads from PA 423 to the right and is also grassy. Continue straight ahead for a short distance; then veer left along the grown-over earthen dam bank. Here you encounter a view across Tobyhanna Creek and the wetland area that used to be the artificial pond. Follow the trail downstream for a short distance to the falls. Farther downstream, you cross Tobyhanna Creek. At the trail intersection, follow the gravel road to the left across the creek on a bridge and back to PA 423 to complete the loop.

Pond Swamp and Huckleberry Marsh (3 miles): The trailhead for this hike is on a game land service road. Take PA 423 west for 1.3 miles from PA 611. Turn right on the dirt service road and follow it north for 3.5 miles. The trailhead is on the left just past a swampy area; park off the road. An old dry grassy woods road, shown as No. 3 Trail on the game land map, leads into Pond Swamp. At a quarter mile, take the right fork and continue following No. 3 Trail. At the next fork, take the trail on the right, still No. 3 Trail, to Octave Spring. At the trail junction, turn right onto Half Moon Trail and proceed to Huckleberry Marsh. At 2 miles, veer left off Half Moon Trail; then take the left trail at the second fork. The trail leaves Huckleberry Marsh and reconnects with No. 3 Trail along Pond Swamp. Follow No. 3 Trail back to the trailhead.

Rauscher Run (2.5 miles): The trailhead for this hike is located on the right side of a game land service road, 1.3 miles south of PA 507. The service road is the first left turn off PA 507 west of I-380. Walk down the open grassy woods road through a northern hardwood forest with thick understory. Avoid a woods road to the left at about .5 mile; then at 1 mile turn left onto the next woods road. (The road you just turned off eventually leads to the Lehigh River.) After the left turn, go a couple hundred yards to a small pond on the right along Rauscher Run. To return, retrace your steps. This is a good cross-country ski route with a couple hills.

Brady's Lake (4.5 miles): Access this hike via PA 940, 2.5 miles west of the junction with PA 423 at Pocono Lake. Turn right onto the Brady's Lake access road, and follow it for 3.5 miles to the parking area. To begin the hike, cross the dam, and then turn right onto a woods road, following it parallel to the lake. Several trails cross this road. The road later veers away from the lake; continue to the old Wilkes-Barre and Eastern Railroad grade. This is the same railroad grade that goes around Big Pocono State Park and through State Game Lands 38 and 135.

You can create an extended hike by following the railroad grade north (right) for approximately 2 miles. For the hike described here, turn left onto the grade.

After 1 mile, among views of swamps, turn left onto a grassy woods road and follow it back to the first woods road. Then turn right and return to the dam and parking area. This is also a good cross-country ski loop.

17

Gouldsboro State Park

Within the 2,800-acre Gouldsboro State Park are the 101-acre Gouldsboro Lake and 10 miles of hiking trails. The park entrance is .5 mile south of Gouldsboro; via PA 507, that village is 2 miles north of I-380 and 13 miles south of I-84. State Game Land 127 is to the west and south of the park. You can make a loop hike via the park entrance road, Prospect Rock Trail, and Old 611 Trail. Another trail along Gouldsboro Lake is a couple miles long. The red-blazed Frank Gantz Trail connects with Tobyhanna State Park. For additional information, contact Gouldsboro State Park, c/o Tobyhanna, P.O. Box 387, Tobyhanna, PA 18466, (570) 894-8336, www.dcnr.state.pa.us/stateparks/parks/gouldsboro.aspx.

18

Tobyhanna State Park

The 5,440-acre Tobyhanna State Park in northern Monroe County is adjacent to Gouldsboro State Park and State Game Land 312. The state park contains 12 miles of hiking trails. The focus of the park is the 170-acre Tobyhanna Lake, encircled by an excellent 5-mile loop trail marked with blue blazes. Other trails extend throughout the park's northern hardwood forest. The Frank Gantz Trail, marked with red blazes, connects to Gouldsboro State Park. For more information and a recreational guide, contact Tobyhanna State Park, P.O. Box 387, Tobyhanna, PA 18466, (570) 894-8336, www.dcnr.state.pa.us/stateparks/parks/tobyhanna.aspx.

19

State Game Land 312
4 miles

The 3,912-acre State Game Land 312 is located at the headwaters of the Lehigh River. To reach the parking area, take Exit 13 off I-380 and go east on PA 507 for 2.7 miles, passing through Gouldsboro and across the railroad tracks (used for excursions for Steamtown USA National Park in Scranton). Turn left onto the first road after the tracks. Go 1.6 miles to the game land parking area on the left.

Walk down the grassy woods road through a northern hardwood forest and swamps to the West Fork of the Lehigh River. Cross the stream and continue until the woods road ends. Return to the parking area via the woods road. This trail is great for cross-country skiing in the winter.

20
State Game Land 221

The 4,615-acre State Game Land 221 consists of mixed oak forest and is located between the town of Mount Pocono and Mountainhome. No trails are marked, but the area offers many good hiking opportunities.

Devil's Hole (4 miles): This hike follows Devil's Hole Creek to the waterfall of the same name. It involves numerous stream crossings, so prepare to get your feet wet. To access the trail, follow PA 940 east from the junction with PA 611 in Mount Pocono. At less than a mile, turn left onto Devil's Hole Road. After 1 mile on that road, park at the game land parking area located at a sharp bend in the road. Walk down a woods road lined with thick mountain laurel, which blooms in June, to Devil's Hole Creek. After crossing the creek, follow the woods road up the creek through hemlock, beech, and birch trees, crossing the creek several more times. In this 600-foot-deep gorge, jack-in-the-pulpits bloom in spring and rhododendron bloom in July. The woods road becomes indiscernible in places. You encounter the remains of a homestead at 1 mile among towering pines. Local legend has it that the spot was used as a speakeasy during Prohibition in the 1920s. Soon the woods road crosses the creek and ascends the side of the gorge. Turn onto a trail along the creek. This trail is sometimes indiscernible and becomes very rocky and difficult to follow, crossing the creek several times. A small tributary comes in from the right; a short, steep climb up this tributary leads to a small waterfall. Continue up the main creek over rocky terrain, eventually reaching beautiful Devil's Hole Creek Falls, nestled against the rocky gorge wall amid rhododendron, with a large pool at the base. Retrace your steps to return to the parking area. The hike can be especially challenging and beautiful in winter.

Devil's Hole to Cresco Heights (10 miles): The beginning of this hike is the same as the Devil's Hole hike above, from the parking area to the homestead ruins. From there, stay on the woods road and ascend through switchbacks up Seven Pines Mountain. The vegetation changes from a northern hardwood forest with rhododendron, to a mixed oak forest with mountain laurel, and then to scrub oak at the top. Where the woods road levels at the top, you can see Blue Mountain, Delaware Water Gap, and Big Pocono. Continue on the woods road as it passes a small, shallow pond near a stand of pines. At approximately 3 miles, turn right on another woods road, which soon crosses Mill Creek amid large hemlocks with springs emerging from their roots. After hiking .8 mile from the last junction, follow a woods road that veers left. It leads for about a mile to Cresco Heights, where rocky ledges provide views of High Knob, Cresco, and Mountainhome. Here you can retrace your steps to your car or descend Cresco Heights to Mountainhome.

Rattlesnake Creek Falls (1.5 miles): From Mountainhome, take PA 191 north. Take the first left; then veer right onto Monomonock Road. Follow this road to the game land parking area at end of the road. Hike the dirt woods road uphill for .75 mile, and look for a trail to the left. Follow this trail down to Rattlesnake Falls. Return to the parking area via the woods road.

21
State Game Land 38
(Wolf Swamp and Deep Lake)
4 miles

The 3,943-acre State Game Land 38 is adjacent to Big Pocono State Park (see separate entry below) along the edge of the Pocono Escarpment. It contains numerous woods roads and jeep trails that you can combine into many possible hiking routes. A significant feature of this game land is Deep Lake, one of the most famous of Pennsylvania's kettle lakes.

Start the hike at the game lands parking area on the only road that climbs to Big Pocono State Park (follow the signs from Tannersville and Exit 299 off I-80). Walk up the gravel road by the towers on the ridge. The surrounding area is very rocky, with scrub oak and stunted pines on the ridgeline. Bear right onto another dirt road, where a rock indicates the direction to Wolf Swamp and Deep Lake. This road crosses the earthen dam on Wolf Swamp. Turn right onto the next dirt road, which leads a short distance to the beautiful, circular Deep Lake. A trail to the left leads to the outlet, which flows when the water is high. The wild azalea is particularly beautiful in the spring. Backtrack to the parking area or continue down the road to Sand Spring Run.

22
Big Pocono State Park

The 1,306-acre Big Pocono State Park sits atop the rugged slopes of Camelback Mountain. State Game Land 38 (see separate entry above) is adjacent to the park on the west. Big Pocono is virtually the top of the Pocono Plateau escarpment and is one of the area's most prominent natural features. The summit is covered with scrub oak, gray birch, blueberry, and multitudes of mountain laurel, which blooms in mid-June. The mountaintop offers tremendous views of Blue Mountain from Lehigh Gap to High Point in New Jersey, the route of the Appalachian Trail. You can also see all the way to Delaware Water Gap and the Catskill Mountains in New York. A paved scenic drive encircles the top and offers views in all directions. Parking Lot 4 and the nearby picnic and restroom facilities are handicapped-accessible.

Ten miles of hiking trails marked with blazes of different colors extend throughout the park. North Trail, Indian Trail, and the section of South Trail that descends the east side of the mountain are steep and rugged. The section of South Trail on the south face of the mountain is relatively flat. The level Old RR Grade Trail, on the abandoned Wilkes-Barre and Eastern Railroad grade, extends around the mountain and is ideal for cross-country skiing. On the north side of the mountain, this trail passes through hemlock and rhododendron, which blooms in July. At the park's high point, the Old RR Grade Trail passes through a cut in the mountain.

The trails are all closed to mountain biking. No camping is allowed in the park. *Caution:* The road to the park is very steep and should not be attempted by vehicles with trailers. For more information, contact Big Pocono State Park, c/o Tobyhanna, Tobyhanna, PA 18466, (570) 894-8336, www.dcnr.state.pa.us/stateparks/parks/bigpocono.aspx.

23

Tannersville Cranberry Bog

Created during the last ice age, the Tannersville Cranberry Bog is a national natural landmark owned by The Nature Conservancy. The North Woods Trail and Fernridge Trail are open to the public. The boardwalk into the bog is accessible only when accompanied by a guide from the conservancy or the Bog Preserve Committee or by the Monroe County naturalist. For directions, a schedule of boardwalk hikes, and other information, contact Monroe County Conservation District, 8050 Running Valley Rd., Stroudsburg, PA 18360, phone (570) 629-3061, www.mcconservation.org/EnvironEducation/abouteecenter.html.

24

Kettle Creek Wildlife Sanctuary

The 166-acre Kettle Creek Wildlife Sanctuary, site of the Monroe County Environmental Education Center, has several short loop hikes on interconnecting trails, some of which lead to Swink Pond. At 1 mile, the Deer Trail is the longest loop trail. The Songbird Trail is .5 mile. Several connecting trails allow you to construct various loops. From PA 33, take PA 611 north to the traffic light in Bartonsville. Turn left onto Rimrock Drive and proceed for .4 mile. Bear right onto North Easton-Belmont Pike; then after .2 mile, bear right onto Running Valley Road. Follow this road for .7 mile to the sanctuary on the left. For more information, contact Monroe County Conservation District, 8050 Running Valley Rd., Stroudsburg, PA 18360, (570) 629-3061, www.mcconservation.org/ EnvironEducation/abouteecenter.html.

25

Delaware Water Gap
National Recreation Area

No guide to enjoying the Poconos would be complete without describing the hiking opportunities in Delaware Water Gap National Recreation Area, under the management of the National Park Service. Forty miles of the Delaware River, one of the last free-flowing rivers in the eastern United States, have been designated a national scenic and recreational river, flowing through approximately 70,000 acres of recreation area lands in Pennsylvania and New Jersey.

Camping is available for canoeists on various islands in the river, for hikers along the Appalachian Trail (see the Long-Distance Trails chapter), and for all visitors at Dingmans Campground. Camping along the Appalachian Trail is only for hikers who plan trips of two or more days, and the selected spot must be more than halfway between the two nearest access points if the distance is too great to be covered in one day. Private land exists within the boundaries of the park, and hikers must obey posted signs. Hunting in accordance with state laws is permitted throughout the recreation area, so exercise extreme caution during deer season, and be alert to hunting year-round.

The park is primarily used for day hiking, though the Park Service has a long-range plan for the development of a backcountry trail system. Several day hikes are described below.

McDade Recreational Trail: This is a planned multiuse recreational trail on the Pennsylvania side of the park. A 5-mile section, extending from Hialeah Picnic Area to the Turn Farm Trailhead on River Road, is now open for hiking, biking, and cross-country skiing. A total length of 37 miles is proposed.

Mount Minsi (4.6 miles): From the Lake Lenape parking area, the white-blazed Appalachian Trail leads 2.3 miles to the summit of Mount Minsi, on the Pennsylvania side of Delaware Water Gap. This trail is rocky and steep, leading to the summit through hemlock, rhododendron, and mixed oak forest, and features several vistas. At more than 1,000 feet above the river, you can view Mount Tammany and Kittatinny Ridge in New Jersey and the Pocono Plateau in Pennsylvania. A .5-mile side trail leads to Table Rock, with another beautiful view of the Water Gap. Another .5-mile side trail loops around Lake Lenape and Lake Latini.

The Lake Lenape parking area is on the south side of Mountain Road, a quarter mile from PA 611 in the borough of Delaware Water Gap.

Pocono Rim (3 miles): This very rough and unmarked route, which is difficult to follow in early summer, climbs steeply on a woods road that starts behind two white barns at a parking area on US 209, 4.5 miles north of the blinking light in Bushkill. At the rim, follow the woods road south, bearing left at a double intersection with another woods road. At the end of the road is Cactus Bluff, a rocky opening with views of the Delaware River and valley. After backtracking, turn at the second left. The woods road leads to Terrace Pond, then bears right and descends steeply from a vista to the parking area.

Tumbling Waters Trail (3 miles): This orange-blazed trail starts near the office at the Pocono Environmental Education Center (PEEC) and follows a woods road that eventually becomes a trail as it descends into a hemlock ravine, with waterfalls on Mill Creek. The trail ascends out of the ravine, goes by two ponds, and loops back to the parking area. The trailhead is located at PEEC, along Briscoe Mountain Road off US 209, 6 miles north of Bushkill.

Sunrise Trail (5 miles): This yellow-blazed trail starts at the PEEC parking lot and forms a pleasant loop through the forest.

Scenic Gorge Trail (2 miles): This red-blazed trail leaves the Sunrise Trail along a woods road, and then follows a trail along Spackman's Creek in a hemlock gorge, before looping back to the PEEC parking lot.

Tom's Creek Trail (1.9 miles): This is an easy walk along Tom's Creek, offering bird watchers and hikers a quiet stroll through a mixed hardwood forest with lush vegetation. The trail starts at Tom's Creek Picnic Area, on US 209 3.5 miles north of Bushkill.

Dingmans Ferry Trail (1 mile): From the Dingmans Falls visitors center, follow this trail through a hemlock and rhododendron ravine to Silverthread Falls, in a narrow cleft in the rocky ravine wall. The trail then leads to the powerful, rushing Dingmans Falls, plunging from high above the hemlocks. The falls are worth seeing in the winter, but use extreme caution, as the trail is usually ice-covered. From US 209 just south of the traffic light in the Dingmans Falls, take Johnny Bee Road to the Dingmans Falls access road. The trailhead is at the end of this road.

Childs Park Trail (1.8 miles): This is a wide trail through a hemlock forest. From the parking area, the trail leads across Dingmans Creek, through the picnic area, and along the creek to three beautiful waterfalls. Factory Falls, Fulmer Falls, and Deer Leap Falls are all nestled in the rocky, hemlock-laden ravine. Several small cascades between the falls add to the beautiful scenery. To reach the parking area from the Dingmans Ferry traffic light on US 209, go north on PA 739 for 1.2 miles; then take Silver Lake Road 1.6 miles to the parking area.

Raymondskill Falls Trail (.1 mile): This trail leads 300 feet to the powerful and beautiful Raymondskill Falls, amid hemlocks in a rocky ravine. The parking area is .4 mile up Raymondskill Road from US 209, 5.1 miles north of the Dingmans Ferry traffic light.

The Cliff (5 miles): This hike follows a woods road from the Raymondskill Falls parking area (see above for directions) up to the ridgetop. A rocky cliff amid cedar trees provides a view across Raymondskill Creek valley to Pow Wow Hill, Indian Point, the Delaware River valley, and High Point in New Jersey. Hike north for 2.5 miles along the cliff; along the way, a woods road to the right leads to Milford Cemetery. Return via the same route.

Hackers Falls Trail (.6 mile): This trail follows a woods road about a third of a mile to a side trail along Raymondskill Creek to Hackers Falls. To reach the parking area, follow US 209 for 5.1 miles north of Dingmans Ferry, and turn onto Raymondskill Road. Continue for 1.7 miles; then turn right and follow Long Meadow Road for 1 mile. This road leads to a parking area.

The Park Service has issued a useful brochure with maps and descriptions of hiking trails, available at the visitors centers at Bushkill (570-588-7044), Dingmans Falls (570-828-2253), and Kittatinny Point (908-496-4458), which is closed at the time of this writing but is scheduled to reopen in the future. For the Delaware Water Gap National Recreation Area's quarterly newsletter, *Spanning the Gap,* brochures on the AT and the river, and other information, contact Chief of Visitor Services, Delaware Water Gap National Recreation Area, Bushkill, PA 18324, (570) 426-2452, www.nps.gov/dewa.

26
Thunder Swamp Trail System
45 miles

Thunder Swamp Trail System is in Delaware State Forest, in southern Pike County just north of the Monroe County line, and it extends into Pennel Run and Stillwater Natural Areas. Suitable for both day hikes and backpacking trips, the system consists of a blue-blazed main loop trail of 30 miles, plus 15 miles of red-blazed side trails to many natural features. The trail system was built in the 1970s by the Youth Conservation Corps and is now maintained by Pocono Outdoor Club and state forest volunteers. The trails cross streams, pass through wetlands, and are very rocky in many areas, so sturdy footwear is a necessity. You may encounter many species of Pocono Plateau wildlife on the trails. Near the northern end of the trail system is the site of the first tree planting in Pennsylvania. Free camping permits are available from the district forest office. Primitive campsites should not be located within 50 feet of the trail or within 300 feet of buildings, roads, or water sources. Fires are prohibited during the fire seasons, from March 1 to May 25 and from October 1 to December 1.

Access the Thunder Swamp Trail System via PA 402, about 14 miles south of Exit 30 off I-84. The main parking area is on the left. For more information and an excellent map of the trail system with distances included, as well as camping permits, contact Delaware State Forest, HC 1, Box 95A, Swiftwater, PA 18370, (570) 895-4000, www.dcnr.state.pa.us/forestry/hiking/thunder.aspx.

27
Grey Towers

Grey Towers was the home of Gifford Pinchot, who served two terms as governor of Pennsylvania and was later the first chief forester for the U.S. Forest Service. There are several trails through the property, with one leading to the estate's waterfalls. Grey Towers is located on US 6, .5 mile west of the intersection with US 209 in Milford. Turn left at the sign for Grey Towers; the entrance is .2 mile on the left. For more information, contact US Forest Service, Grey Towers National Historic Landmark, P.O. Box 188, Milford, PA 18337, (570) 296-9630, www.fs.fed.us/na/gt/.

28
Buckhorn Natural Area

Buckhorn Natural Area is a pristine 535-acre parcel within Delaware State Forest and near State Game Land 209. The state forest and game land parcels add nearly 9,000 acres of wilderness along the Delaware River, and within the natural area are many opportunities for hiking. Old stone quarries, overgrown with the passage of time, abound along the trails. Some have become ponds hosting aquatic species and supplying water for wildlife.

Yellow Pine Trail (5 miles): This trail follows a grassy woods road that leads over Dimmick Meadow Brook and Pinchot Brook. Upon reaching the state forest boundary, turn around and follow the woods road back to the parking area.

Buckhorn Fire Tower Trail (1 mile): Follow the grassy woods road to the fire tower, amid a mixed oak forest. Then retrace your steps back to the parking area.

Lost Camp Trail (5 miles): This trail follows a grassy woods road that crosses Pinchot Brook and a tributary of Bush Kill. Upon reaching the state forest boundary, turn around and retrace your steps back to the parking area.

Pond Trail (4.6 miles): Starting at the game land parking area, follow the grassy woods road through a mixed oak forest. At about 2 miles, veer left at a fork in the trail. At a T intersection, turn left and follow the grassy woods road as it weaves through old, overgrown stone quarries. To the left is a small pond with day lilies amid white pines. Next, pass a larger pond to the right in an old quarry carving. The woods road ends at the shore of a large pond speckled with many hummocks. After enjoying the view, return to the parking area via the woods road. This trail is excellent for cross-country skiing.

Pond Eddy Creek Trail (7.4 miles): The beginning of this hike is the same as the Pond Trail hike above. After following the grassy road for about two miles, veer right at the fork in the trail. This trail descends through a mixed oak and white pine forest, and later hemlock, on very rocky footway. Bear left on a faint woods road down through rhododendron, eventually reaching Pond Eddy Creek. (The previous woods road descends steeply to Pond Eddy Creek, passing a large stone quarry and rock ledge on the right, with a limited view up the valley from a massive pile of stone slag on the left.)

To lengthen this hike by 2.7 miles, turn left and follow the creek upstream several hundred yards, bear right, and cross the creek. Ascending on a faint woods road, the trail passes by many overgrown stone quarries and reaches a ridge offering limited views into New York across the Delaware River on the right. The woods road descends through a hemlock forest to the edge of the game land. Do not trespass on the adjacent private property. Retrace the woods road back to Pond Eddy Creek.

At the creek, continue downstream; the woods road dwindles to a trail before widening again as it follows the cascades. This road then veers away from the creek, ascends a ravine, and disappears adjacent to the massive pile of stone slag mentioned earlier. A short hike along the stone pile leads to the original woods road. Turn right and ascend the woods road back to the parking area.

To reach Buckhorn Natural Area and the majority of the hiking trails leading into the adjacent state forest and state game land, take Exit 46 off I-84, proceed 1 mile east on US 6, and turn left onto Schocopee Road. Go .7 mile, crossing under I-84 along the way, and turn right onto Fire Tower Road (TR 430). After 1.6 miles, you reach the end of the macadam; continue on the stone road into the state forest. The trailhead for Yellow Pine Trail is on the left at 2.3 miles. On the left at 4 miles is the woods road to the fire tower. On the right at 4.3 miles is the trailhead for Lost Camp Trail. The game land parking area is at 4.5 miles. For more information, contact Delaware State Forest, HC 1, Box 95A, Swiftwater, PA 18370, (570) 895-4000, www.dcnr.state.pa.us/forestry/stateforests/delaware.aspx.

29

State Game Land 180

The 11,372-acre State Game Land 180 is located on US 6, 13 miles east of Hawley and 12 miles west of Milford. Its focal point is a 1,150-acre lake created by a small dam on Shohola Creek. There are parking areas adjacent to the dam, overlooking a beautiful set of waterfalls that flow into a scenic gorge.

Shohola Falls and eastern side of Shohola Lake (2 miles): From the parking area on the south side of US 6 and the east side of Shohola Creek, follow the access road a short distance to the boat launch near the dam. Hike the trail downstream a short distance to the base of Shohola Falls. Enjoy the falls; then backtrack to the boat launch parking lot. From the opposite side of the lot, backtrack on the access road and follow the grassy woods road on the east side of the lake. The road leads into the woods and away from the lake. Hike several hundred feet; then turn right onto another grassy woods road. (The road straight ahead leads about .5 mile to the edge of the game land.) The woods road on the right passes through a mixed hardwood forest to the Game Land Propagation Area. Entry into this area is prohibited by the Game Commission. Turn right and proceed to the end of the woods road. The lake is visible from this point. Backtrack to the parking area.

Loop hike to southern end of Shohola Lake (7.2 miles): Reach parking for this hike by following PA 739 for .7 mile north of I-84. Turn right onto SR 4004 and go 1.4 miles. A game land parking area is on the right. Hike down the grassy woods road through a mixed hardwood forest. Continue downhill, bearing left and crossing a small creek. At 2.5 miles, you reach a dirt road. (The road to the right goes down a short distance along Shohola Creek and ends at a Game Land Propagation Area, entry into which is prohibited by the Game Commission.) Turn left and follow the dirt road for about a mile. Turn right on a grassy woods road prior to a bridge over a small creek. Follow the woods road to the edge of Shohola Lake for a beautiful view of the lake and islands. If you are lucky, you will get some impressive bird sightings. Backtrack on the dirt road to another woods road and follow it uphill, away from the dirt road. Soon it passes a view on the right to a small beaver pond. Farther on is another beaver dam across the creek and woods road. Select a dry route around the wet area and continue uphill on the woods road. At the bend, another pond is visible through the woods on the right. The woods road continues through thick birch saplings back to the road that descends from the parking area; turn right and climb back to your car. This hike is good for viewing fall foliage and for cross-country skiing in the winter.

Trail to small pond (3.5 miles): Reach parking for this hike by following PA 739 for .7 mile north of I-84. Turn right onto SR 4004 and go .7 mile. A game land parking area is on the left. From the trailhead, follow the woods road through a white pine forest. At the last food plot planted by the Game Commission, veer left on the woods road. A small pond lies to the right. Farther on, the woods road leads to another small pond, amid white pine and black spruce, and crosses the dam. After crossing a small seep from a swamp, the road continues through a white pine forest and ends at the edge of the game land. The trail continues into Delaware State Forest through a mixed hardwood forest, and then ends at private property. Do not trespass. Backtrack to the parking lot. This trail is great for cross-country skiing in the winter.

Billings Pond (.3 mile): Reach parking for this hike by following PA 739 for 1.7 miles north of I-84. A game land parking area is on the left side of the road. Walk on the woods road for a short distance through white pine, hemlock, and mountain laurel, until you reach a stone dam at Billings Pond. A beaver dam atop the stone dam has raised the water level. Below the dam, the trail crosses the creek over a stone arch bridge and soon degenerates into deer trails in the woods. Enjoy the view of the pond and backtrack to the parking area.

30
State Game Land 316
4.6 miles

Reach the 2,715-acre State Game Land 316 by following PA 590 east for 6.5 miles from its intersection with US 6 at the northern end of Hawley. Turn left and follow SR 4003 for 3.5 miles; then turn right and follow SR 1014 for 1 mile. Turn left onto a game land dirt road, cross Masthope Creek, and follow the road for .3 mile to a grassy parking area.

To start this loop hike, walk down the dirt road to a woods road at Masthope Creek. Turn left and follow the gravel road along the creek through white pine, hemlock, and spruce. The gravel road becomes grassy. Where Masthope Creek meanders through a field, turn left and continue on a woods road uphill. Upon reaching private property, do not trespass. Turn left and follow the game land boundary over rocky terrain, turn right and follow the boundary uphill, and then turn right again and follow the boundary back to the woods road. Turn left onto the woods road and ascend. Looking behind, you can see Point Peter, a knob on the hillside across Masthope Creek valley.

The first woods road on the right leads down a steep slope amid old shale pits to a small creek that descends to the Delaware River. In late fall and winter, there are views of the Delaware Valley into New York. Back on the main woods road, continue along the ridge. Soon there are winter views of Point Peter and the ridge to the west. When you reach the dam at Cobey Pond, turn right and follow the woods road around the pond to the opposite side of the dam. To shorten your hike by 1.1 miles, simply cross the dam breast. Upon reaching the opposite side of the dam, descend a woods road to the parking area.

31
Blooming Grove Trail System

The Blooming Grove Trail System, in Delaware State Forest, was built by the 4-H Club of Pike County with the cooperation of the Bureau of Forestry and is maintained by Pocono Outdoor Club. It consists of three loops that can be combined for a 7-mile hike. The 2-mile-long red loop skirts Blue Heron Swamp, where deer, beavers, blue herons, and other wildlife have been spotted. The White Deer Trail,

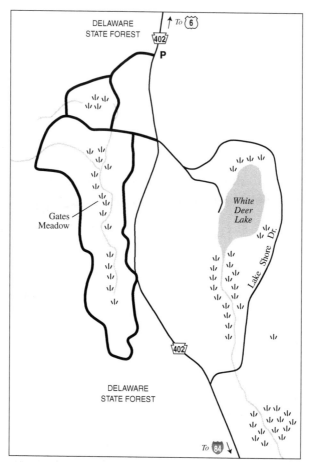

Blooming Grove Trail System

1.5 miles in length, of which .5 mile is coincident with the red loop, connects PA 402 and the blue and red loops. The 4-mile-long blue loop encircles Gates Meadow, Blue Heron Swamp, and Gates Meadow Run. Reach the Blooming Grove Trail System via PA 402, about 1 mile south of US 6 and 4 miles north of I-84. A large parking lot with a sign is on the west side of the road. For more information, visit the Pocono Outdoor Club website at poconooutdoorclub.org.

32

Promised Land State Park, Bruce Lake Natural Area, and Pine Lake Natural Area

The 2,971-acre Promised Land State Park and more than 8,000 acres of adjacent Delaware State Forest, which includes Bruce Lake and Pine Lake Natural Areas, provide many hiking opportunities. Numerous trails in the state park connect to trails extending into the state forest, forming a 50-mile network. The forest consists of northern hardwoods, with beech, birch, maple, cherry, and hemlock trees. Groves of white pine, planted in the days of the Civilian Conservation Corps, abound in many areas of the park. Camping is not allowed except in designated areas.

Bruce Lake Natural Area features Egypt Meadow Lake and Bruce Lake, both beautiful glacial lakes. To reach the natural area, take Exit 26 off I-84 and proceed south on PA 390. The parking area is a short distance on the left. Promised Land State Park is farther south on PA 390. You can also access Bruce Lake from Promised Land Park via Bruce Lake Trail.

Although the lake at Pine Lake Natural Area cannot be easily accessed because of the thick underbrush, you can hike into the area via a woods road and power line. Reach Pine Lake Natural Area by taking Exit 20 off I-84. Follow PA 507 south to Greentown, and turn left onto Brink Hill Road. Continue on this road after it becomes Old Greentown Road. Turn left onto Beaver Dam Road (TR 389). Park at the woods road on the right after entering the state forest.

For more information on the state park and a recreational guide with maps, contact Promised Land State Park, RR 1, Box 96, Greentown, PA 18426, (570) 676-3428, www.dcnr.state.pa.us/stateparks/parks/promisedland.aspx. To obtain a state forest map showing the natural areas, contact Delaware State Forest, HC 1, Box 95A, Swiftwater, PA 18370, (570) 895-4000, www.dcnr.state.pa.us/forestry/stateforests/delaware.aspx.

33

Lake Wallenpaupack, Shuman Point Natural Area, and Ledgedale Natural Area

The large Lake Wallenpaupack was built and is managed by Pennsylvania Power and Light Company, which also manages the adjacent Shuman Point Natural Area and Ledgedale Natural Area.

The 250-acre Shuman Point Natural Area contains the 3-mile Blue Trail, a loop through a mixed oak forest where you are likely to encounter wildlife. The trail provides excellent views of the lake. Next to the natural area is the 60-acre Beech House Creek Wildlife Refuge, where you can see evidence of beaver activity and aquatic wildlife. Reach Shuman Point Natural Area via PA 590, 2.1 miles west of US 6. Trail maps are available at the trailhead parking area.

Ledgedale Natural Area, adjacent to Ledgedale Recreation Area, has been set aside for hiking, birding, and photography. If you are lucky, you may sight diverse wildlife as you walk through the hardwood and hemlock forest. You can hike a system of four blazed trails, ranging from .3 to 1.5 miles in length, in a variety of combinations. To reach Ledgedale Natural Area, take Exit 20 off I-84 and go .5 mile north on PA 507; then turn left onto Ledgedale Road. After 1.8 miles, turn left onto Kuhn Hill Road and continue .3 mile to the parking area on the left. There is an alternate parking area on Ledgedale Road before Kuhn Hill Road. Trail maps are available at the trailhead.

For maps and brochures for both natural areas, contact Lake Wallenpaupack Preserve, P.O. Box 122, Hawley, PA 18428, (800) 354-8383, www.pplweb.com/lake+wallenpaupack/things+to+do. Brochures are also available at the Ledgedale Store.

34
Lacawac Sanctuary

Lacawac Sanctuary is in Wayne County next to Lake Wallenpaupack (see separate entry above). The main attraction of this 510-acre natural landmark is the 52-acre Lake Lacawac, one of the least disturbed glacial lakes in the United States. The Maurice Brown Nature Trail and the Lake Lacawac Nature Trail are open to the public during daylight hours. Three miles of other trails are available for hiking by appointment with a Lacawac interpretive guide. To reach the sanctuary, take Exit 20 off I-84, and follow PA 507 north for .5 mile. Turn left onto Ledgedale Road. At a stop sign, turn right (toward Hawley). Proceed 1 mile and turn right onto St. Mary Church Road. Go .2 mile and turn right onto Lacawac Road. After about half a mile, turn right onto a dirt road at the Lacawac Sanctuary/Sanctuary Road sign. Follow this road to the main entrance, marked by a stone gate. Parking for the nature trail is ahead on the right. For public programs, continue to the Carriage House. For more information, contact Lacawac Sanctuary, 94 Sanctuary Rd., Lake Ariel, PA 18436, (570) 689-9494, www.lacawac.org.

35

State Game Land 310

5.4 miles

Reach the 1,120-acre State Game Land 310 by following PA 196 north for 2 miles from the intersection of PA 590 in Hamlin. Turn left onto Fernwood Road, then right onto Freight House Road, which becomes Lake Henry Road. Turn right onto Bob Black Road (TR 387) and proceed .2 mile to a blind bend, where the parking area is on the left. From the parking area, cross Bob Black Road, walk past the Game Commission gate, and follow the abandoned railroad grade into the game land. The abandoned stone railroad leads through a cherry, maple, and birch forest, crossing a number of small creeks that flow down the hillside on the left into Silkmans Swamp on the right. The foliage and views in the fall are especially rewarding, and the trail is excellent for cross-country skiing in the winter. At 2.7 miles, you reach a gate. Farther on, the grade becomes overgrown and ends at a road after passing through a cut in a hillside. The fill from the road blocks the cut in the hill, and water accumulating in the cut forms a small pond that submerses the railroad grade. At the gate, turn around and follow the grade back to the parking lot.

36

Lake Scranton

3.5 miles

A beautiful 3.5-mile loop trail leads around Lake Scranton. This trail is not for those who want solitude, because it is very popular with residents of the Scranton/Wilkes-Barre metro area. From I-81, follow PA 307 south for about 2 miles to a parking area on the right.

Bibliography

In addition to the many trail-specific guidebooks published by volunteers and trail clubs throughout Pennsylvania, there are many regional and statewide guides to hiking as well. Some, like this book, are for the general hiking enthusiast, whereas others are dedicated to particular interest groups. Some local guides are discussed throughout this book in conjunction with particular trails of interest. In addition, a selection of regional and statewide guides appears below. Not all of these books are intended to guide hikers specifically, and many do not contain trail descriptions, but all are of interest for those hikers looking for new opportunities or wishing to learn about new areas to explore.

Aron, Jean. *The Short Hiker: Small Green Circles*, 3rd Ed. State College, PA: Aron Publications, 1999.

Bonta, Marcia. *More Outbound Journeys in Pennsylvania: A Guide to Natural Places for Individual and Group Outings.* University Park: Pennsylvania State University Press, 1995.

———. *Outbound Journeys in Pennsylvania: A Guide to Natural Places for Individual and Group Outings.* University Park: Pennsylvania State University Press, 1995.

Brown, Scott E. *Pennsylvania Moutain Vistas: A Guide for Hikers and Photographers.* Mechanicsburg, PA: Stackpole Books, 2008.

———. *Pennsylvania Waterfalls: A Guide for Hikers and Photographers.* Mechanicsburg, PA: Stackpole Books, 2005.

Dillon, Chuck. *Short Hikes in God's Country.* Wellsboro, PA: Pine Creek Press, 1995.

———. *Short Hikes in Pennsylvania's Grand Canyon.* Wellsboro, PA: Pine Creek Press, 2006.

Fergus, Charles. *Natural Pennsylvania: Exploring the State Forest Natural Areas.* Mechanicsburg, PA: Stackpole Books, 2002.

Golightly, Jean. *Circuit Hikes in Virginia, West Virginia, Maryland, and Pennsylvania*, 7th Ed. Vienna, VA: Potomac Appalachian Trail Club, 2004.

Gross, Wayne E., ed. *Guide to the Appalachian Trail in Pennsylvania*, 10th Ed. Cogan Station, PA: Keystone Trails Association, 1998.

Miller, E. Willard, ed. *A Geography of Pennsylvania.* University Park: Pennsylvania State University Press, 1994.

Mitchell, Jeff. *Backpacking Pennsylvania: 37 Great Hikes.* Mechanicsburg, PA: Stackpole Books, 2005.

——. *Hiking the Allegheny Natural Forest: Exploring the Wilderness of Northwestern Pennsylvania.* Mechanicsburg, PA: Stackpole Books, 2007.

——. *Hiking the Endless Mountains: Exploring the Wilderness of Northeastern Pennsylvania.* Mechanicsburg, PA: Stackpole Books, 2003.

Ostertag, Rhonda, and George Ostertag. *Hiking Pennsylvania.* 2nd ed. Guilford, CT: Falcon, 2002.

Owen, Jim and Ginny Owen. *Hiker's Guide to the Bucktail Path.* Cogan Station, PA: Keystone Trails Association, 1998.

Rivinus, Willis M. *The Complete Guide to the Delaware and Lehigh National Heritage Corridor: Where to Go, What to See.* Bethlehem, PA: Lehigh River Foundation, 1994.

——. *Guide to the Delaware Canal: Along the Delaware River Between Bristol and Easton, Pennsylvania,* 8th Ed. Self-published, 1994.

Seeley, Ralph. *Greate Buffaloe Swamp: A Trail Guide and Historical Record for the Quehanna Plateau and the Moshannon State Forest.* Karthaus, PA: Quehanna Area Trails Club, 2001.

Sexton, Tom, and Pamela Hamer. *Pennsylvania's Rail-Trails.* 10th ed. Harrisburg, PA: Rails-to-Trails Conservancy, 2005.

Sierra Club Pennsylvania Chapter. *A Hiker's Guide to the Laurel Highlands Trail.* Pittsburgh: Laurel Highlands Conservation and Development Project, 1981.

Thwaites, Tom. *50 Hikes in Central Pennsylvania: Day Hikes and Backpacking Trips.* 4th ed. Woodstock, VT: Backcountry Guides, 2001.

——. *50 Hikes in Eastern Pennsylvania: From the Mason-Dixon Line to the Poconos and North Mountain.* 4th ed. Woodstock, VT: Countryman Press, 2003.

——. *50 Hikes in Western Pennsylvania: Walks and Day Hikes from the Laurel Highlands to Lake Erie.* 3rd ed. Woodstock, VT: Backcountry Guides, 2000.

Trepanowski, Sally, and John Trepanowski. *Best Hikes with Children in Pennsylvania.* Seattle, WA: Mountaineers Books, 1996.

Whiteford, Richard D., and Michael P. Godomski. *Wild Pennsylvania: A Celebration of Our State's Natural Beauty.* St. Paul, MN: Voyageur Press, 2006.

Young, John. *Hike Pennsylvania.* Guilford, CT: Outside America, 2001.

About the Editors

Ben Cramer, general editor and Three Rivers Region editor, has hiked nearly 3,000 miles on Pennsylvania's hiking trails, and has completed many of the state's long-distance backpacking trails. He is a lifetime member of Keystone Trails Association, a member of Quehanna Area Trails Club, and an executive committee member for Sierra Club at both the local and state levels. He is the author of a forthcoming hikers guide to the Allegheny Front Trail, contributes to a monthly outdoor recreation column in *Centre Daily Times,* and writes regularly for several volunteer publications. He lives in State College, Pennsylvania, and is currently pursuing a Ph.D. at Penn State University.

Henry Frank, Piedmont and Great Valley Region and Blue Mountain Region editor, enjoys a quiet walk in the (mostly) civilization-free woods. He is a public member and secretary of the Snowmobile and ATV Advisory Committee for the Pennsylvania Department of Conservation and Natural Resources. He questions every move that introduces noisy and air-polluting "fun" into his quiet walks. Henry and his spouse of thirty-five years, Elaine, live in Philadelphia.

Wayne Gross, Pocono Highlands Region editor, is Publications Chairman for Keystone Trails Association and has received several KTA hiking awards. He is a founder and past president of Pocono Outdoor Club and has through-hiked the Appalachian Trail and a number of the other trails listed in this guide. He serves as the editor for *Pennsylvania Appalachian Trail Guide,* and a number of his photographs have been published in the official *Appalachian Trail Calendar.* He has served for fifteen years as a scoutmaster, teaching Leave No Trace principles for a Boy Scout troop that has backpacked on the Appalachian Trail and at Philmont Scout Ranch in New Mexico. He lives in Canadensis, Pennsylvania.

Joe and Lorraine Healey, Endless Mountain Region editors, have been members and leaders of Keystone Trails Association since the 1980s. The Healeys have been hiking together for more than twenty-five years and have completed the Appalachian Trail. Joe currently manages the KTA trail care and summer maintenance programs and is also a regional manager for the Mid State Trail. Joe and Lorraine lead several KTA maintenance projects each year. They live in Laflin, Pennsylvania.

Mike Lipay, Laurel Highlands Region editor, has been hiking since the late 1960s, when he acquired his love for the outdoors as a Boy Scout. Over the years, he has returned his appreciation by maintaining trails and introducing both youngsters and adults to the outdoors. He is president of the Allegheny Trails Hiking Club in southwestern Pennsylvania. He lives in Plum, Pennsylvania.

Jim Ritchie, Northwest and Allegheny National Forest Region editor, was involved with the Pittsburgh Council of American Youth Hostels from 1988 to 2002 and served as chair of Hiking Programs, chair of Trail Systems, Rachel Carson Trail manager, and Baker Trail manager. Jim edited several editions of AYH's *Baker Trail Guide Book* and *Hiker's Guide to the Rachel Carson Trail.* He has been a member of Keystone Trails Association and Sierra Club since 1990 and frequently leads organized hikes in and around southwestern Pennsylvania. His most noteworthy achievements include resurrecting the Rachel Carson Trail, creating the successful Rachel Carson Trail Challenge, acting as the primary maintainer for the Baker Trail, and advising the Baker Trail UltraChallenge. Jim's greatest hiking experience was a twelve-day backpacking trip in the Canadian High Arctic, reaching 80 degrees north latitude. Jim is the director of institutional research and planning at Duquesne University and resides in Oakmont, Pennsylvania, with his wife, Susan, and their two children.

Ralph Seeley, Pennsylvania Wilds Region editor, started advising and leading students of the Penn State Outing Club on cross-country ski and hike outings in the late 1960s. He found the experience to be negatively affected by the then deficient quality of trails in central and northern Pennsylvania. Thus began Ralph's accomplished history of trail maintenance, which started out by helping Tom Thwaites build the Mid State Trail. He then moved on to the Quehanna Plateau and started recruiting trail maintainers; he now oversees more than fifty maintainers for about 180 miles of blazed trails. He also consults with the Bureau of Forestry in the design and construction of footbridges in Moshannon and Sproul State Forests. Ralph is the author of *Greate Buffaloe Swamp,* with local history and trail descriptions for Moshannon State Forest. He is a member of Mid State Trail Association, Quehanna Area Trails Club, and Keystone Trails Association. He lives in Bellefonte, Pennsylvania.

Tom Thwaites, Seven Mountains Region editor, was for twenty-nine years the faculty advisor to the hiking division of the Penn State Outing Club. An accomplished trail builder and maintainer, he is a past president of Mid State Trail Association and an active member of Keystone Trails Association, and he has personally scouted many of Pennsylvania's premier hiking trails. Tom has had a section of the Mid State Trail dedicated in his honor, and the recently constructed T-Squared Trail is named after him. He is the author of *50 Hikes in Western Pennsylvania, 50 Hikes in Central Pennsylvania,* and *50 Hikes in Eastern Pennsylvania.* He lives in State College, Pennsylvania.

Index